WATER FOR POOR WOMEN

WATER FOR POOR WOMEN
Quest for an Alternative Paradigm

Sayeed Iftekhar Ahmed

LEXINGTON BOOKS
Lanham • Boulder • New York • Toronto • Plymouth, UK

Published by Lexington Books
A wholly owned subsidiary of The Rowman & Littlefield Publishing Group, Inc.
4501 Forbes Boulevard, Suite 200, Lanham, Maryland 20706
www.rowman.com

10 Thornbury Road, Plymouth PL6 7PP, United Kingdom

British Library Cataloguing in Publication Information Available

Library of Congress Cataloging-in-Publication Data

Library of Congress Cataloging-in-Publication Data Available
ISBN 978-0-7391-7527-9 (cloth : alk. paper) -- ISBN 978-0-7391-7528-9 (electronic)

∞™ The paper used in this publication meets the minimum requirements of American National Standard for Information Sciences—Permanence of Paper for Printed Library Materials, ANSI/NISO Z39.48-1992.

Printed in the United States of America

For the Women
Who suffer the most when water is scarce

Table of Contents

List of Tables

List of Figures

Acknowledgments

Although I was born in a country where there are abundant water resources, I have witnessed a severe potable water crisis in Dhaka and other parts of Bangladesh. Although water problems bothered me back home, I did not seriously start thinking about the crisis until 2002 when my dissertation committee chair, Professor Carol Thompson, asked me to write a report on the debate over water privatization for the Advocacy Network for Africa, and the Washington Office on Africa. She deserves special thanks for providing me the opportunity to work on this project through which, for the first time, I became familiar with the literature about the problems and debates regarding the management of water resources as well as the nuances and complexities associated with it. Later, after obtaining the Merriam Powell Graduate Fellowship for working on water privatization in Morocco, I seriously began to think about writing a dissertation on water governance issues. When I completed my dissertation, I wanted to transform it into a book because through this I would be able to reach a wide range of readers, especially those who are concerned about the unavailability of water in the developing world.

As I witnessed the plight of poor women due to the lack of access to water in Bangladesh, I decided to work on the water governance issues of Dhaka. I wanted to compare the water governance in Dhaka with a different type of governance system from another developing country, located in Asia. I chose Manila because it is practicing a different type of water governance system than in Dhaka. I requested Professor Thompson to be my committee chair, and she kindly agreed. All these years her patient guidance, moral support, and thoughtful comments on my drafts have been very helpful in completing my dissertation.

I would also like to acknowledge the support and guidance of the other committee members. Their expertise and diverse points of view have helped me to understand the complexities of water governance from multiple perspectives. Dr. Zachary Smith generously gave his knowledge and expertise to help me comprehend the complex issues related to water management. Dr. David Schlosberg's critical feedback helped me to understand Amarya Sen's capability approach and other theories that I've used in this dissertation. Dr. Karen Bakker's knowledge of governance was also very helpful in trying to grasp the intricacies of various governance paradigms.

The poor women living in the slums and other parts of Dhaka and Manila deserve special thanks. They are the individuals who assisted me in understanding the kinds of impacts that people might face as a result of the lack of access to potable water. Moreover, they also helped me to grasp the necessity of poor women's participation in the decision-making process. I would also like to acknowledge the following DWASA (Dhaka Water Supply and Sewerage Authority), MWSS (Metropolitan Waterworks and Sewerage System), MWCI (Manila Water Company, Inc.), and MWSI (Maynilad Water Services, Inc.) staff and workers: Md. Ishaq Dewan, Engineer, DWASA; Mizanur Rahman, Deputy Chief, Revenue, DWASA; A.K.M. Jafar Ullah, Superintending Engineer and Project Director, Water Supply System Expansion & Rehabilitation Project (WSSERP), DWASA; Zaber Hossain, General Secretary, CBA, DWASA; Carla May Berina-Kim, Planning and Communications Officer, Regulation & Corporate Development Group, MWCI; Randolph A, Sakai, Manager, Tariff Control and Monitoring Department, MWSS and Carmen Vilasqnes, Secretary, Customer Service, MWSI.

It is my pleasure to also acknowledge the following NGO activists in Dhaka and Manila for clarifying various issues regarding supplied water resources in the metropolitan areas of Dhaka and Manila: Hemantha Withanage, Environmental Scientist, Executive Director, Center for Environmental Justice; Foyzun Nahar, Field Trainer, Association for Realisation of Basic Needs (ARBAN); Md. Mubashir Hossain, Project Engineer Sustainable Environmental Sanitation, ARBAN; Azahar Ali, Governance Adviser, Water Aid (Bangladesh); Md. Shahidul Islam, Porgramme Coordinator, Directorate Team, Water Aid (Bangladesh); Zakir Hossain Senior Project Coordinator, Water & Sanitation Project DSK (*Dustho Sastho Kendro*); Raquibul Amin, Programme Cordinator, IUCN (International Union for Conservation of Nature); Bubut D. Palattao, Team Cordinator, Campaign on Human Rights to Water and the Privatization of Water Services, Freedom from Debt Coalition; Xavier Sku, Associate Documentation Officer, Advocacy & Information

Cell, NGO Forum for Drinking Water Supply and Sanitation; J. Ronald D. Masayda, Advocacy and Campaign Coordinator, NGO Forum on ADB; and Khondokar Shamim Ara, Receptionist IUCN. Special thanks to all of them.

I would also like to acknowledge the kind help of my tour guide and translator in Manila, Lemuel Espra A. (Dodo). Without his help, it would have been difficult for me to communicate with the women living in various slums in the city. Moreover, I would like to thank Monirul Islam, an architect in Dhaka, who assisted me in visiting poor women's households in various parts of Dhaka. Many thanks to my aunt, Kawsar Chowdhury, and uncle, Fuad Zaman, for their warm hospitality in Manila.

I am grateful to my parents, Mamin Uddin Ahmed and Sayeeda Ahmed, for their continuous encouragement and for instilling in me the passion for political studies. The ambience they fostered for me in the home shaped my decision to study politics later in life.

My beloved wife Chella read every page of the manuscript with her natural acumen and interest, and made invaluable comments. She is the person who bears with me the daily hardships of a graduate student's life. My debt to her endures forever.

Finally, Louella Holter did excellent work while editing this book and she deserves special thanks for that. I am grateful to everyone who helped in so many ways while conducting my research. But of course I bear the sole responsibility for the shortcomings/views expressed in this book.

Glossary

ADB = Asian Development Bank

BOT = Build-Operate-Transfer

BT = MWSS's Board of Trustees

BT Project = *Bayan Tubig* (Water for the Community)

CA = Concession Agreement

DCA = DWASA Cooperative Association

DCC = Dhaka City Corporation

DENR = Department of Environment & Natural Resources

DOH = Department of Health

DWASA = Dhaka Water Supply and Sewerage Authority

EPC = Engineering, Planning and Consultant

FDC = Freedom from Debt Coalition

IFC = International Finance Corporation

IWRM = Integrated Water Resource Management

LGUs = Local Government Units

MDG = Millennium Development Goal

MLD = million liters of water per day

MMDA = Metropolitan Manila Development Authority

MWCI = Manila Water Company, Inc.

MWSI = Maynilad Water Services, Inc.

MWSS = Metropolitan Waterworks and Sewerage System

NAWASA = National Waterworks and Sewerage Authority

NRW = Non-Revenue Water

NSO = National Statistic Office

PNSDW = Philippine National Standards for Drinking Water

PPI = Project Performance Improvement

PRA = Participatory Reflection and Action

PSI = Pounds per Square Inch

PSP = Private Sector Participation

RO = Regulatory Office

SEA = South East Asian

TPSB Project = *Tubig Para sa Barangay* (Water for the Poor)

VAT = Value Added Tax

WHO = World Health Organization

1

Introduction

The next world war will be over water.

— Ismail Serageldin, Vice-President of the World Bank[1]

Access to safe drinking water is crucial for human existence. In contrast to the common belief of an infinite supply of water, only 0.5 percent of the earth's water is available for drinking.[2] Also, this water is not evenly distributed among various populations and regions. Usually, rich people are "twice as likely" to use safe drinking water as the poor.[3] People living in urban areas have more access to water than those in rural areas. According to one estimate, 1.1 billion people (about 1 in 6 human beings) in 2000 did not have access to potable water. Among them, 63 percent live in Asia and 28 percent in Africa.[4]

The Millennium Development Goal's aim for water (Goal 7, Target 10) is to "halve by 2015 the proportion of people without sustainable access to safe drinking water." Meeting the MDG targets would save millions of children's lives from water-borne diseases such as cholera and diarrhea, although it would not completely eliminate the deaths related to water, especially in the developing world, and would still leave hundreds of millions of people without access to their basic needs. To achieve the 2015 target, it is necessary to provide water access to 1.5 billion more people by the end of that year.[5] In order to accomplish this task, it is essential to supply water to 280,000 new people every day.[6] Over the coming decades, one of the biggest challenges will be to ensure water and sanitary facilities, especially in Africa, Asia, and Latin America, due to the expected dramatic increase in population.[7]

Water is not merely a chemical substance.[8] Religious, political, social, economic, and cultural issues are associated with water. Equitable access to water is a basic human right and is pivotal for sustainable development. However, it is not a legally recognized universal human right, although in 2010, the United Nations General Assembly passed a resolution[9] affirming water and sanitation as a fundamental human right; the Assembly recognizes that access to clean drinking water and sanitation comprises an important prerequisite for the realization of all human rights. This resolution regarding the right to water and sanitation presents a legal predicament for many nation-states through international law. In South Africa and some other countries, access to water is now a legal human right and can therefore be interpreted as such in legal cases (Appendix, Table 2). In California and in other places around the world, legislation is being considered to recognize water as a human right. The right to water is related to the user's political capability to participate in the decision-making process regarding the distribution of water; otherwise, it would not be possible to execute the water rights of the users.[10] In reality, economically, politically, and socially powerful individuals and those who have technological know-how are in advantageous positions, and hence are more able to participate at the decision-making table. Moreover, they have more material capability to access supplied water resources than those who belong to the lower rank of the social ladder, such as the urban poor or marginalized women.

In the developing world, the majority of the marginalized women and the urban poor do not have access to safe, potable water sources. The World Bank statistic shows that 220 million urban dwellers in the developing world do not have potable water sources near their residences.[11] This study defines marginalized women as those who live below the poverty line. "Woman" is not a monolithic conception; there is stratification among women, although almost all the women in my study in Dhaka came from the same ethnic background. In both Dhaka and Metropolitan Manila the women who were deprived of water services were economically marginalized women. I did not come across any case in these two cities where women were deprived because of their ethnic backgrounds. Hence, this study is based solely on economically marginalized women.[12]

Lack of access to water has different impacts on women's lives, especially marginalized women, living in big cities, like Dhaka and Metropolitan Manila. In these two cities, most marginalized women live in the slum areas and are thus deprived of "household water security."[13] Also, poor women have less access than poor men do to safe potable water.[14] Poor sanitation, inadequate washing facilities, and contaminated water supply are regular features in the slums.[15] Moreover, due to the unavailability of water, there is no proper sanitation system in many slum areas.[16] In Dhaka and Metropolitan Manila, women usually take primary responsibility for fetching water for their families from distant places, as well as for washing clothes. This tedious time-consuming work deters women's involvement in other productive activities.

These marginalized women in Dhaka and Metropolitan Manila, who suffer the most as a result of the lack of water supply, are what Arjun Appadurai calls the "citizens without a city" who are nevertheless "a vital part of the urban workforce."[17] Across political, social, religious, ethnic, or class affiliations, economically marginalized women are the most disadvantaged and vulnerable. Often, they are also invisible in the eyes of both the states and the markets.

Due to the gender division of labor in South and South East Asia, the role of women, especially marginalized women, is vital in collecting, distributing, and safeguarding water. In rural and poor urban areas in Bangladesh and the Philippines, women take the main responsibilities for "fetching water for use in the home, of coping when there is not enough water for domestic needs, and of caring for those made sick by poor-quality water."[18] In contrast, they have "a much less influential role than men in [spaces created by the governance systems], problem analysis and the decision making processes related to water resources."[19]

In comparison to other women, economically marginalized women can play almost no role in the areas mentioned above. The usual pattern of distributing water in the various cities of South and South East Asia is paternalistic, where marginalized women and the urban poor have almost no chance to participate in the decision-making spaces because of their subaltern location in society. The governance spaces are occupied by the various forms of local elites who have more political capability to participate. As a result of their greater capability, in most cases they can influence the decisions in their favor. The services that marginalized women and the poor receive from the water boards are the outcomes of a paternalistic governance pattern where their political capability to participate in decision-making spaces is usually ignored or very limited.

In Dhaka and Metropolitan Manila, water supply sectors are managed by the state and by Public-Private Participation (PPP) governance mechanisms, respectively. State-led governance refers to the mechanism that is run mainly by government-appointed bureaucrats. The Dhaka Water Supply and Sewerage Authority (DWASA) has utilized state-led governance since its establishment in 1963. This type of mechanism is usually hierarchical; hence decisions are made and implemented using the top-down approach.[20]

Although the Metropolitan Waterworks and Sewerage System (MWSS) in Metropolitan Manila originally followed state-led governance, it transformed its governance mechanism to PPP in 1997 with the promise of ensuring effective service and universal access to everyone living in the city. PPP governance means "a reworking of the management institutions (rules, norms, and customs)" which entails cooperation of the state and private corporations "as allocation mechanisms, market-simulation decision-making techniques," and an effort to combine Keynesian-welfarism with neo-liberal principles in policy making and distribution.[21] It opened up an avenue to transfer partial ownership from the public (state) to the private sector.

In PPP governance, there is less interference by the state in managing and distributing resources. It was expected that in Metropolitan Manila this strategy would ensure more efficient distribution of water as well as improved water quality.

Statement of the Problem

The state-led governance in Dhaka might not necessarily ensure marginalized women's capabilities to participate in decision-making spaces and to access supplied water resources. As a result of the prevalent hierarchy in the society, local elites are in advantageous positions when it comes to the issue of participation. They could also be the beneficiaries of most of the state's services and subsidies. The majority of the population living in poverty or below the poverty level, including marginalized women, might not have the material capability to receive an equitable share of the state's services because of the governance policies and the structural arrangement of the society. This situation is also more or less applicable to the water services.

Because the state-led water governance system in Dhaka might not create a separate space for marginalized women to participate in decision making, this study hypothesizes that given their subaltern location in society, marginalized women might have less political capability or no capability at all to participate in these decision-making spaces. This study also hypothesizes that under this governance system, their basic material capability to access supplied water resources might also not increase as a result of the absence of an equitable distribution policy.

In a city where most people live in poverty, the introduction of PPP governance might also not ensure marginalized women's participation in the spaces where decisions are made. The PPP governance system might not create a space for marginalized women to participate, or it might not create an environment conducive to their participation in the existing spaces. Therefore, this study hypothesizes that in Metropolitan Manila, under the PPP governance system, marginalized women might not be able to establish their political capability to participate in the decision-making spaces. Moreover, it might also fail to guarantee an equitable distribution system that would establish their relative material capability over resources.

Most of the private enterprises are run on a completely commercial basis.[22] Hence, what neo-classical economics describes as a "natural monopoly" may arise in the water business.[23] These enterprises always seek to expand their service areas to ensure more profit. Thus, under the PPP governance in Metropolitan Manila, the material capability of marginalized women to access supplied water resources might increase moderately, although not equitably in comparison to other sections of society, as a result of the policies of the private enterprises that are expanding water services to ensure more profit.

As argued by Amartya Sen, "capabilities have intrinsic importance" to establishing equality in any society, which is a fundamental prerequisite for social justice.[24] Reducing "capabilities" decreases a person's functioning, which ultimately deprives a person of his or her rights. This study therefore compares the intended and unintended effects of the two types of governance systems on marginalized women's political and basic material capabilities to participate in decision-making spaces and to access supplied water resources. I have thus defined social justice in water distribution in terms of the capability to participate in the decision-making process (political capability) as well as the capability to obtain water (basic material capability).

There can be "good" governance, which could deliver water equitably to every citizen without their participation in the decision-making spaces. However, the capability approach does not stand for the paternalistic distribution of resources. "It leaves room for individuals to decide for themselves how useful or important are the capabilities that [the governance system] secures for them." The concept of capability egalitarianism envisions "an active participation of citizens at different levels in the formulation, revision and effective realization of the plan."[25]

The capability approach is not satisfied merely by citizens benefiting as a result of a good governance system. It argues for creating opportunities for every citizen to implement their agency aspect in protecting their well-being and freedom, as well as that of other fellow citizens. Capability egalitarianism is more choice-centered and less paternalistic. Therefore, even in cities with excellent water delivery, justice is not necessarily served unless all sectors of the population are involved in governance. Thus, this study defines social justice in water distribution in terms of equitable capabilities for the marginalized women to participate in the decision-making spaces as well as to access supplied water resources.

The two cities—Dhaka and Metropolitan Manila—were chosen for comparison for the following reasons. Both cities have large populations living in poverty, and both have reputations for badly managed water systems. Metropolitan Manila has the largest PPP water governance mechanism in Asia, and it has been in operation for a relatively long time (1997 to the present); most PPP water governance systems in developing countries have not been in place this long. Dhaka's state-led system has of course been well established over a long period of time. Since the birth of the state in 1971, the water sector in Dhaka has been managed under the state-led governance mechanism.[26]

Research Questions

The central questions of this research are as follows: How do two different types of governance systems—the state and the PPP—affect the political capability of marginalized women to participate in the spaces where decisions are made regarding the distribution of supplied water resources in Dhaka and Metropolitan Manila? How do these systems affect their basic material capability to access supplied water resources in these two cities?[27]

Theoretical Framework

The main theoretical framework for this study is Amartya Sen's capability approach. Marginalized women's *political* and basic *material* capabilities under the state-led and the PPP governance systems are measured through the lens of the capability approach. Drawing on the typologies of various scholars, David Crocker developed participatory typologies, which I used in this study to examine the patterns of participation in these governance mechanisms. Moreover, I also applied John Gaventa's "power cube" theory to comprehend the role of power in the participatory process that determines the patterns of women's participation (or non-participation) in the spaces created by the governance systems mentioned above.

The Capability Approach

Amartya Sen's theory of capabilities offers an alternative perspective to the utilitarian theory that is generally used in microeconomics.[28] The utilitarian theory postulates that a person's well-being depends on the control of personal utilities. Utility has been defined as the happiness or pleasure or satisfaction of preference. In contrast, capability theory does not address happiness or preference. It also does not address the significance of goods in a person's life, or the pleasure a person derives from the use of those goods. Instead, capability theory addresses a person's "opportunities" and "freedoms" to make use of the resources to secure well-being.[29] Rather than paying attention to people's satisfaction, according to Martha Nussbaum, it focuses on "what they are actually able to do or to be," that is, whether the person has "agency freedom" to do something that would lead to "achievement of well-being."[30]

Following Sen, capability signifies the ability of a person to achieve basic and desired "functionings." Capabilities refer to opportunities and the freedom or choice to achieve something, and functionings refer to the outcomes or the achievements. These concepts are related to the concepts of "well-being freedom" and "well-being achievement." Functionings are, according to Sen, "doings or beings"—both tangible and intangible. These represent the real achievements of a person—concrete and abstract—such as being well educated, well nourished, and obtaining proper health care, or attaining social status due to community involvements or intellectual development. *Basic* capabilities are those related to a person's existence, such as the ability to obtain the required amount of potable water or food. *Desired* capabilities are those that are associated with human development, such as the ability to achieve education or to participate in the decision-making process.

A "capability set" allows people to achieve the various functionings that they choose. The concept of a capability set provides a means of explaining why different individuals are able to mobilize specific commodities differently to achieve certain functionings. It emphasizes the agency aspect of individuals—individual choices, values, and preferences—which are indeed central; they are what individuals use to decide how to apply the various available capabilities to the functions that they choose for their own lives.

The fundamental argument of the capability approach is thus to "measure the well-being of a person" by considering his or her ability in "doing" and "being."[31] Sen uses "the notion of capability" to indicate "a space within which comparisons of quality of life [or, as he sometimes says, standard of living] are most fruitfully made."[32] The expansion of the capabilities depends on (1) the elimination of oppression and exploitation combined with the power to make choices, and (2) the assurance of the provisions of basic facilities, such as education, health care, and social safety nets.[33]

Sen's theory, which originated from liberalism, pays attention solely to the individual, or the individual's capacity to achieve functionings. The individual is the basic unit of analysis in the capability approach. Sen defines capabilities as "the capability to function, i.e., what a person can do or can be."[34] Although not ontologically, it is ethically and normatively an individualistic liberal theory. Ethical individualism refers to individuals, not groups or households, as the units of normative judgments.[35] However, Sen's theory does not focus exclusively on "atomistic individuals," nor are the capabilities and functionings independent of societal concerns or the interactions of other individuals.[36]

Sen emphasizes the process aspect of capabilities, or exercising agency, which matters a great deal in achieving social choice and distributive justice. Sen's perception of agency is very much similar to that of Anthony Giddens—that is, the capacity of an individual to act.[37] This concept is related to the ability of an individual to attain well-being; more specifically, it refers to the subjective capacity of an individual to attain well-being. Establishing a subjective capacity is related to the power of an individual to function.

The concept of agency helps to understand the expansion of individuals' capabilities by increasing their choices, or "freedoms." However, this is still a weak version of agency because it does not take into account the unequal power structure of society. The idea of agency is not autonomous; spatial and temporal domains determine the nature of agency. As a result of "structural social and economic inequalities," powerful individuals are in advantageous positions regarding exercising their agencies.[38]

Therefore, to attain political or basic material capabilities, marginalized women "require collective action," because as individuals they have less ability to exercise their subjective roles.[39] Collective action, or what Martha Nussbaum calls "affiliation," is one of the basic capabilities, as defined by her. Collective agency is thus a condition for achieving individual agency because the former refers to a sense of exercising a shared influence over the social provisions of an individual's life. This could be achieved "by joining or participating in a group with similar goals, [where] the person acts in concert with the others to achieve these goals."[40] It is also an important means to exercising "agency achievements," which "may be realized whether one is a unique decision-maker or a participant in a group decision, as in the case of participation."[41]

It is essential to develop the conditions necessary for exercising agencies. Sen's major focus is on individual freedom and political participation.[42] Without favorable conditions, it might not be possible for a person to exercise individual or collective agencies through political participation in a way that could lead to what Sen describes as "agency achievement" or individual freedom.[43] Therefore, to fulfill the goal of the capability approach—that is, to transform a person from a passive recipient to an active subject—the necessary conditions must be created to achieve this objective. However, people can exercise their agencies, although in a very limited way, even under extremely constrained situations. They can impact the situation to improve their conditions.

Collective participation has intrinsic value for exercising agencies. The work of both Sen and Jean Dreze suggests that participation is a manifestation of agency.[44] Therefore, to achieve a desired functioning, whether under favorable or restricted conditions, it is crucial for the marginalized women to exercise their collective agencies through collective participation. It is important to mention here that in a society where asymmetrical power relations (gender, class, race, or religious) prevail, it might not be possible for marginalized women to exercise their agencies (either collectively or individually) without participation.

Sen's theory assesses capability from the perspective of the individual. My study takes the perspective of the economically marginalized women, as a group, who live in subaltern locations in Dhaka and Metropolitan Manila.[45] The reason behind focusing on women as a group rather than as individuals is that an individual's "well-being depends heavily on other people's well-being."[46] Moreover, "larger units of analysis ... are useful and even necessary under certain contexts and circumstances in order to evaluate the structural or institutional support for individuals."[47] The women I interviewed in both Dhaka and Metropolitan Manila almost always expressed concerns about the expansion of their capabilities to obtain supplied water in relation to the other members of the community as a group. Their understandings of well-being and agency are constructed in "relational terms."[48]

Capability theory links a vital physical need (water) with a vital political need (participation) in order to provide for the larger functioning of life. Thus, this study investigates the intended and unintended effects of both the state and PPP governance mechanisms in providing the basic capability of water to marginalized women. It investigates whether under these governance systems there is a space for marginalized women to play the role of active agents through participation (active and passive). My research further suggests that marginalized women comprise a significant category for assessing the capability of an individual to access the water supply and to participate in the space where decisions are made about supplying water.

Organized collective agencies—for example women as a collective group—are crucial for obtaining both political and basic material fucntionings. Hence, marginalized women's capabilities with regard to supplied water resources can be seen as their abilities to participate in the decision-making process regarding water distribution as well as their ability to access the minimum requirement of supplied water—that is, their capabilities regarding the quantity, quality, and price of water.

Nussbaum's List of Human Capabilities

In reviewing Sen's contributions on the capability approach, Nussbaum has created a framework for measuring social and gender justice.[49] She is particularly concerned about gender justice, which does not receive due attention in Sen's analysis. However, Sen refused to identify a particular set of human capabilities because it would ultimately limit an individual's capabilities, which he did not intend to do. In contrast, for Nussbaum, it is essential "to take a more definite stand on which capabilities are important in our ethical judgments and our conceptions of justice."[50] Moreover, the two authors have different understandings of capabilities. For Sen, capabilities are "real opportunities" and for Nussbaum "they also include talents, internal powers and abilities."[51] Her capability lists are "based on a universalistic account of central human functionings."[52]

In her list of human capabilities, Nussbaum calls for "normative guidance for gender justice."[53] The capabilities Nussbaum identifies are (i) life, (ii) bodily health, (iii) bodily integrity, (iv) senses, imagination, and thought, (v) emotions, (vi) practical reason, (vii) affiliation, (viii) relationship to the world of nature, and (ix) control over one's environment: (a) political, (b) material.[54] Although Nussbaum discusses the 10 types of "central human functional capabilities," my study concentrates on women's capabilities to control their "environment: political and material"— their capability to participate and to obtain supplied water resources. I have adopted a narrow definition of "political" and *basic* "material." Political refers to the capability of women to participate (directly or indirectly through deliberation) in decision-making spaces. *Basic* Material refers to the capability to obtain the minimum requirement of supplied water in terms of the quantity, price, and quality of water.[55] Hence, my research pays attention to only one aspect of the basic and political capabilities of marginalized women in Nussbaum's capabilities list.

One empirical study cannot capture the complexity of a theoretical concept, especially as delineated in all its diversity by Nussbaum. This study therefore investigates mainly the political and material capabilities of marginalized women in terms of participation and obtaining water.[56] Water sustains life and health; without access to sufficient quantity and quality, children quickly succumb to lethal diseases. Adults may also die, but certainly they are somewhat incapacitated, less capable of attending to work or family exigencies. Ready access to water reduces the time a household (most often women) requires to gather water, releasing adult/youth energy for other economic activities. Therefore, I have chosen access to water as the *basic* material capability from Naussbaum's set of such capabilities. This study also investigates the capability of marginalized women to participate in the decision-making spaces. Participation is a political capability for women who want to play the vitally important role of active agents.

Participation and Marginalized Women's Capabilities

Participation is a popular concept among development scholars.[57] The partic

ipatory approach to development has been practiced since the 1970s. Partici-

patory methodologies, especially participatory reflection and action (PRA),

have shifted from NGO-centered approaches in the 1980s to mainstream

development approaches in the 1990s. The United Nations, the World Bank,

and other large international donor agencies are now encouraging and pre-

scribing PRA and related methods in development programs and projects.[58] It

is assumed that participatory methods are important for implementing pro-

people development and that they provide significant means for incorporat-

ing local communities and grassroots people into the development process as

well as expanding their capabilities.

There are multiple meanings of participation, which "fall along an axis be-

tween 'light' interactions," where the participants' role is to provide informa-

tion, to "deep participation," where participants can influence the decision-

making procedures and establish command over resources.[59] These different

types of participation overlap in decision-making spaces as the actors shift

between different types of participation because actors are differently empow-

ered and thus are able to enact different kinds of participation.

Sabina Alkire discusses participation in terms of participants' command

over their resources, but this study argues that marginalized people can estab-

lish only a limited command over resources due to the prevalence of asym-

metrical power relations. Societal power relation patterns are usually reflected

in the system of governance. Hence, it may not be possible for marginalized

people to establish absolute capabilities over their resources under a particu-

lar governance framework, despite creation of a space for their participation.

The created space can help the marginalized to play a role in the decision-

making process, but due to their subaltern location in society, they can play

only a limited role.

The elites (the bureaucrats, experts, or influential persons) are definitely

in an advantageous position to influence the decisions in their own favor.

This is due not only to their powerful position in the society, but also to

their "technical supremacy" in terms of implementing development agen-

das. Therefore, under current power structures, the goal of incorporating

the marginalized into the governance system is to establish their relative

command over resources.

Creating or providing access to participation in the existing space (condi-

tionality) in the governance system is necessary for implementing participa-

tory methodologies, where "the micro is set against the macro, the margins

against the center, the local against the elite, and the powerless against the powerful."[60] Access to this space would provide opportunities for the marginalized and excluded groups to engage in public life and to build their capacity to "express their voices."[61] It is thus assumed that participation is also an important method for expanding capabilities, more specifically what Sen mentions as basic political capabilities or "political freedoms." Political freedom refers to a person's ability to participate—actively or passively—in the decision-making process through deliberation. The term political freedom, coined by Severine Deneulin, is used here to describe the ability to take part in the democratic and participatory mode of decision-making.[62]

According to Alkire, "'Participation' refers to the process of discussion, information gathering, conflict, and eventual decision-making, implementation, and evaluation by the groups directly affected by an activity." It is a process of making decisions in which the choices are made by the participants "who are directly affected by an action."[63] She further points out four major features of participation: (i) it enhances participants' agency, (ii) it is the basis for ensuring the "well-being freedom of participants," (iii) it is an important way of making participants aware of "value-information" because discussion helps them to realize the "effects" of certain "values," and finally, (iv) it allows "identity formation," which is shaped by participants' "own choices, rather than by inertia or the choices of more powerful others."[64] However, she does not discuss the necessity of creating conditionality or spaces for the marginalized women or for the less powerful individuals to ensure their participation. The necessity of a group effort for ensuring participation in unequal power relations is also missing in her discussion.

Marshall Wolfe explains participation from a group perspective, and mentions the significance of a group effort to ensure participation. According to Wolfe, participation consists of "the organized efforts to increase control over resources and regulative institutions in given social situations, on the part of groups and movements hitherto excluded from such control."[65] Therefore, for excluded people, the group effort is an important means for increasing their capabilities.

Dharam Ghai writes that the practice of participation is significant for the "expansion" of people's moral, intellectual, technical, and manual capabilities.[66] Nevertheless, in practice, under various governance systems, despite the incorporation of the grassroots people into development activities, whether they can exercise political capabilities under asymmetrical power relations to impact decision-making procedures is questionable.

There is a difference between participatory and democratic decision-making processes. Deneulin mentions that Sen does not differentiate between democratic and participatory decision-making processes.[67] Democratic decision-making refers to making a decision through existing political structures, such as parliaments or local-level electoral bodies. Participatory decision-making means incorporating the local or marginalized people into the development process through ad hoc participatory structures, and thereby bypassing conventional democratic procedures.

In hierarchical socio-economic arrangements, usually those who are in the upper echelons of the social ladder are the beneficiaries of democratic participation and governance systems. Therefore, in democratic governance/participation, more privileged groups or segments are able to manipulate the situation in their own favor because of their hegemonic location in terms of their voices, views, knowledge, and concerns. According to Iris Young, it is a kind of "vicious circle," where asymmetrical socio-economic and political relations "often reinforce more than undermine those injustices."[68]

In a participatory decision-making process, although there is a space for the locals or the marginalized to be represented in the ad hoc structures, the local elites are the chief beneficiaries in most cases. They can exercise their influences and voices over others, especially over women, who are even more "marginalized" than their male counterparts. Like in a democratic decision-making process, this process is not only unable to challenge deep-rooted existing power relations, but also "sometimes reproduces social inequalities" within the local communities.[69]

Andrea Cornwall has noted that even if women participate in formal decision-making structures, their voices have far less influence than their dominant male counterparts.[70] This also applies to informal structures. Therefore, most of the time, despite their representation, women's voices are excluded from the decision-making process. Bina Agarwal refers to "participatory exclusions" and explains the causes behind these exclusions in the context of disadvantaged community forestry groups in India and Nepal.[71] However, the basic difference between these two types of participation is that in a democratic decision-making process, there is less space for the marginalized women to participate; although they are unable to play a greater role, there is more space for them in ad hoc structures.

None of the participatory processes ensure that the most marginalized people would reach the level of "agency achievements." Several scholars have pointed out the negative aspects of the participatory approach in an effort to highlight the exclusionary and elite-centered nature of the so-called democratic or participatory decision-making process.[72] Creating a space for marginalized groups to exercise their agencies may give a false sense of inclusion. Decisions taken by the elites may be presented in such a way that they seem to represent the aspirations of the people or the entire local community, and as a result, national/communal moral authority is established that is difficult to overturn. Thus in asymmetrical power relations, participation "may simply add a more 'democratic' face of *status quo*" and undermine marginalized women's capabilities of genuine achievements.[73]

In a book edited by Bill Cooke and Uma Kothari, all the contributors came to the conclusion that participatory development methods in general, contrary to the popular belief, are not conducive to the empowerment of grassroots people. Instead, they reproduce "tyranny."[74] However, the purpose of pointing out the limitations of participation is not to argue against participation. Participation is overall better than non-participation. The point is to highlight the limitations of the participatory approaches and how these approaches, in reality, reshape and reproduce the existing power relations with the help of local elites.

Those who can participate definitely have more political capabilities or freedoms than those who cannot. If the participants cannot alter the existing power structures or their participation does not lead to agency achievements, even then any minimal form of participation certainly has the ability to influence the decision-making process. It opens up an avenue for bargaining with the power holders. Moreover, it also gives them a sense of inclusion. A sense of minimal participatory inclusion is better than the sense of complete structural exclusion. Despite all the limitations mentioned above, I am still in favor of women's participation in decision-making spaces. It is necessary, however, to mention here that despite having the capability to participate, many will still choose not to participate—which is a topic for another research. The focus of this study is to analyze whether women have the capability to choose to participate or not in the decision-making space.

Denis Goulet characterizes the participation of marginalized people as "non-elite participation in development decision-making."[75] The purpose is to ensure marginalized people's participation—not local elites' access to natural resources and control over institutions.[76] Participation "can have a range of levels," depending on the structure and the nature of the organizations as well as the level of empowerment of the actors.[77]

Sherry Arnstein identifies "a ladder of participation" in which she categorizes participation on the basis of the degree of empowerment, rising from non-participation to tokenism to citizen's power. Those who are less powerful can participate only at the bottom rung of the ladder, which she identifies as non-participation. Those who have capabilities to participate in the decision-making process are identified as having "citizen power" and those who are in between represent tokenism.

Arnstein further subcategorizes each category based on the level of empowerment.[78] The strength of her analysis is that this categorization is helpful in understanding how the degree of empowerment determines the level of participation. However, a major drawback of her analysis is the juxtaposition of the powerless and the powerful on the same ladder, whereas in reality, they might not always have the opportunity to act in the same space. Moreover, referring to those who have capability to participate on the top rung of the ladder as "citizen control" might create confusion regarding the distinction between the elites and the marginalized section of society. Her ladder is also not helpful in comprehending the role of the least powerful, who are completely excluded from the ladder.

Drawing on the typologies of Jules N. Pretty, Jay Drydyk, Gaventa, and Agarwal, Crocker develops the following participatory typologies.[79]

Minimal Participation: Participation through group membership. Participants do not play any role besides attending the meetings or sometimes not even attending the meetings.

Unreceptive Participation: Group members attend meetings passively and merely to be informed what the decisions are that have already been made by the elites. A group member's maximum role is to ask questions or make comments.

Reflexive Participation: Non-elite participants are being asked their opinions regarding specific issues, without the assurance of changing any decisions that were already made by the elites.

Petitionary Participation: Non-elites petition to the elites regarding certain decisions. Although the elites are in a privileged position to decide, the non-elites can exercise their agencies by sending their petitions to the elites. This method of participation is often used in traditional decision-making processes.

Participatory Implementation: The objectives and goals are determined by the elites. The role of the non-elites is to implement the goals and decisions. In this mode, non-elites can play a larger role than just listening, commenting, and endorsing.

Interactive Participation: Non-elites can express their voices and opinions and can exercise their relative agencies by influencing the decisions taken by the elites.

Deliberative Participation: Non-elites have greater autonomy in exercising their agencies through deliberation with themselves and with the elites as well as having the ability to alter proposals. In this type of participatory pattern, non-elites can establish their control over the use of resources, although they might not have the ability to alter the prevailing system of inequitable allocations of assets and authorities.

Participation can promote not only political capabilities but also economic. It supplies "the set of navigational skills needed to move through political space, and the tools to re-shape these spaces."[80] Marginalized women who can participate definitely have more capabilities than those who cannot; however, the point is whether they would be able to establish their relative capabilities over resources through participation or could contribute to the final decision regarding resource allocation. However, this study does not focus on whether their political capabilities or freedoms (participation) lead to physical/material capability, such as access to water resources in the water governance systems in Dhaka and Metropolitan Manila. Instead, it investigates whether they have political capabilities to participate in the decision-making space to decide for themselves, which is one of the important central capabilities identified by both Sen and Nussbaum. Or do we need to redesign the governance structures to provide them a space to enhance their both political and basic material capabilities? This study argues that redesigning the governance system would improve the quality of participation and fulfill the conditionality for achieving the political and basic material capabilities as well. Hence, I suggest that governance systems should be redesigned to make them more deliberative and reflexive as well as marginalized women centered. Redesigning would moderately increase both the political and material capabilities—participation in the decision making process and access to the minimum requirement of water per day per person.

Power Analysis: Spaces and Patterns of Power in the Participatory Process

Although creating spaces (or providing access to the existing spaces) might ensure greater inclusion of the excluded groups, it does not help to equalize the socio-economic and political inequalities, nor does it challenge the prevailing power structures. Gaventa's "power cube" theory helps us to understand the limitations of the participatory spaces, and the patterns of interactions (permutations of power relations) among the powerful and less powerful in these created (or existing) spaces.[81]

Gaventa has developed the power cube model, like a Rubik cube, for interpreting the three dimensions of power: spaces, levels, and forms.[82] He argues that each dimension is related to one another; and hence, any of the blocks of the cube could be picked for analysis. To bring meaningful changes in power structures, it is important to realign the pieces of each dimension with others simultaneously. Therefore, to initiate a fundamental transformation in social relations, it is necessary to open up the previously closed spaces through engagement with the excluded groups. They can do this by pressing their demands, which he describes as horizontal alliances.

The initial process of transformation usually starts in the excluded groups' existing spaces rather than in created or invited spaces. Political activism in their existing spaces leads to the necessity of opening new spaces in the formal governance structure. Marginalized groups and women's engagement are needed to challenge visible, hidden, and invisible power structures, and at the same time to build communication across local and global activists/groups, which Gaventa refers to as vertical alliances. The three dimensions of power, described below, affect each other through simultaneous interactions; hence, tactics for building alignment through participation along one dimension may cause misalignment on another.

Spaces of Power

The idea of space is used widely in texts on policy, power, development, citizen participation, and democracy. These texts refer to, for example, political spaces, policy spaces, and democratic spaces.[83] Cornwall argues that spaces used for participation are not neutral; they are shaped and reshaped by multiple power relations, which "both surround and enter them."[84] She draws her idea from French social theorists Henri Lefebvre, Michel Foucault, and Pierre Bourdieu, who revealed the linkages between the notion of power and the notion of space. According to Lefebvre, space is the outcome of social interactions. It is "not simply 'there,' a neutral container waiting to be filled, but is a dynamic, humanly constructed means of control, and hence of domination, of power."[85] Those who created a particular space are more powerful than those who were invited to participate in the space.

The image of boundary is also related to the idea of space. Power relations play a significant role in shaping the boundaries of spaces and determining who is entitled to enter inside the boundaries, with "which identities, discourses and interests."[86] Therefore, the capability in terms of participation could be defined as "the capacity to participate effectively in shaping the social limits that define what is possible."[87] In this meaning, the capability to participate is not only the ability to participate effectively, which could lead to the agency achievements in a particular space, but also the ability to redefine and reshape the given space. Therefore, the discussion of space should address the nature of engagement among different power groups, the way the space was created, and whose interest is served. Gaventa uses the following terminologies to describe various spaces. However, he was aware that there might be other variations of spaces depending on the "context and historical setting."[88]

Closed Spaces: Closed spaces refer to those where a group of actors make decisions "behind closed doors." The actors do not incorporate or invite marginalized groups into the decision-making procedures. At the state level, Gaventa refers to these spaces as "provided spaces," where the elites (bureaucrats, technical experts, or elected officials) make and implement decisions for the people without the requirement for discussion or any kind of involvement of the people.

Invited Spaces: Spaces are sometimes created for participation, what Gaventa refers to as "invited spaces." People or citizens are invited to participate in these spaces by the elites as well as by government authorities, transnational agencies, and non-governmental organizations. The spaces may be "institutionalized, ongoing, or more transient," as "one-off forms of consultation."[89] These spaces are visible at various levels of local and national governments and even in global policy round-tables.

Claimed/Created Spaces: These spaces are "claimed" by "less powerful actors from or against the power holders, or created more autonomously by them."[90] Cornwall mentions that "common concerns or identifications" as well as popular mobilization creates these spaces, which she refers to as "organic spaces." Soja mentions these as "third spaces," where underprivileged actors decline hegemonic spaces and make their own spaces to participate.[91] There are wide ranges of these spaces outside of the institutionalized structures, from spaces created by social movements and associations to the places where people can gather to debate, discuss, and resist the powerful elites.

Finally, the transformative prospects of spaces could be assessed in terms of the relationship with other spaces that surround them. The newly created spaces might also be captured by the already powerful elites from different spaces due to the absence of countervailing power spaces. This study investigates the types of space allocated to marginalized women so they can participate in the decision-making process under the state or PPP governance systems in Dhaka and Metropolitan Manila, relative to their capability to achieve the political functioning.

Levels of Power

The levels of power refer to the places or levels where "critical social, political, and economic power resides."[92] Gaventa identifies three levels of power: local, national, and global. He further mentions that these levels are "increasingly" interconnected. Local structures and expressions of power are constantly being shaped and reshaped by their interactions with global actors and powers; in turn, local activism influences and forms the patterns of global power. This "vertical dimension" of the levels of participation is also a "flexible, adaptable continuum," not a "fixed set of categories."

The transforming nature of local, national, and global levels of power determines the pattern of engagements, that is "where and how to engage."[93] This study focuses on the level of engagement of marginalized women at the local level (only the formal spaces created by the governance systems), or whether there is any engagement at all at this level, when it comes to the issue of water distribution in Dhaka and Metropolitan Manila.

Forms of Power

The third component of Gaventa's power cube relates to the forms of power, or the dynamics of power that play the decisive role regarding the inclusion of various groups in each space. Gaventa's three forms of power—visible, hidden, and invisible—are adapted from Lisa Veneklaseen and Valerie Miller.[94]

Visible Power: This refers to observable structures of political power as well as decision-making procedures. This form of exercising power is relatively democratic and accountable because the approaches that follow are usually attempts to alter the "who, how and what" of policymaking.

Hidden Power: In this type of power relation, a certain group of influential people maintain their authority through institutions "by controlling who gets to the decision-making table and what gets on the agenda."[95] Less powerful people's agendas and participations are "excluded" and "devalued" in this power dimension.

Invisible Power: This is the most "insidious" form of power dimension, which "shapes the psychological and ideological boundaries of participation." Important agendas and concerns are not placed on the decision-making table, but rather are kept away from the psyches and perceptions of the different actors, even from those who deal directly with the agendas. Powerful persons use this dimension of power to shape "people's beliefs, sense of self and acceptance of the *status quo*, even their own superiority or inferiority" by influencing their thought process regarding their role in the society.[96] Even stakeholders' or actors' voices in the "invited spaces" are controlled and echoed according to the powerful persons who created or shaped the spaces.

My research investigates these forms of power to understand the nature of decision-making procedures in the spaces created by both the state and PPP governance systems in Dhaka and Metropolitan Manila.

Literature Review

Although a good number of books and articles have been written on the management of water resources, none have yet conducted a comparative study regarding the issue of marginalized women's capabilities over supplied water resources in Dhaka and Metropolitan Manila from the perspective of Sen's "capabilities" approach. Also, none of them have discussed the necessity of developing an alternative governance model to incorporate the inputs of marginalized women into the governance mechanism. Almost all of the studies in general either deal with the role of the transnational corporations in managing water sectors, or examine the privatization policies of the World Bank, the IMF, the WTO, and various agreements of the international water trade.

Some of the studies discuss the laws related to water rights, whereas others concentrate on analyzing the efficiency or inefficiency of water markets. For example, Peter Gleick and colleagues discuss various issues related to water resources, such as the efficient use of water, the quality of bottled water, water conservation, and the assessment of the worldwide supply of groundwater. The authors propose some "principles" for water corporations and the governments. They assert that water companies and governments should recognize water as a "social good," and that water and water-related services should be distributed at "fair and reasonable rates."[97] However, they do not elaborate upon the meaning of fair and reasonable rates. They do not examine whether the governments and water corporations are conducting business according to their proposed principles. Gleick et al. are also not interested in the human capability to establish command over water; rather they pay attention to the formulation of policy guidelines for the governments and water corporations, based on the assumption that water is a "social good," not simply a commodity.

Vandana Shiva analyzes various conflicts camouflaged as ethnic or religious wars in modern times, which were basically conflicts about establishing authority over a valuable natural resource—water. By paying special attention to "the historical erosion of communal water rights," she examines how transnational water trade, damming, mining, and aqua farming not only caused environmental degradation, but also deprived people of their rights to water resources.[98]

Like Shiva, Jeff Rothfeder also argues against the process of water privatization. He considers water to be a right rather than a commodity or "need."[99] Therefore, private management of water would not ensure this right due to the profit motives of water companies. In addition, using an example from Cochabamba, Bolivia, Rothfeder argues that privatization of water might lead to a "water war" between local residents and private corporations.

Matthias Finger and Jeremy Allouche advocate for the "re-regulation" of the water sector instead of management by transnational corporations.[100] In contrast, by reviewing the policy details about the world's largest water privatization initiative in Metropolitan Manila, Mark Dumol argues for privatization.[101] Narelle Martin adopts a different approach to privatization. After examining the "corporatization" of the water industry in Victoria, Australia, he concludes that in addition to privatization, it is imperative to develop corporate accountability for the "substantial improvement" of water services.[102]

On the issue of public policy toward water management, Raul Rodriguez suggests an alternative proposal. Instead of supporting or opposing water privatization, he argues for "a refined model" of public-private partnership with the involvement of local stockholders. However, in this joint venture, Rodriguez asserts that governments should play "major roles" to ensure "affordability and equity for the poor."[103] Although his discussion mentions the issue of equity, the issue of the capability to ensure equity is ignored.

By examining water privatization efforts in France and the United Kingdom, Mohammed H. I. Dore and coauthors draw the conclusion that private management of water sectors does not have an "absolute efficiency advantage" in producing drinking water.[104] Maria Luisa Corton argues for some kind of regulatory action in water sectors rather than completely relying on corporations for distribution.[105] She advocates for regulation because, in the context of Peru, her study shows that after 8 years of the privatization process, 50 percent of water companies have experienced financial losses. Corton believes that regulatory action would prevent such losses in the water business.

Like Corton, Karen Bakker also prefers public-sector management of water resources because water is "not only physically produced, but also socially enacted." According to her, the concept of scarcity of water is a construction that is "both structural to and highly functional for capitalism" and thus opens up avenues for marketization.[106]

Finally, in comparison to others, Paul Trawick presents a completely novel argument for managing water sectors. According to him, state, corporate, and public-private partnership are all unable to ensure equity in the distribution of water. Instead, after reviewing water privatization in Peru, he proposes community management based on the experience of the indigenous Andean community, which he defines as the "Andean model of management."[107]

Methodology

This study employs a comparative method to analyze the effects of the two governance systems on the two capabilities that are central to women's functioning—participation in the decision-making spaces and access to supplied water resources. This research investigates the space, levels, and forms of power interacting within the governance systems to understand the types of marginalized women's participation in these systems. The purpose of this investigation is to understand the role of marginalized women in the governance systems, whether they are active agents or passive recipients (or recipients at all), when it comes to the issue of obtaining water resources.

Political capability refers to marginalized women's capabilities to contribute to final decisions through participating in formal decision-making spaces. A *basic* material capability refers to women's relative control over the quantity, price, and quality of supplied water. Therefore, the social justice in water distribution is measured in terms of marginalized women's capabilities to participate in the formal decision-making spaces and to obtain a minimum requirement of water, that is, the minimum quantity, affordable price, and acceptable quality of water.

Although qualitative analysis is the basic approach in this research, empirical data are used to operationalize important concepts such as minimum quantity and price. In other words, the purpose of combining the two methodologies is to verify the qualitative findings through the empirical scrutiny of quantitative data. In addition, I use causal analysis to examine under what type of governance—state or PPP—marginalized women have more capabilities to participate and to obtain water.

The central concept in this study is "capabilities." The general meaning of this concept closely follows Sen, but indicators for the concept vary across the cases because of the different political-economic contexts. In contrast, the concepts of social justice and of state and PPP governance systems remain the same regardless of the context. The minimum distribution of water also varies depending on the publicly acceptable definitions for each city; however, the research carefully follows the definition that has been worked out by the people, their governments, and NGOs for each location.

The major limitation of this study is the problem of controlling important factors in "small n" research, such as legislative requirements, political culture, and others. This research also has the problem of selection bias (here comparing two cities from different countries). The advantage of small n research is the opportunity to establish some controls by selecting case studies from different countries: both the cities belong to developing states, for example, and they have both experienced a military regime. In this research, I established control on factors that are similar across the countries, while concentrating on other factors that are different but significant for the outcome. I use the following capability indicators.

Political Capability: Participation

Participation is an important indicator for marginalized women's capabilities, especially for political capabilities. If there is a high level of participation in governance systems, there are relatively higher political capabilities for women, and vice versa. Marginalized women's participation may also influence the other indicators: the quantity, quality, and price of water. Women's participation in the water boards (active or passive) means that they have access to the spaces created by the boards. Participation in these spaces promotes and enhances their interests and reflects their relatively higher political capabilities. Lack of participation means that they have relatively lower political capabilities and as a result, they do not have the ability to influence the indicators mentioned below.

Basic Material Capability: The Quantity, Price, and Quality of Water

1. Quantity
 • The indicator of quantity is directly related to the concept of material capability because a decrease in quantity reduces women's capabilities to obtain water and vice versa. This study uses the minimum supply of water per person per day as defined by the WHO.
 • The number of hours per day that water is available (minimal interruption) directly affects women's capabilities; less interruption indicates that women have higher capabilities, and vice versa.

2. Price
 • The price of water is directly related to women's capabilities. If the price of water goes up, their access goes down, and vice versa.

3. Quality
 • A supply of low-quality water reduces women's capabilities because, in such a context, they have to spend extra time, energy, and money to collect potable (suitable for consumption) water from other sources. Therefore, the supply of low-quality water ultimately reduces their capabilities regarding obtaining water.

I employ Gaventa's power cube theory—space and forms of power typologies—in this research to measure the political capability of marginalized women, that is, their capability to participate in the decision-making spaces created by the state and PPP governance systems in Dhaka and Metropolitan Manila, respectively. The governance mechanisms of these two cities provide examples that illustrate the space and forms of power within the systems. The purpose of the study is to understand the nature of engagement among different groups in a particular space and how powerful players determine the inclusion of various groups in each space. The nature of engagement and the role of power determine the patterns of women's participation or non-participation in the spaces created by the governance mechanisms mentioned above.

The fieldwork for this research mainly involved conducting interviews with economically marginalized women living in slum and non-slum areas, local NGO activists, water board members, and water company officials. Marginalized women were defined as women living in slum areas or women who are paid low wages. The easiest way to locate marginalized women in Dhaka and Metropolitan Manila is therefore to visit the slums, where a good number of women are doing all kinds of low-paid jobs. I collected data that would quantify distribution priorities, including planning documents versus actual distribution to users, as well as data regarding the quantity, quality, and pricing of water (e.g. sliding scale vs. contracted pricing vs. actual prices).

Significance of the Study

The significance of this study is that it contributes to the discussion of the interplay between governance and equitable people's capacities, further facilitating the analysis of the effects of governance on the expansion of marginalized women's capabilities. No research has yet been conducted in the contexts of Dhaka and Metropolitan Manila that analyzes the relationship between governance systems and marginalized women's capabilities with regard to their participation in the decision-making spaces and their access to supplied water resources through the lens of Sen's capability approach.

Perhaps the most important contribution of this study is to analyze capabilities from the perspective of marginalized women. Further, this study offers marginalized-women centered deliberative, reflexive alternative governance paradigm to include the input of the marginalized women in the governance system.

Limitations of the Study

One of the major limitations of this study was that I was not able to systematically interview the poor women and people in various slums across Metropolitan Manila to obtain an overall understanding of their opinions regarding the private sector involvement in the distribution process. Another major limitation of this study was the communication problem with the women in Metropolitan Manila, due to the language barrier; I had to rely on a translator. In addition, a good number of people in slums considered me to be an outsider, and therefore, it appeared to me that they were not that willing to talk about the negative aspects of their country (problems of managing water resources by the private corporations). I was thus not able to communicate with them as efficiently as I communicated with the women in Dhaka. Therefore, I had to rely on a small number of women to understand the political and material capabilities of the marginalized women living in the city. Concerning the material capabilities of women in Dhaka, I was not able to determine exactly how much water they were able to collect per day from DWASA sources for meeting their daily needs.

I was also unable to collect detailed information about the grassroots organizations active in the claimed spaces in either Dhaka or Metropolitan Manila. As my focus was on the formal spaces in the two cities, I did not directly investigate the nature of political organizing (e.g., degree of participation, hierarchies) in the informal spaces. This study did address the interaction between the informal and formal, with the findings demonstrating that it is sporadic; most often, those operating in the informal sectors are reduced to protests in order to try to change formal policies.

Overview of Chapters

The second chapter discusses various governance paradigms and their limitations in providing the minimum requirements of supplied water to marginalized women and the urban poor. It also indicates that the major shortcoming is their inability to create spaces for people who are economically marginalized in society to take part in the decision-making process. The third chapter focuses on marginalized women's capabilities under the state-led governance in Dhaka in terms of their participation in decision-making spaces and their access to supplied water resources. The fourth chapter examines the capabilities of marginalized women in Metropolitan Manila under PPP governance. The fifth, concluding chapter proposes an alternative paradigm to integrate the inputs from the marginalized women into the governance system.

Notes

1. Cited in Jeffrey Rothfeder, *Every Drop for Sale: Our Desperate Battle over Water in a World About to Run Out* (Washington, DC: International Thompson Publishing, 2001), front flap.

2. Another estimate shows that only 0.0008 percent of the world's water is fit for drinking (see Rothfeder, back flap). By 2000, the total withdrawal of freshwater had tripled in comparison to 1950, from 1365 km3/yr to 3773 km3/yr. The values includes Asia at 2297 km3/yr, Europe at 377 km3/yr, Africa at 207 km3/yr, North and Central America at 708 km3/yr, South America at 164 km3/yr, and Oceania at 20 km3/yr. (data for the year 2000, computed by the author). Peter Gleick et al., *The World's*

Water: The Biennial Report on Freshwater Resources, 2004–2005 (Washington and London: Island Press, 2004) 265–271 and UNDP *Human Development Report 1998* (Oxford and New York: Oxford University Press, 1998) 55. The availability of fresh water also decreased severely from about 16,800 km3 per capita per year in 1950 to 7,300 km3/yr in 1995. Due to groundwater over-pumping and aquifer depletion, it is not possible to replenish the depleted water. In Beijing, in the past 40 years, the water table has declined by 37 meters. As a result of over-pumping, in and around Bangkok, the land has sunk 5–10 centimeters per year for the last two decades. In the Middle East and North African regions, there has been more use of water than recharge. If the current trend of water use persists, within 50 years there will be absolutely no ground water in these regions (UNDP 55).

3. UNICEF, WHO, "Meeting the MDG Drinking Water and Sanitation Target," (UNICEF, WHO 2004). 3 Feb 2005 <http://www.unicef.org/wes/mdgreport/dispari-ties2.php>.

4. Water Supply and Sanitation Collaborative Council, *Global Water Supply and Sanitation Assessment 2000 Report* (United States of America: WHO, UNICEF, 2000) 9.

5. Gleick 2.

6. UNICEF, WHO 1.

7. In Latin America and the Caribbean region, over the same period, there would be a 50 percent increase of population (UNICEF, WHO 1). If the present trend of population growth persists, by 2025, there would be 5.0 billion people who would not have access to clean water. Currently 1.7 billion people, who constitute one third of the developing world's population, live in countries that are under water stress. A water-stressed country is defined as a country using more than 20 percent of its renewable water resources each year (UNDP 125). According to one estimate, by 2020, two thirds of the world population will run short of potable water, if the current rates of population increase and developing infrastructures continue. Public Citizen, "Water Privatization Backgrounder," *Public Citizen,* 1 May 2007. http://www.citizen .org/ cmep/Water/activist/articles.cfm?ID=9589>.

8. Gleick xv.

9. United Nations General Assembly Resolution 64/292, United Nations. Water is a "common pool resource;" it could also be used as an economic good. However, under certain circumstances, a "common property regime performs bet-ter than private property." Thomas Dietz et al., "The Drama of the Commons," In Elinor Ostrom et al., eds., *The Drama of the Commons* (Washington, DC: National Academy Press, 2003) 15. Those who consider water as a human right believe that water is a public good, and argue for decentralization of water management for "local development (and) human environmental needs." Those who consider water as a commodity stand for market-led governance of water resource management and support "profit over social welfare and environmental quality concerns." Bar-bara Rose Johnston, "The Political Ecology of Water: An Introduction," *Capitalism, Nature, Socialism* 14 (2003) 73–90. WHO, UNICEF, and FAO are in favor of ad-dressing water issues as a basic human right. On the contrary, the World Bank con-siders water an "economic good" rather than a fundamental right, "subject to the rules and power of markets, prices, multinational corporations, and international

trading regimes." According to the Bank, market-led governance would ensure more efficiency in the distribution of water and improve the quality of water. The United Nations Economic and Social Council states that "the human right to water entitles everyone to sufficient, safe, acceptable, physically accessible and affordable water for personal and domestic use." Cited in general comment 15 (2) of the Committee on Economic, Social, and Cultural Rights; Economic and Social Council of the United Nations (Gleick 45). The 1992 International Conference on Water and the Environment adopted four principles, known as the Dublin Principles: 1 – Fresh water is a finite and vulnerable resource, essential to sustain life, development, and the environment. 2 – Water development and management should be based on a participatory approach, involving users, planners, and policy-makers at all levels. 3 – Women play a central part in the provision, management, and safeguarding of water. 4 – Water has an economic value in all its competing uses and should be recognized as an economic good. Including the World Bank, various international, multilateral and bilateral agencies have accepted the Dublin Principles. Karen Bakker, "Archipelagos and Networks: Urbanization and Water Privatization in the South," *The Geographical Journal* 169.4 (2003) 339. http://www.un.org/ga/search/view_doc.asp?symbol=A/RES/64/292

10. World Water Assessment Programme, *Water, a Shared Responsibility: The United Nations World Water Development Report 2* (Paris, New York: UNESCO and Berghahn Books, 2006) 61.

11   The World Bank, "Access to Safe Water" (26 July, 2012). <http://www.worldbank.org/depweb/english/modules/environm/water/print.html>

12. In 1999, the Asian Development Bank defined poverty as "a deprivation of essential assets and opportunities to which every human is entitled." Quoted in Junio M. Ragaragio, "The Case of Metro Manila, Philippines," Massachusetts Institute of Technology (22 Mar 2008). <http://web.mit.edu/ sigus/www/NEW/challengecourse/pdfs/pdfscities/Manila.pdf>. The "highest number of poor" lives in South Asia. Position Paper of the South Asia Sub-Region, "Towards Reducing Poverty and Vulnerability in South Asia." Asia-Pacific Regional Document of the 4th World Water Forum (16–22 March 2006) 5. Only one percent of the population belongs to the other ethnic groups in Bangladesh. They mainly live in the other parts of the country, not in Dhaka. Therefore, there is no ethnic discrimination issue involved as far as Dhaka is concerned. I also did not come across any cases in Manila that indicated some households are not receiving water because they belong to different ethnic groups. In fact, I have not come across any literature about this issue. "Class" invokes relation to production and general consumption. I am referring to marginalized women in terms of their residence and non-access to water. "Residence" is not the only indicator of class. Therefore, instead of class, I use the term "marginalized" in my study.

13. "Household water security" is a new concept which means "timely availability of safe water in adequate quantities to meet household water requirements." Position Paper of the South Asia Sub-Region, 5.

14. Begum Shamsun Nahar, "Gender, Water and Poverty Experiences from Water Resource Management Projects in Bangladesh," presented in *Regional Workshop on Water and Poverty*, Dhaka (22–26 Sept 2002) 4.

15. In addition, because women are mainly taking care of sick children, this responsibility may also increase "their exposure to disease-causing organisms," which mainly spread through water. UNDP 80.

16. Lack of proper sanitation leads to health problems, such as urinary tract infections and chronic constipation. It poses more problems for the sick, pregnant, and post-partum women living in the slum or poor areas of the cities. For the types of water-borne diseases, see Appendix, Table 3.

17. Arjun Appadurai, "Deep Democracy: Urban Governmentality and the Horizon of Politics," *Public Culture* 14.1 (2002) 26.

18. John Soussan, *Water and Poverty: Fighting Poverty through Water Management* (Manila: Asian Development Bank, 2004) 3.

19. Anges Balota, *Water Advocates' Resource Book: Planning for Community-Based Integrated Water Resource Management, Vol. 3* (The Philippines: Tambuyog Development Center, Water Commons Institute, 2005) 11.

20. State and market-led governance mechanisms are discussed in detail in the next chapter.

21. Karen Bakker, "Archipelagos and Networks: Urbanization and Water Privatization in the South," *The Geographical Journal* 169.4 (2003) 331.

22. Although privatization often refers to commercialization, commercialization and privatization are not always "concomitant." Some public water sectors also run on a fully commercial basis, for example in Amsterdam, the Netherlands. On the contrary, in the developing world, most of the cases of public-private partnerships set up an arrangement for providing concessions "in the form of direct or cross subsidy" to the consumers who are unable to pay for water. Without any form of private control of infrastructure, competition may take place for the market. In France, water supply infrastructures are controlled by the municipalities and they "may choose to tender water services out to private companies who compete for long-term contracts." Thus privatization and commercialization may be a different form of transfiguration of water sector management. See Bakker 331.

23. In economics, a "natural monopoly" arises if it is not profitable for a second company to enter into the competition because of the highly fixed cost of capital goods. In such a situation, a single company is the sole provider of a specific type of manufactured good or a particular service. There is a "natural" reason for some industries to become a "monopoly, namely that the economies of scale require one, rather than several, firms. Small-scale ownership would be less efficient." See Fred E. Foldvary, "Natural Monopolies," Jan 1999. *The Progress Report* (27 Feb 2005). <http://www.progress.org/archive/ fold74.htm>. Usually, natural monopolies arise in public utilities, such as water, electricity, sewerage, and natural gas. It is very expensive to construct these infrastructures in a city. Their delivery service "has a high fixed cost and a low variable cost." See Flodvary. Typically, one or two companies have cost advantages over other competing companies, thus barring other competitors entering the market.

24. Martha Nussbaum, "Capabilities As Fundamental Entitlements: Sen and Social Justice," *Feminist Economics* 9.2 (2003) 47.

25. John M. Alexander, "Capability Egalitarianism and Moral Selfhood," *Ethical Perspectives* 10.1 (2003) 16.

26. In this study, the words system and mechanism are used interchangeably.

27. The terms political and basic material capabilities are explained in the Capability Approach section. However, "everybody's needs" is a relative term, which varies from person to person and also depends on a person's preference for using water. According to WHO, 7 liters per person per day(lpcd)—which includes 3–4 lpcd for drinking and 2–3 lpcd for food preparation and clean up—is the "minimum survival allocation," while 15–20 lpcd is the "medium term allocation" of water (as above plus 6–7 lpcd for personal hygiene and 4–6 lpcd for laundry). See WHO, "Minimum Water Quantity Needed for Domestic Use in Emergencies," *Technical Note* 3 (2005) 2–3. NGOs working to supply potable water in slum areas in Dhaka accepted 20–40 lpcd as the minimum requirement of water. Based on interviews with Zakir Hossain, Senior Project Coordinator, Water and Sanitation Project, Dushtha Shaystha Kendra (DSK) and Mobasser Hossain Ripon, Engineer, Association for Realization of Basic Needs (ARBAN).

28. Amartya Sen, "Equality of What?" In Sterling M. McMurrin, ed. *Tanner Lectures on Human Values* (Cambridge: Cambridge University Press, 1980).

29. Manoj Sharma, "Capability Theory for Use in Alcohol and Drug Education Research," *Journal of Alcohol & Drug Education* 48.1 (2004); see also Ingrid Robeyns, "Sen's Capability Approach and Gender Inequality: Selecting Relevant Capabilities," *Feminist Economics* 9.2–3 (2003) 61–62.

30. Martha Nussbaum, *Women and Human Development: The Capabilities Approach* (United Kingdom: Cambridge University Press, 2000) 12; Jerome Ballet, Jean-Luc Dubois, and Francois-Regis Mahieu, "Responsibility for Each Other's Freedom: Agency As the Source of Collective Capability," *Journal of Human Development* 8.2 (2007) 192; see also Amartya Sen, *On Ethics and Economics* (Oxford: Blackwell, 1987).

31. Pinar Uyan-Semerci, "A Relational Account of Nussbaum's List of Capabilities," *Journal of Human Development* 8.2 (2007) 203.

32. Nussbaum 12.

33. Peter Evans, "Collective Capabilities, Culture, and Amartya Sen's Development As Freedom," *Studies in Comparative International Development* 37.2 (2002) 55.

34. Amartya Sen, *Commodities and Capabilities* (India: Oxford University Press, 1999) Preface.

35. Uyan-Semerci; also Robeyns, and also Thomas W. Pogge, "Can the Capability Approach be Justified?" *Philosophical Topics* 30.2 (2002).

36. Robeyns 65.

37. Jerome Ballet, Jean-Luc Dubois, and Francois-Regis Mahieu 192; see also Anthony Giddens, *The Transformation of Intimacy: Sexuality, Love, and Eroticism in Modern Societies* (California: Stanford University Press, 1993).

38. Sony Pelisesery and Sylvia I. Bergh, "Adapting the Capability Approach to Explain the Effects of Participatory Development Programs: Case Studies from India and Morocco," *Journal of Human Development* 8.2 (2007) 285.

39. Evans 56.

40. Ballet, Dubois, and Mahieu 199.

41. Alkire 131.

42. Amartya Sen, *Development as Freedom* (New York: Knopf, 1999) 10–17.

43. Alkire 131.

44. Jean Dreze and Amartya Sen, *Hunger and Public Action* (Oxford: Clarendon Press, 1989); Jean Dreze and Amartya Sen, *India: Economic Development and Social Opportunity* (Delhi: Oxford University Press, 1995).

45. In Dhaka and Metropolitan Manila, the term subaltern refers to people who belong to the marginalized groups (economic, political, religious, or ethnic) and the underclasses. The location of subalternity is "relational and relative; therefore in some local or regional situations or under certain circumstances any of them could act as or for the 'elite.'" Sayeed Iftekhar Ahmed, "Resurgence of Islam in Bangladesh Politics," *South Asian Journal* 11 (2006) 159. Economically (and other) marginalized women in Dhaka and Metropolitan Manila live in extreme subaltern locations in comparison to their male counterparts.

46. Uyan-Semerci 205. Frances Stewart analyzes capabilities from a group instead of an individual perspective because "the quality of groups with which individuals identify forms an important direct contribution to their well-being, is instrumental to other capabilities, and influences people's choices and values." Frances Stewart, "Groups and Capabilities," *Journal of Human Development* 6.2 (2005) 185.

47. However, the problem of focusing on a group instead of an individual is that it could hide many forms of inequality and deprivation to the individuals "belonging to the collectives." Alexander 11.

48. Alexander 205.

49. Besides Nussbaum, Alkire and Black also develop a universal list of capabilities. For details, see Sabina Alkire and Rufus Black, "A Practical Reasoning Theory of Development Ethics: Furthering the Capabilities Approach," *Journal of International Development* 9.2 (1997).

50. Bina Agarwal et al., "Exploring the Challenges of Amartya Sen's Work and Ideas: An Introduction," *Feminist Economics* 9.2–3 (2003) 6.

51. Robeyns 75.

52. Uyan-Semerci 203.

53. Uyan-Semerci 6.

54. For details, see Nussbaum 78–80.

55. Sabine Alkire argues that "some capabilities may be so basic to human welfare" compared to others. Basic capabilities are part of "the full capability set," although the definition of the basic is relative and depends on spatial and temporal domains. This study suggests that the capability of accessing a minimal requirement of supplied water in Dhaka and Metropolitan Manila is a basic material capability for marginalized women because this is clearly related to their "life/health security." Sabina Alkire, *Valuing Freedoms: Sen's Capability Approach and Poverty Reduction* (New York: Oxford University Press, 2002) 154, 162, and 166. The water supplied by the water boards is the major source of obtaining potable water for the residents living in Dhaka and Metropolitan Manila. Therefore, access to supplied water resources is a basic material capability for the marginalized women living in these two cities.

56. Alexander identifies nourishments, health as well as some "more complex" functionings such as self-respect and participation as basic capabilities. Alexandar 4–5. However, this study argues that participation is a desired capability instead of

basic because it is not an important functioning to sustain or survive like water or health care.

57. The World Bank refers to participation as engaging local communities at all phases of planning, execution, and development procedures. World Bank, *The World Bank: Participation Source Book* (Washington DC: The World Bank, 1996).

58. James Blackburn and Jeremy Holland, "General Introduction." In James Blackburn and Jeremy Holland, eds., *Who Changes? Institutionalizing Participation in Development* (London: International Technology Publications, 1998) 1. The acronym PRA has long been known as participatory rural appraisal. A consensus has been developed among the scholars that the two words rural and appraisal are no longer sufficient to explain the approach because their implementations are no longer limited to rural areas, and are also not restricted in territorial vicinity. This approach is now used in urban areas and for explaining institutions. PRA is used not only for appraisal, but also for implementation, monitoring and evaluation, and related activities.

59. Alkire 129.

60. Uma Kothari, "Power Knowledge and Social Control in Participatory Development." In Bill Cooke and Uma Kothari, eds., *Participation: The New Tyranny* (London: Zed Books, 2001) 140.

61. Lisa Veneklasen and Valerie Miller, eds., *A New Wave of Power, People & Politics: The Action Guide for Advocacy and Citizen Participation* (UK: Practical Action Publishing, 2007) 2.

62. Severine Deneulin, "Promoting Human Freedoms Under Conditions of Inequalities: A Procedural Framework," *Journal of Human Development* 6.1 (2005) 77.

63. Alkire 129–130.

64. Alkire 131–143. She further mentions that participation "can also have intrinsic value" because it is the significant means of attaining "friendship, sociability, and sense of community," 131.

65. Marshall Wolfe, *Participation: The View from Above* (Geneva: UNRISD, 1983) 2.

66. Dharam Ghai, "Participatory Development: Some Perspectives from Grass-Roots Experiences," *UNRISD Discussion Paper* 3 (1988) 14.

67. Deneulin.

68. Iris Marion Young, "Political Debate and Social Justice," *Maitree* 4 (206) 3.

69. Jay Drydyk, "When Is Development More Democratic?" *Journal of Human Development* 6.2 (2005) 261. For describing the context of exclusion of women from the development process in Gambia, Alamgir discusses how difficulties arose in a smallholder project there because land allocation committees were unable to provide assurance for the right of entry for poor women to the newly cleared swampland. "This was because the committees, designed to give women full representation, were gradually co-opted by the men who did the clearing work." Mahiuddin Alamgir, "Participatory Development: The IFAD Experience." In W. Lineberry, ed., *Assessing Participatory Development; Rhetoric Versus Reality* (Boulder: Westview Press, 1989) 16.

70. Andrea Cornwell, "Whose Voices? Whose Choices? Reflections on Gender and Participatory Development," *World Development* 31.8 (2003) 1329–1330.

71. For details, see Bina Agarwal, "Participatory Exclusions, Community Forestry, and Gender: An Analysis for South Asia and a Conceptual Framework," *World*

Development 29.10 (2001) 1626. Agarwal identifies the following causal factors that excluded (marginalized) women from participation: formal statutes that bar women from being a part of a group; social norms, such as gender segregation in public places; the gender division of labor that keeps women busy in household work, hence, they have very little time to participate in activities outside their households; gendered behavioral patterns that stress "self-effacement, shyness and soft speech;" social perception regarding inferior participation ability of women; men's traditional authority over social structures; and women's lack of personal possessions.

72. For examples, see Sanjay Kumar and Stuart Corbridge, "Programmed to Fail? Development Projects and the Politics of Participation," *The Journal of Development Studies* 39.2 (2002); Glyn Williams, "Evaluating Participatory Development: Tyranny, Power, and (Re)politicization," *Third World Quarterly* 25.3 (2004); Cooke and Kothari; Majid Rahnema, "Participation," in Wolfgang Sachs, ed., *The Development Dictionary: A Guide to Knowledge as Power* (London: Zed Books, 1992); William Easterly, *The White Man's Burden: Why the West's Efforts to Aid the Rest Have Done So Much Ill and So Little* (New York: Penguin Press, 2006).

73. John Gaventa and Andrea Cornwell, "Challenging the Boundaries of the Possible: Participation, Knowledge and Power," *IDS Bulletin* 37.6 (2006) 126. Rahnema (see previous note) expresses doubts whether participatory approaches can bring any "substantial change" in the development process by "halting the processes of domination, manipulation and colonization of the mind" or is it simply a substitute of the old pattern of participatory process in a more subtle way, which simply reproduces the domination of the elites.

74. For the discussion of how participatory development can produce tyranny and reinforce "oppressions and injustices in their various manifestations," see Cooke Kothari (3), who wrote that "tyranny is both a real and a potential consequence of participatory development, counter-intuitive and contrary to its rhetoric of empowerment though this may be." The pitfall of participatory approach is that it "reinscribes power relations between expert and other." Mohan Giles, "Beyond Participation: Strategies for Deeper Empowerment," 158.

75. For details, see Denis Goulet, *Development Ethics: A Guide to Theory and Practice* (London: Zed Books) 1995.

76. Crocker 2.

77. Agarwal (2001), 1624.

78. For details, see Sherry R. Arnstein, "A Ladder of Citizen Participation," *Journal of the American Institute of Planners* 35.4 (1969) 216–224.

79. David Crocker "Deliberative Participation in Local Development," *Journal of Human Development* 8.3 (2007) 432–433. See Jules N. Pretty, "Alternative Systems of Inquiry for Sustainable Agriculture," *IDS Bulletin* 25.2 (1994); John Gaventa, "The Scaling-Up and Institutionalization of PRA: Lessons and Challenges," in James Blackburn and Jeremy Holland, eds., *Who Changes? Institutionalizing Participation in Development* (London: Intermediate Technology Publications 1998); Agarwal (2001); and Drydyk (2005). In addition, also see, Sarah C. White, "Depoliticising Development: The Uses and Abuses of Participation," *Development in Practice* 6.1 (1996), pp. 6–15.

80. Glyn Williams, "Evaluating Participatory Development: Tyranny, Power and (Re)politicization," *Third World Quarterly* 25.3 (2004) 567.

81. John Gaventa, "Finding the Spaces for Change: A Power Analysis," *IDS Bulletin* 37.6 (2006) 23–33.

82. Rubik's cube is a mechanical cube invented by a Hungarian architect, professor, and sculptor named Erno Rubik in 1974. It was marketed worldwide as a puzzle. The sides of the cube can spin, although the entire body remains intact.

83. For the concept of political spaces, see N. Webster and L. Engberg-Petersen, eds., *In the Name of the Poor: Contesting Political Space for Poverty Reduction* (London: Zed Books, 2002); for policy spaces, see Rosemary McGee, "Unpacking Policy Actors, Knowledge and Spaces," in Karen Brock, Rosemary McGee and John Gaventa, eds., *Unpacking Policy: Actors, Knowledge and Spaces in Poverty Reduction in Uganda and Nigeria* (Kampala: Fountain Press, 2004) 16; and for democratic spaces, see Andrea Cornwell and V. Coehlo, eds., *Spaces for Change? The Politics of Citizen Participation in New Democratic Arenas* (London: Zed Books, 2006).

84. Quoted in Gaventa 26; see also Andrea Cornwall, "Making Spaces, Changing Places: Situation Participation in Development," *IDS Working Paper* 170 (2002).

85. Henri Lefebvre, *The Production of Space* (London: Verso, 1991) 24.

86. Gaventa.

87. C. R. Hayward, "De-Facing Power," *Polity* 31.1 (1998) 2.

88. Gaventa 27.

89. Gaventa 26.

90. Gaventa 27.

91. E. Soja, *Third Space: Journeys to Los Angeles and Other Imagined Places* (Cambridge, MA: Blackwell, 1996).

92. Gaventa 27.

93. Gaventa 28.

94. For details, see Veneklasen and Miller 47–50.

95. Veneklasen and Miller 29.

96. Veneklasen and Miller 29.

97. Gleick et al.

98. Vandana Shiva, *Water Wars: Privatization, Pollution and Profit* (Cambridge, MA: South End Press, 2002), back flap.

99. Rothfeder.

100. Matthias Finger and Jerremy Allouche, *Water Privatization: Transnational Corporations and the Re-Regulation of Water Industry* (UK: Spon Press 2001).

101. Mark Dumol, *Manila Water Concession: A Key Government Official's Diary of the World's Largest Water Privatization* (Washington DC: World Bank Publications, 2000).

102. Narelle Martin, "Corporations As a Means of Improving Water Quality: The Experience in Victoria, Australia," *Journal of Toxicology and Environmental Health: Part A*, 67 (2004) 1889.

103. Raul Rodriguez, "The Debate on Privatization of Water Utilities: A Commentary," *International Journal of Water Resources Development* 20 (2004) 107.

104. Mohammed H. I. Dore, Joseph Kushner, and Klemen Zumer, "Privatization of Water in the U.K. and France—What Can We Learn?" *Utilities Policy* 12 (2004) 41–51.

105. Maria Luisa Corton, "Benchmarking in the Latin American Water Sector: The Case of Peru," *Utilities Policy* 11 (2003) 133–143.

106. Karen J. Bakker, "A Political Ecology of Water Privatization," *Studies in Political Economy* 70 (2003) 49, 51.

107. Paul Trawick, "Against the Privatization of Water: An Indigenous Model for Improving Laws and Successfully Governing the Commons," *World Development* 31 (2003) 77–97.

2

Governance Paradigms and the Capabilities of Marginalized Women

> *Creating participatory institutions for public service provision is inherently political. The process will take time and cause conflict, and it will not result in perfectly representative governance.*

Tim Kessler, Citizen's Network on Essential Services[1]

> *We cannot only defend the maintenance of the status quo, which is not very good in developing countries. We can change reality, improving the quality of public services through popular participation, through mechanisms of social control.*

Antonio da Costa Miranda, Municipal Director for
Water and Sanitation in Recife[2]

An important criticism of the conventional paradigms of governance is that they are not successful in recognizing the marginalized women's needs. They are not successful because poor women's participation in the decision-making process is very limited or nonexistent in the conventional governance systems. Even the Integrated Water Resource Management (IWRM) approach, which prescribes the increased involvement of women in drinking water and sanitation projects, fails to distinguish the needs of the marginalized women, who belong to the bottom rung of the social ladder, from those of "the people."[3] As mentioned in the previous chapter, as a social category, marginalized women are the poorest of the poor and they have less access to water compared to poor men and middle or upper class women.[4] Their role as "legitimate stakeholders in water-related decision-making" and their inputs and interests related to the networked-water supply are completely denied in typical water governance paradigms.[5]

This chapter discusses the various paradigms of governance with the goal of assessing the capabilities of marginalized women in terms of their participation in decision-making spaces and access to supplied water resources under the state and PPP governance systems in Dhaka and Metropolitan Manila.[6]

Governance and the Capability Approach

Governance plays an important role, and it "matters instrumentally" for socio-economic accomplishments, i.e. the mechanism and the objectives of the governance determine the patterns of achievement.[7] There is a strong relationship between governance—the allocation mechanism—and the capability of an individual to obtain access to resources.[8] The main criticism of the capability approach, which addresses the capabilities of individuals, is that "it leaves too many evaluative issues unresolved."[9] For example, despite its concern for actual opportunities to obtain resources, it does not pay enough attention to the allocation mechanism, which is crucial for determining the patterns of resource distribution—that is, who will get what and how. However, it stands for a choice-oriented and less paternalistic form of distribution. It "leaves room for individuals to decide for themselves," instead of distributing resources through "brilliant bureaucratic planning."[10]

This study argues that without proper institutional support (i.e. creating a space for all sections of the population in the governance system) it would not be possible to execute the idea of equitable popular capabilities. The capability approach ignores the issue of power in a hierarchical society, where the powerful have more capabilities than the less powerful. Establishing equitable access to supplied water is related to the issue of power because controlling the water supply is itself an act of power, and "those who control the flow of water in time and space can exercise this power in various ways."[11] Hence, the challenge is to empower women in a hierarchical society through their involvements (active or passive) in governance.

What Is Governance?

There is no single understanding of governance; it includes multiple forms. Society, economics, politics, culture, traditions, and the legislative practices of a particular country all shape the patterns of governance. Julius Court has stated that although it is "possible to identify concepts and principles of governance that are universal, they make no sense without contextual references."[12] The specific circumstances of a particular society, country, or organization determine "both constraints and opportunities to improve governance."[13] Financial accountability, administrative efficiency, participatory process, democratic management, transparency, responsiveness, inclusiveness, and politico-ecological systems are all associated with governance. It is also related to "the broader social system of governing," which incorporates the constricted view of government as the core "decision-making political entity"; however, it does not solely rely on it.[14]

A major responsibility of governance is the development of structures (institutional and administrative) and practices within which people from different strata of a society can peacefully negotiate their interests and organize activities on the basis of a broader consensus. Bob Jessop defines governance as the intricate maneuvering of various agencies, institutions, and systems that are both functionally independent from one another and organizationally connected through multiple forms of mutual interdependence.[15] Governance is focused on the process—"how things are done, not just what is done."[16]

Decision-making is another central aspect of governance. Governance is a complex issue; it has to deal with multiple forms of "inter-personal," inter-institutional, and "inter-systemic relations."[17] Governance is a holistic and dynamic concept, with precise goals. An inability to transform its mechanisms in changing socio, economic, political, and environmental contexts can lead to underperformance.

Governance entails *distributive* and *regulatory* mechanisms to manage economic and social resources. It also extensively appropriates the formal and informal traditions and institutions through which power and authority are exercised.[18] There is a profound element of political and social power involved in governance networks that is pivotal for allocating resources and maintaining equilibrium among different interests.[19] Thus, the challenge of placing the needs of the marginalized women at the hub of the governance as well as creating a space for them to participate in the decision-making process is to combine both the *"balance of power* and the balance of actions at *different levels of authority."*[20] Hence, governance is defined for this study as a complex dynamic mechanism that has the ability to maneuver various agencies, where multiple forms of social and political power play significant roles in the decision-making process for resource allocation and participation in decision-making spaces.

Paradigms of Governance

Because different paradigms of governance affect the distributive mechanism and management of resources in different ways—that is, who is entitled to get what and how—there is no ideal type of governance; social, economic, cultural, and political contexts as well as spatio-temporal domains shape the patterns of governance. Peter Rogers and Alan W. Hall have identified three models of governance: hierarchical, market-led, and distributed.[21] Karen Bakker refers to them as the planning model, market model, and hybrid model respectively. The distributed or hybrid model can also be known as a public-private partnership (PPP). This study refers to them as *state-led, market-led,* and *PPP* respectively.

The major characteristics of *state-led governance* are a centralized structure and "top-down" approach. The positive side of this governance system is that it could prevent the monopolies of the private corporation, when it comes to the issue of service or resource distribution. Moreover, like private corporations in market-led governance, this governance system is not profit-driven; hence, it may ensure services to a wider range of the population than market-led governance. Roger and Hall state that "there is a growing dissatisfaction with ineffective but costly state machinery, lack of vision or leadership, weak financial discipline and political dictates crippling administrative functions."[22] These phenomena are more or less prevalent in Bangladesh and the Philippines.

In emphasizing the causes of the failure of the planned model of state-governance, James C. Scott highlights four conditions that are, according to him, more or less common to any kind of state-led planning model: the state's endeavor to impose administrative regulation on nature and society; "a high-modernist ideology" that believes scientific intervention would eventually bring a positive change in society; the state's use of authoritarian power to "effect large-scale innovation"; and a "prostrate" civil society that is unable to oppose the state's development plan.[23] Moreover, this model of governance embraces a paternalistic form of distribution, and the state apparatus plays a significant role in this distribution pattern. Citizens under this mechanism are mainly the beneficiaries of the system as a result of good bureaucratic planning, rather than a part of it. Therefore, what Sen describes as "political freedoms" of the citizens—the possibility of developing this aspect of human capability—is low under state-led governance. Dissatisfaction with state-led governance has resulted in a growing worldwide trend of shifting towards "horizontal, hybridized, and associational forms of governance."[24]

The key features of *market-led governance* are less involvement by the public sector in resource distribution, reduction in government command of economic management, and "institutional restructuring" that will allow "private enterprises and the market" to take charge of resource allocation.[25] After the collapse of the Soviet Union and East European "socialist systems," many countries in the world have adopted a "free" market economy as the dominant path for economic development. Denationalization, deregulation, greater involvement of the private sectors, foreign direct investments by transnational enterprises, and removing trade "barriers" are major features of a free-market economy. These types of structural reform have helped to integrate national economies into the global capitalist economy. Theoretically, to achieve economic integration, market-friendly governance should reduce the role of the state in managing the economy, opening up new avenues for the private sector and the Transnational Corporations, and making the market the major mechanism for resource distribution. Market-led governance mainly pays attention to efficiency rather than the distributive aspect of governance.

Market-led governance advocates a market economy, yet a market economy might not fulfill the goal of relatively equitable distribution, although it has brought economic growth to a good number of less-developed countries. Despite economic growth and an abundance of commodities in the market, as a result of the absence of a fair distributive mechanism, marginalized people in the less-developed countries do not have adequate access to resources, which ultimately may lead to "demand failure."

In most developing economies the absence of a redistributive mechanism leads to the vast majority of the population being deprived of the benefits of a good supply of commodities in the market. The upper or middle class is the chief beneficiary of market-led governance, whereas the majority of the population lives in poverty. For example, if we consider $2 income per day as the poverty line, 80 percent of the population in India, Bangladesh, and Nepal, and 73.6 percent in Pakistan and Sri Lanka, are still poor.[26] As a result, these people are unable to articulate their demands in the market place and are unable to access the market, which ultimately leads to demand failure in the market-led governance system.

In contrast, *state-led governance* might create both "demand and supply failures." The absence of a redistributive mechanism and, as a result, the failure of the vast majority of the people to articulate their demands in the market place leads to the "demand failure." In addition, poor financial management, and the lack of supply of commodities in the market place might also lead to "supply failure" in many less-developed countries. The market-led, profit-driven governance system is not inclusive and thus, not interested in including all sections of the people in the decision-making process. Therefore, the "political capabilities" of individuals might not increase under the market-led governance system. Mainly a section of economically or politically powerful citizens are the beneficiaries of the market-led governance system in terms of political capability.

The inability of both state and market-led governance to ensure fair re-distribution, particularly in developing countries, brought forth the issue of replacing the existing networks of distribution. The role of the state in managing the economy and the ability of the market to allocate resources, especially to those who live below the poverty line, were being questioned by the members of national and global civil society and by NGO activists. The belief that neither the state nor the market was able to address social, economic, or environmental problems, or the needs of the poor, as well as the failure of the state and the market to ensure equity in distribution, has led to a new form of paradigm that Roger and Hall identified as *distributed governance*, and that Bakker calls the *hybrid model* of governance.[27] This paradigm is also known as a *public-private partnership* (PPP). Roger and Hall define distributed governance as "an institutional response to the changed environment. Distributive governance is thus the empirical manifestation of state adaptation to its external environment. It is the conceptual representation of the co-ordination of social systems and specifically the role of the state in that process."[28]

Therefore, we can say that the *PPP governance* system is the empirical manifestation of state management of the external affairs of private companies or corporations. The state sometimes manages these external affairs through a regulatory body; hence, PPP governance is a manifestation of public-private joint management—the adjustment of state and private enterprises, and the reorganization of distributive systems for the benefit of the customers or citizens depending on the context. In this system, both the state and private enterprises are in charge of distributing resources, and price plays an important role in determining who accesses water, although the state exercises regulatory control. Therefore, who will get what and how are decided by both the market and the state.

PPP governance, however, does not place socially and economically marginalized people or women at the center when it comes to the issue of resource distribution. There is no inherent mechanism in the framework of PPP governance through which the inputs of marginalized women could be included in the decision-making process. The focus of this model is the *customer* or *citizen*. In the developing world, especially in the Philippines and Bangladesh, marginalized women do not always have the capabilities to act as customers. Moreover, their citizenry role in the state and society is also invisible and peripheral. Therefore, the possibility for marginalized women to develop political capabilities is very limited in PPP governance. Moreover, it might not be possible to fulfill their minimum requirements of essential resources, such as supplied water, through PPP governance because their needs are not the prime focus of this governance system.

Besides the governance paradigms mentioned above, Bakker refers to another type of governance paradigm, a *community model*,[29] where both leaders and the members of the community make major decisions regarding the allocation of resources. Community members are also the owners and the managers of the assets. The community model focuses on the participation of community members, but the limitation of this model is that it ignores the unequal power (both economic and political) relations and social, economic, and gender stratifications within the community. Those who are powerful are still the main beneficiaries of the community. Hence, it is not possible to understand the needs of the marginalized within the structure of the community model and there is almost no chance that their inputs will be included in the decision-making process.

Creating a framework solely for community participation (more specifically, local communities) does not guarantee that marginalized women can participate in decision-making spaces. In local governmental bodies or in local communities, only people who are economically or politically powerful have the ability to represent these organizations. Although women have representations in these bodies in Bangladesh and the Philippines, their role is peripheral. There is almost no representation of marginalized women in any of the local bodies there. Therefore, involving local bodies or communities in water distribution would not ensure minimal distribution of water to the marginalized women because this approach ignores unequal power relations at the lower structure of the government body and the community. As a result of stratification and unequal power relations, mainly the local elites and the middle class are the beneficiaries of most of the decisions taken by the local government bodies and community organizations.

The community model of governance could also not ensure what Sen describes as political freedom for marginalized women through participation. Thus, the challenge is to involve the communities of the marginalized women in water governance along with the local communities as a whole. None of the paradigms (state-led, market-led, PPP, or community) address the necessity of including the inputs of the people who live on the bottom rung of society. These paradigms are exclusionary in general, where the voices of the marginalized are denied or minimalized.

It is necessary to note here that besides the conventional paradigms mentioned above, the Integrated Water Resource Management (IWRM) approach is also not successful in addressing the needs of marginalized women. This approach recommends "stakeholder's participation and decision-making at the lowest appropriate level."[30] Although the IWRM approach stands for the key role of women in "provision, management and safeguarding of water," it does not particularly prescribe incorporating the inputs of the marginalized women. Moreover, it does not place marginalized women's needs at the center of governance; instead, it addresses women's needs in general. Therefore, the IWRM approach is not sufficient to address the needs of marginalized women. This approach is not vocal about the political capabilities of the marginalized women specifically, and hence there is little opportunity for them to participate in decision-making spaces. Therefore, the important aspect of Sen's capability approach—securing the freedom aspect for marginalized women through implementing the idea of the equality of capability—might not be achieved under the IWRM approach.

Conventional approaches to participation "mean approaches that utilize processes to inform, consult, involve, collaborate with, and empower the public."[31] The major drawback of the conventional paradigms of governance is that they are not successful in addressing the needs of marginalized people/women separately; instead they address the public in general. They are precluded from contributing their inputs into the policy-making processes that affect their lives. Conventional paradigms are interested in including the inputs of the public or local communities, but do not refer to marginalized woman as a distinct category. There is also no space for them to participate in the decision-making process, an important component for an individual to achieve political capability. Marginalized women's well-being and freedom, both aspects of capabilities, are generally ignored in the conventional paradigms. They constitute a significant portion of the total population in Dhaka and Metropolitan Manila but are the most deprived in terms of well-being and freedom compared to the other sections of the population. Therefore, to establish their capabilities it is imperative to recognize their needs specifically and to create a space for them (or provide them access to the existing space) to participate in the decision-making process. Addressing all citizens as the "public" might not ensure marginalized women's fair share of water resources or their capability to participate in the decision-making spaces of the governance system in the cities, where societies are widely stratified along class lines.

The next chapters discuss the state-led and PPP governance systems in Dhaka and Metropolitan Manila for assessing the capabilities of marginalized women to participate in decision-making spaces and to access supplied water resources under these two governance systems.

Notes

1. Tim Kessler, "Who's Taking Risks? How the World Bank Pushes Private Infrastructure and Finds Resistance in Some Surprising Places," July 2004, *Citizen's Network on Essential Services,* 20 Jan. 2007 <http://www.servicesforall.org/html/infrastructure/Taking%20Risks-FINAL.pdf>.

2. Brid Brennan, Bernhard Hack, Oliveir Hoedeman, Satoko Kishimoto, and Phillip Terhorst, *Reclaiming Public Water! Participator Alternatives to Privatization* (The Netherlands: Transnational Institute, 2004) 9.

3. The IWRM approach considers water as an "economic good" rather than a common pool resource.

4. For poor women's access to water in Bangladesh, see Begum Shamsun Nahar, "Gender, Water and Poverty Experiences from Water Resource Management Projects in Bangladesh," presented in *Regional Workshop on Water and Poverty*, Dhaka (22–26 Sept 2002) 4.

5. *Water a Shared Responsibility: The United Nations World Water Development Report 2* (Paris, New York: UNESCO and Berghahn Books, 2006) 46.

6. Although equitable distribution is the basis for measuring justice in resource allocation, this principle was not implemented in any of the service sectors in the Philippines or Bangladesh. Yet, it might not be possible to implement the policy of equitable allocation solely in the supplied water sector; instead, it might be possible to supply the minimum requirements of water to every household. In this study, the basis for measuring justice in water distribution is to supply the minimum requirement of water to the marginalized women in Dhaka and Manila. The concept of minimum requirement is a relative term that is subject to spatial and temporal domains.

7. Julius Court, "Governance, Development and Aid Effectiveness: A Quick Guide to Complex Relationships," *ODI Briefing Paper* (London: Overseas Development Institute, March 2006) 1.

8. For the causal relationship between governance and development outcomes, see Daniel Kaufmann, Aart Kraay, and Pablo Zoido-Lobatón, "Governance Matters," *Policy Paper 2196* (World Bank Institute, October 1999).

9. David Crocker, "The Capability Approach and Deliberative Democracy," *Maitreyee* 4 (Feb. 2006) 6.

10. John M. Alexander, "Capability Egalitarianism and Moral Selfhood," *Ethical Perspectives* 10.1 (2003) 16.

11. UNESCO, *Water a Shared Responsibility* 47.

12. Court 1.

13. Court 1.

14. Peter Rogers and Alan W. Hall, "Effective Water Governance," *TEC Background Papers*, No. 7. (Stockholm: Global Water Partnership, 2003) 7.

15. Bob Jessop, "The Governance of Complexity and the Complexity of Governance: Preliminary Remarks on Some Problems and Limits of Economic Guidance," in *Beyond Market and Hierarchy: Interactive Governance and Social Complexity*, eds. Ash Amin and Jerzy Hausner (Cheltenham and Lyme: Edward Elgar, 1997) 95. According to the Institute of Governance, an Ottawa-based think tank, "Governance is the process by which stakeholders articulate their interests, their input is absorbed, decisions are taken and implemented, and decision-makers are held accountable."

16. Court 1.

17. Jessop 101.

18. Jessop 7; see also Daniel Kauffman, "Rethinking Governance: Empirical Lessons Challenge Orthodoxy," *Discussion Draft* (The World Bank, March 11, 2003) 5.

19. For a discussion of governance as networks, see R.A.W. Rhodes, "Governance and Public Administration," *Debating Governance: Authority, Steering, and Democracy*, ed. John Pierre (New York: Oxford University Press, 2000) 60–61.

20. Global Water Partnership, "Effective Water Governance: Learning from the Dialogues" (Global Water Partnership, March 16–23, 2003).

21. Rogers and Hall 11–13. There are many forms of governance, such as network governance, corporate governance, participatory governance, multi-level governance, and the list goes on. However, it is not possible to cover all the forms of governance in one study. Therefore, this study discusses the forms of governance that are relevant to this research.

22. Rogers and Hall 11–12.

23. James C. Scott, *Seeing Like State: How Certain Schemes to Improve the Human Condition Have Failed* (New Haven and London: Yale University Press, 1998) 1–8. However, natural monopoly can also arise under private ownership or operation.

24. Carolyn J. Hill and Laurence E. Lynn, Jr., "Is Hierarchical Governance in Decline? Evidence from Empirical Research," *Journal of Public Administration Research and Theory* 15:2 (2005) 173.

25. Hill and Lynn 12.

26. Imtiaz Alam, "Growth and Poverty in South Asia," *South Asian Journal* 15 (2007) ii.

27. Karen Bakker, "Good Governance in Restructuring Water Supply: A Handbook," *Federation of Canadian Municipalities*, 18 Feb. 2006 <http://www.sustainable-communities.ca/Home/>.

28. Roger and Hall 13.

29. Bakker 18.

30. Court 4–8. For details about IWRM, see "Tool Box," *Global Water Partnership* 19 Nov. 2006 <http://www.waterland.net/index.cfm/site/Toolbox%20-%20en/pageid/4663B313-A25C-8A9B-5C1C99D060C92B62/page/1/objecttype/mark.apps.nwp.contentobjects.tool/objectid/1991C019-0284-467B-9CCC9CC25D4EA057/index.cfm>. See also "Integrated Water Resources Management," *Cap-Net* 16 Nov. 2006 <http://www.cap-net.org/iwrm_tutorial/mainmenu.htm>. IWRM is "a process which promotes the coordinated development and management of water, land and related resources in order to maximize the resultant economic and social welfare in an equitable manner without compromising the sustainability of vital eco-systems" ("Sharing Knowledge for Equitable, Efficient and Sustainable Water Resources Management," 2003) *Global Water Partnership* 19 Nov. 2006 <http://www.waterland.net/gfx/content/ToolBox%20text%20book%20Ver2%20Eng.pdf>. For IWRM principles also see Asim Das Gupta, Mukund Sungh Babel, Xavier Albert, and Ole Mark, "Water Sector of Bangladesh in the Context of Integrated Water Resources Management: A Review," *Water Resources Development* 21.2 (2005): 385–86.

31. Libor Jansky, Dann M. Sklarew, and Juha I. Uitto, "Enhancing Public Participation and Governnace in Water Resource Management," in *Enhancing Participation and Governance in Water Resources Management: Conventional Approaches and Information Technology*, eds. Libor Jansky, Juha I. Uitto (Tokyo, New York, Paris: United Nations University Press, 2005) 6.

3

State-Led Water Governance and Marginalized Women's Capabilities: A Perspective from Dhaka

The [Bangladesh] Government's goal is to ensure that all people have access to safe water and sanitation services at an affordable cost.

Since women play a crucial role in water management and hygiene education at the household level, recognition of women's role will contribute to the overall development of the [water] sector.

Government of the People's Republic of Bangladesh

National Policy for Safe Water Supply and Sanitation 1998[1]

The growing scarcity of water is a severe problem in Dhaka, and it becomes worse during summer. Except in some rich areas of the conurbation, 90 percent of the city faces a water shortage in summer; 60 percent of city dwellers face acute crisis during that time.[2] There is no regular water supply in most of the neighborhoods even in "normal" times. Moreover, residents are also not satisfied with the quality of the water supplied to their households.

The Dhaka Water Supply and Sewerage Authority (DWASA), a public water company, is in charge of supplying water to the Dhaka and Narayanganj area, which has approximately 15 million people.[3] As mentioned in the previous chapter, since its establishment in 1963, it has adopted state-led governance for making and implementing decisions regarding the city's water supply.

The goal of this chapter is to examine the political and material capabilities of marginalized women; that is, their capabilities to contribute to final decisions through participating in formal decision-making spaces as well as to access the water resources supplied under the state-led governance of DWASA. Before analyzing their capabilities, it is important to first portray the living conditions of the marginalized women in Dhaka.

Marginalized Women's Households in Dhaka

The concept of marginalized women's households in Dhaka is complex. The major difference between marginalized women's households and those of upper, middle, or lower-middle class households is the problem of "very poor sanitation and inadequate water access" in the households of the marginalized women.[4] Most reside in slum areas, where the concentration of households varies; some areas are denser than others (Table 3.1). Marginalized populations live not only in slum clusters, but also in other parts of the city.[5]

According to Anu Muhammad, a Bangladeshi economist, there are 6 million people living in slum areas, on sidewalks, in rail-stations, in garages, and inside sewer pipes. Among these, more than 100,000 people live on the sides of street, along sidewalks, in market verandas, in rickshaw vans, and inside marketplaces. Those who are relatively privileged live in the slum areas.[6]

TABLE 3.1.
Number of Households by Slum Cluster (in percentage) in Dhaka

Households	Cluster Percentage
Up to 10	7.2
11–20	29.7
21–30	14.7
31–40	8.5
41–50	6.0
51–100	12.5
101–150	5.5
151–200	3.3
201–250	1.9
251–500	5.3
501–750	1.6
751–1000	1.3
1000+	2.4
Total Percent	100
N (hh only)	4,814
Clusters with mess units only	152
Total Clusters	4,966

Source: Islam et al. 37.

A slum is defined as a neighborhood or residential area with a minimum of 10 households, or a mess unit (mess housing) with at least 25 members, with four of the following five conditions prevailing within it:

- Predominantly poor housing
- Very high population density and room crowding
- Very poor environmental services, particularly water and sanitation facilities
- Very low socioeconomic status for the majority of residents
- Lack of security of tenure[7]

One study suggests that more than 3.4 million people live in roughly 4,966 slum clusters in Dhaka.[8] The total area of these slum clusters is only 3,840 acres.[9] The population density is very high in slum clusters—891 persons per acre, whereas the city population is 121 per acre (Table 3.2).[10] No accurate statistics are available on how many people live in slum clusters; most of the statistics are based on estimation because slum populations are highly mobile. Moreover, in a good number of cases, the residents also face the problem of eviction, either by the government or by local authorities.

The population living in slum areas is estimated to have increased by about 100 percent between 1996 and 2005 (from 1.5 million to 3.4 million). The expansion of garment factories encouraged village populations, especially women's populations, to migrate from the villages to the capital city around that time. Although slums have been in existence for a long time

TABLE 3.2.
Population Size in Slum Clusters

Slum Population Size (Persons)	Percentage of Clusters
Up to 100	39.0
101–200	22.3
201–300	9.4
301–400	4.9
401–500	3.2
501–1000	8.4
1,001–2,500	7.3
2,501–5,000	2.8
5,001–10,000	1.6
Above 10,000	1.0
Total Percent	100
N	4,966

Source: Islam et al. 38.

in Dhaka, massive migration by the rural poor to urban areas is the major reason for the rapid increase of the slum population, especially after the liberation war of 1971.

Roughly 37.4 percent of the city's population now lives in the 4,966 slum clusters.[11] The slum population is still growing in Dhaka, and both "the rate of growth … and their tendency to emerge in more peripheral locations are likely to persist in the near future with continuing heavy rural to urban migration in the face of an ongoing dearth of land for cheap housing in more central locations."[12]

More than 75 percent of households in slum clusters comprise "single room family occupancy," and 77.2 percent of households are rentals.[13] In these households, on average, 5 persons live in one room in more than half of the clusters (55.2 percent; Table 3.3).[14] Although most slum households do not have water connections, there are both "illegal" and legal electricity connections in most of the households there.[15]

Most of the marginalized women share their households with other family members and friends. Some women (and males also) live with non-relatives in "mess" housing. Low-income people also live in this type of "mess" housing in other parts of the city not considered slum areas. The numbers of people living in slum households and in slum mess units are 3,286,770 and 133,751 (96.1 and 3.9 percent respectively).[16] In the slum clusters, there are 673,883 households and mess units; 80.6 percent are households and 3.1 percent are mess units (Table 3.4).[17] Most of the households in slum clusters are women-centered, although men are the figureheads.

TABLE 3.3.
Number of Persons Residing per Room in Slum Clusters

Persons per Room	Percentage of Clusters
1	0.0
2	0.0
3	1.5
4	31.8
5	55.2
6	7.4
7	0.3
Above 7	0.5
Don't Know	3.2
Total Percent	100
N	4,966

Source: Islam et al. 40.

Although some slum clusters consists of only 10 households, there are some with more than 1,000 households. Karail in Mohakhali is the "largest single slum" in the city, with more than 100,100 residents. In the Kamrangirchar area, where "the single largest concentration of slums" is located, 265,000 of the 300,000 residents live in slum clusters. Large concentrations of slums are also located in Khilkhet, the Badda-Satarkul area, Hazaribagh, West Moham-madpur, and along the Narayanganj to Tongi railway line.[18]

The majority of the marginalized women living in slum clusters are gar-ment factory workers, domestic workers, vendors, day laborers, factory workers, and housewives. The men of these households work as rickshaw pullers, drivers, factory workers, day laborers, and vendors. Causal inquiries suggest that the daily income of both the women and men is very low—less than a dollar per day.[19] The average income of a man is slightly higher than that of a woman because of the gender discrimination in wage distribution in most cases. More than 50 percent of the households and 75 percent of the people live below the poverty line. The monthly income of most households in slums is only $71.[20]

DWASA is in charge of supplying water to all city dwellers, including the poorest women living in slums and other areas of the city. Therefore, the critical questions to be asked regarding DWASA'a state-led governance system are these:

- When it comes to the issue of water distribution, who in DWASA decides what is to be distributed and for whom?
- Do the marginalized women have the necessary capabilities to participate at any level of the decision-making spaces in DWASA?
- Or, is DWASA relying on "hidden" or "invisible" forms of power struc-tures to meet the necessities of a certain group of people?
- Do marginalized women have the same capability to access the water supply as the relatively wealthy citizens living in the same conurbation?

TABLE 3.4.
Percentage of Slum Clusters by Household Pattern

Clusters With	Percentage
Total Households	673,883
Households Only	80.6%
Mess Units Only	3.1%
Households and Mess Mixed	16.3%
Total Percentage	100%
Number of Slum Clusters	4,966

Source: Islam et al. 36.

To address the capability of marginalized women to access the supplied water resources first requires a discussion of their capability to participate in DWASA's decision-making spaces.

Marginalized Women's Capabilities to Participate in DWASA's Decision-Making Process

DWASA has been operating as a public company since its establishment (under EP Ordinance No. XIX, 1963). Although it is a semi-autonomous organization under the Ministry of Local Government and Rural Development, prior to the establishment of DWASA, the Dhaka Municipality and the Department of Public Health Engineering had supplied water to the city's residents. The Dhaka City Corporation (DCC) had been in charge of managing solid waste since its establishment.[21]

At the beginning of the 1990s, DWASA took charge of supplying water to the Narayanganj district, which is adjacent to the city of Dhaka. Under the WASA Act of 1996, DWASA's objectives also changed and it was restructured to set up corporate management "under which mandates for water supply, treatment and disposal of domestic and industrial sewage and storm water drainage were entrusted with DWASA."[22]

DWASA is currently working as a corporate organization. The major goals of DWASA are the following:

- Provide safe and sufficient water for drinking, industrial, and commercial uses.
- Ensure sanitation and good hygiene conditions through proper disposal of domestic and industrial sewerage.
- Ensure efficient storm-water drainage.[23]

At DWASA, there are 3,294 people working hierarchically as first, second, third, and fourth class staff.[24] The managing director is the head of internal management. Three main divisions are responsible for the governance and management of the internal organization: Administration, Finance (F&A), and Engineering (O&M). DWASA's yearly revenue budget is $4.8 million and the yearly development budget is $1.67 million.[25]

DWASA's state-led governance system is hierarchical and centralized, so that decisions are made at the top of the organization (Figure 3.1). Senior DWASA officials are in charge of making decisions for allocating water to the city. They make these decisions in a "closed" or "provided" space, which means that decisions are made behind closed doors by a restricted set of actors (bureaucrats, technical experts, and selected staff). This type of decision-

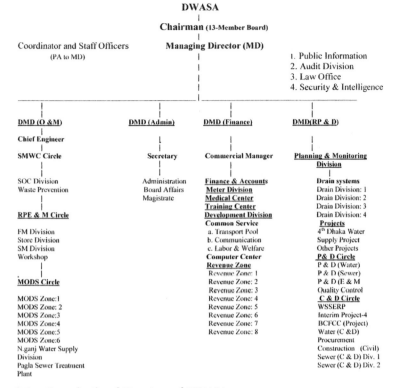

Figure 3.1.   Organizational Structure of DWASA

Notes: MD (Managing Director); PA (Personal Assistant); DMD (Deputy Managing Director); O & M (Opera-
tion and Maintenance); F&A (Finance and Administration); RP& D (Research, Planning and Development);
SMWC Circle (System Monitoring and Waste Control); SOC Division (System Operation and Control) ,
RPE & M (Resource, Plant, Equipment and Maintenance) Circle; FM (Field Maintenance) Division; SM
(Structural Maintenance) Division; MODS (Maintenance, Operation, Distribution and Service); P &D
(Planning and Design) Circle; E & M (Electrical and Mechanical); C& D (Construction and Development)
Circle; WSSERP (Water Supply System Expansion & Rehabilitation Project) .

Source: Jafar Ullah, A.K.M. "Country Report of Bangladesh: Management of Urban Water Environment."
JICA Executive Seminar on Public Works and Management JFY 2004. National Institute for Land and
Infrastructure Management. 27 Oct., 2006 < http://www.nilim.go.jp/english/conference/04.13th/7/13-7-2.
pdf> and based on my phone conversation with the author on March 15, 2007.

making process precludes any kind of involvement or discussion with the
common citizens or women.

The technological elites in charge of the Planning and Monitoring Division of DWASA make the plans regarding the supply of water to the city's
residents. Currently, five members work in the Planning and Monitoring
Division. After developing a plan, they submit it to the office of the managing director for approval. The managing director requires the approval of
DWASA chair before implementation of any plan; the chair may seek suggestions from the DWASA Board.

There are thirteen members on DWASA Board. The chair of DWASA is also the chair of the board and the managing director is one of the members of the board. Twelve other members of the Board are chosen from a wide spectrum of elite backgrounds, such as attorneys, leading industrialists, journalists, doctors, engineers, university professors, or government-appointed joint secretary-level officials. Besides this, one male and one female councilor are chosen from the elected officials of the DCC.[26]

The state-led governance system of DWASA is an example of a "hidden power" structure, as suggested by John Gaventa, wherein a certain group of elites maintain their authority through institutional mechanisms and decide who in the city is entitled to receive what amount of water. Not only do they control the decision-making process, but they also decide who should be invited to the decision-making table and what agendas should be discussed. Economically, socially, and politically less powerful people as well as marginalized women (as a group or as a person) are thus completely excluded from the decision-making space. Their agendas always receive less priority in this governance mechanism. The elites effectively control the "hidden" power structure that decides how the city's water will be distributed. Senior DWASA officials monopolize the decision-making process by controlling whose agendas will proceed, as well as the right of access to decision-making spaces, which is reserved solely for the city's more powerful and influential citizens.

Decisions made by senior DWASA staff regarding water allocation usually do not conflict drastically with the WASA Board, where non-DWASA officials have a limited role in the decision-making process; the Board's role is mainly advisory.[27] Of the thirteen members in the board, currently two are women. However, they do not belong to the category of marginalized women, nor do they represent their needs and interests.

DWASA has no plan for allocating water to marginalized women or for supplying it to slum dwellers' households, which constitute a significant portion of households in the city. DWASA's policy is to supply water only to legal households—those with DCC holding numbers.[28] Marginalized women without such documentation are considered to be living "illegally" in slum areas and are thus not regarded as customers; as a result, they are not entitled to receive water from DWASA.

Eighty women whom I interviewed in various slums in Dhaka informed me that they do not consider themselves to be illegal residents. They believe that it is the government's responsibility to recognize their households as legal households and hence, they should take the necessary steps to supply water to their households or their neighborhoods. They also informed me that they did not grab a single piece of land in the city. If any slum was built on government or illegally occupied land, the owner of the slum should be responsible for it. They simply rented houses that were built in the slums. In this case, the authorities should take proper legal action against the persons who built houses illegally on the land that does not belong to them.

At the same time, these women believe that the government should take the appropriate initiative to rehabilitate them in the city. They think that if the government would come forward with appropriate measures to rehabilitate them or to recognize their households as legal, they would be able to receive water, sewerage, and sanitation services from the government authority. For example Rahima Khatun, who lives in a slum area near Mirpur, told me the following: "How can we be illegal? Me or my family, none of them are the owner of the house or the land where we are staying. We simply rented the house. How can we know whether the owner owns the land legally or illegally? If he owns it illegally, why should we be punished for his fault? If the government wants to punish somebody, punish him, not us. As a citizen of the country, therefore, the government or the Dhaka City Corporation should take an appropriate measure for our housing. Do we not have the right to live in the capital city as legal residents?"[29]

All the women I interviewed informed me that if DWASA would agree to supply water to their households or neighborhoods, they stand ready to purchase water from DWASA at the same rates that other legal residents are paying in the city. Saleha Begum, who also lives in a slum, told me that "It is a misconception that we will not pay for the supplied water. In some slum areas, NGOs are working as subcontractors for DWASA and there is hardly a case where poor people did not pay their water bills on time to the NGO authorities. Most of the defaulters you will come to know in the city do not live in the slum areas."[30]

When I asked them whether they wanted to send representatives to DWASA, all of them told me that they thought it would be the best arrangement for them because only a poor woman can understand the plight of other poor women. DWASA workers have not experienced the plight of living in slums without proper water and sanitation services. Ranu Begum summarized their thinking in the following way: "The rich people who are making decisions for supplying water have no idea what it means to lead an everyday life without having an adequate amount of water. If we could send somebody at least we could explain to them our situation."[31]

These women believed that if there were some poor women representatives in the water board, they at least would be able to inform the authorities about their needs. When I asked whether they believe that simply sending representatives to the formal decision-making space would change their condition, they all told me that at least their representatives could bargain with the authority, and if they were able to successfully convince them they believed that this would help to change their situation. According to them, there is nobody in DWASA to argue for poor people, and nobody is paying attention to their needs.

Matia Khanam told me the following regarding the necessity of representation for poor women in the decision-making space: "DWASA is not supplying water to us because they are not even aware of our needs. How can they know about us? Did they ever talk with the poor regarding their need for water? So how will they know? If there are some representatives from the poor in DWASA, they will come to know our needs and I believe this will change our situation drastically."[32] All the women I interviewed agreed that if DWASA would provide them access to the decision-making spaces, DWASA could then assess their necessities and this would lead to supplying water to their neighborhoods according to their needs. Finally, if any one of them were chosen to attend the board meeting, this person would have to sacrifice her work hours, so I asked how she would manage her daily life when she had only her regular meager income to rely upon. To my utter surprise the common response was that they would like to collect community donations so she could attend the meeting. They further informed me that community management is not a big challenge for them because a good number of water and sanitation facilities in slum areas are currently being managed communally.

The level of engagement of the bureaucrats (outside DWASA) and the wealthy citizenry of the city in the formal decision-making process in DWASA is also minimal. DWASA bureaucrats and the technological bureaucrats are mainly in charge of making and implementing decisions. Not only is any kind of engagement with marginalized women at any level of governance denied, but also their right to access the supplied water is refuted. It is clear from the discussion that they do not have the capability even for "minimal participation" in decision-making spaces. Who is entitled to receive what amount of water in the city is subjected to the sole discretion of the technological and bureaucratic elites, and representatives of the wealthy citizenry. There is no organized deliberative, reflexive network in this state-led governance system to integrate the demands of the marginalized women as well as other customers and the poor living in the city.

To sum up, under the state-led water governance, the poorest women do not have political capability—that is, the capability to participate in decision-making spaces. There is no space or mechanism in this governance system where the poorest women could exercise their agencies or political capabilities even though it might not lead to their "agency achievements" through contributing to the final decision regarding water distribution. In DWASA, decisions are not made on the basis of input from the participants whose everyday lives are directly affected by the actions taken by this water authority.

The elites (the bureaucrats, experts, and influential citizenry) are definitely in an advantageous position in the governance structure and they influence the decisions in their own favor.

Participation is vital for promoting political as well as economic capabilities and freedoms. Those who are able to participate in the decision-making spaces definitely have more political capabilities than those who cannot. In Dhaka, only a few wealthy citizens have political capability, and hence can participate in the decision-making space of DWASA. On the contrary, marginalized women have no political capability to participate because their capability did not increase under the state-led governance in Dhaka. This also denies their basic functioning as citizens in numerous ways.

Capabilities of Marginalized Women to Access Supplied Water Resources

The following paragraphs analyze marginalized women's basic material capabilities, that is, their capabilities to access supplied water resources in terms of quantity, price, and quality under the state-led governance of DWASA.

Quantity of Water

Although roughly 96 percent of slum residents have access to potable water, most households do not have water connections. They are also not connected to the drainage or sewerage systems.[33] Among slum clusters, about 95 percent (4,710 clusters) have water sources within slum areas, compared to about 5 percent (256 clusters) outside of slum.[34] Although most marginalized women have access to water sources, they do not obtain adequate water from these sources to meet their everyday necessities; most have to share their sources of water with other people. In the slums, where 75 percent of households are "single room family occupancy" and on average 5 persons live in one room,[35] only about 5 percent of households do not need to share their potable water sources with other families, whereas 40 percent must share their water sources with 11 other households (Table 3.5 and Table 3.6).[36] Although DWASA has set up some water connections inside slum areas, there are almost no water connections inside the residences of slum dwellers.[37] The existing connections have been set up by the "owners" of the slum clusters and in some cases, by the NGOs working there.[38]

Water demand in Dhaka has been increasing at the rate of 100 mld (million liters per day) per year, as a result of yearly 4.2 percent population growth in the city.[39] DWASA currently supplies water to an area of roughly 292 square miles. According to DWASA, the necessity of water for the city during July

TABLE 3.5.
Sources of Drinking Water in Dhaka Slums

Municipal standpipes	92.3 percent
Tube well	6.5 percent
Other sources	1.2 percent

Source: Islam et al. 45.

TABLE 3.6.
Water Sharing Pattern in the Slum Areas in Dhaka

Number of Households Sharing One Tap	Percentage of Clusters	Number of Households Sharing One Tube Well	Percentage of Clusters
Not Shared	1.4	Not Shared	27.9
2–5	19.6	2–5	6.5
6–10	45.8	6–10	27.4
11–20	21.7	11–20	26.2
21–30	4.7	21–30	5.0
Above 30	6.8	Above 30	7.0
Total Percentage	100	Total Percentage	100
N	4,641	N	401

Source: Islam et al. 45.

2010 to June 2011 was 2,240 mld and it was able to supply an average of 2,150 mld (Table 3.7).[40] However, it was not clear on what basis DWASA determined the necessity of water for the city of 15 million people. The water problem is at its worst in summer.[41] In some parts of the city, DWASA was completely unable to supply water during that time, when 60 percent of the city suffered an acute crisis of potable water.[42]

DWASA mainly relies on ground water to supply water to its consumers. Except for regions in the hilly areas, ground water is "the most important source of water supply" for the entire country.[43] Roughly 87 percent of DWASA water comes from ground water sources, whereas only 13 percent comes from nearby rivers: the Shitolokkha, the Buriganga, the Turag, and the Balu.[44] DWASA currently uses 599 deep tube wells to lift water from underground sources.[45] As a result of too much reliance on ground water sources (Table 3.8), the water table for Dhaka has been dropping by 6–9 feet every year, which has further exacerbated the problem of water availability.[46]

DWASA cannot lift water in accordance with its capacity because in the last 27 years the water level has dropped by 180–210 feet in various parts of the city. The water boards in other places do not rely as much on ground water

TABLE 3.7.
DWASA'S Daily Water Production During Fiscal Year 2005–2011 (million liters per day)

Year	Population Million Approx.	Water Demand (MLD)	Water Supply Capacity (MLD)	Shortage (MLD)	No. of Deep Tube Wells
1963	0.85	150	130	20	30
1970	1.46	260	180	80	47
1980	3.03	550	300	250	87
1990	5.56	1000	510	490	216
1996	7.55	1300	810	490	216
1997	8.0	1350	870	480	225
1998	8.5	1400	930	470	237
1999	9.0	1440	1070	370	277
2000	9.5	1500	1130	370	308
2001	10.0	1600	1220	380	336
2002	10.50	1680	1300	380	379
2003	11.025	1760	1360	400	391
2004	11.567	1850	1400	450	402
2005	12.15	1940	1460	480	418
2006	12.65	1900	1540	460	441
2007	13.15	1980	1660	320	465
2008	13.65	2050	1760	290	490
2009	14.15	2120	1880	240	519
2010	14.50	2180	1990	190	560
2011 (Up to June 30)	15.00	2240	2150	90	599

Source: Dhaka Water Supply and Sewerage Authority, 2011, 41.
Note: There was no explanation from DWASA why the demand for water decreased in 2006 from 2005 despite the increase of the population in the city in 2006.

TABLE 3.8.
Average Water Production per Day (in mld) During the Fiscal Year 2010–2011

Source	Amount of Production	Percent of Production
Ground Water	1,870.50	87%
Surface Water	279.50	13%
Total	2,150.00	100

Source: Dhaka Water Supply and Sewerage Authority, 2011, 34.

sources. For example, in the Sabujbag area of the city, during 1978–2005, the ground water level dropped by 180 feet; in Mohammadpur, during 1977–2005, it dropped by 99 feet; in Dhanmondi, for the same period, by

183 feet; in Mirpur during 1984–2005, by 183 feet; and in the Dhamarai and Keraniganj areas, which are located near the city, the water level dropped by only 21 feet in the last 27 years. Moreover, the extreme pollution of the rivers around Dhaka has polluted the ground water as well because the river water exudes through the soil layers and mixes with the ground water.[47] However, the major problem for DWASA is not supplying contaminated water but its inability to supply adequate water to most of its inhabitants. The deep tube wells could lift water from 1,550–1,800 feet before the water level went down. On average, a deep tube well can lift 3,000–4,000 liters of water per minute, but due to the declining water level, now a good number of them can lift only 2,000–3,000 liters per minute.[48] The problem of decreasing water level thus affects the overall production of water.

During 2010–2011 DWASA produced roughly 143.33 liters of water per person per day, which was higher than the minimum requirement. Therefore, theoretically every person in Dhaka should have the necessary amount of water. However, due to the absence of a proper distribution policy—one that would recognize the needs of marginalized women and slum dwellers—DWASA was not able to supply water equitably to all city residents.

In addition, due to the high system loss, not all the water DWASA produced during that time was available to the consumers.[49] However, over time DWASA has been able to reduce its system losses gradually from about 54 percent to nearly 41 percent (Table 3.9).

TABLE 3.9.
Year-Wise System Loss (in percentages) of DWASA Water

	Dhaka WASA Zones			PPI	Zones		All	Zones		
Fiscal Year	I	II	III	VI	VII	Total	IV	V	Total	(I–VII)
2002–2003	64.25	73.60	53.36	50.29	52.31	58.76	55.32	36.02	45.67	54.25
2003–2004	56.45	69.81	44.76	57.82	41.60	40.71	47.6	36.59	57.07	49.32
2004–2005	47.89	60.05	43.43	65.62	50.84	25.95	32.10	32.77	30.49	40.59

PPI Zones= Project Performance Improvement (Private Participation) Zones.
Source: Dhaka Water Supply and Sewerage Authority, 2006, 17/3.
Note: DWASA Cooperative Association (DCA) is in charge of collecting revenues from PPI zones. All the staff (1st, 2nd, 3rd, and 4th class employees) working in DWASA are members of the Cooperative Association. In 1996, the World Bank set up a condition that in order to receive money for the Saidabad Water Treatment Plant, DWASA should privatize its revenue collection system. Therefore, instead of entrusting the responsibility of collecting revenues to an outside company, in 1997, DCA members decided that they would take charge of Zone V experimentally. At the same year, DWASA also conferred Zone IV to Engineering, Planning and Consultant (EPC), a Bangladeshi private company. However, this company was unable to show much "success" in terms of collecting revenues, like DCA. DCA's apparent "success" later inspired them to take charge of Zones IV and III in 1998 and 2003 respectively. Since then, DCA has been in charge of collecting revenue in these three zones. After one year of experience, EPC did not show interest in renewing their contract with DWASA. It is important to mention here that the posh residential areas in Dhaka fall under Zone V. Based on my conversation with Zaber Hossain, Secretary General, DCA.

In June 2011, the total number of DWASA customers was only 295,516; of these, 273,817 were residential customers. The number of customers has increased over time, although this increase does not match the number of citizens residing in the city. The total number of water connections (including industrial and commercial connections) is only 295,516 for the city (Table 3.10). There are no water connections to the households of 3.4 million people living in slums. As mentioned, DWASA provides water connections only to households with holding numbers, and slum dwellers do not have holding numbers because they are not considered "legal" residents in the city, so marginalized women and slum dwellers are not recognized as customers by DWASA.

DWASA has created seven water supply zones in Dhaka, in addition to the government zone, which includes the secretariat, and government offices and establishments. In these seven zones, DWASA sets up water connections to the households of legal residents, government buildings, private institutions and offices, and educational and religious institutions, such as mosques, temples, churches, and seminaries. None of the other areas has 24-hour water.[50]

During summer, only in Zone V does DWASA supply water almost 24 hours per day. One of the deputy revenue collectors of DWASA, who did not want his name to be revealed, informed me that the reasons behind the continuous supply of water to upper class neighborhoods (Zone V) include their smaller populations and their regular supply of power. Moreover, special attention is paid to these areas because "important" people and diplomats and dignitaries live there. In the old parts of the city and in lower-middle class neighborhoods, even in "normal" times, they do not receive water 24

TABLE 3.10.
Numbers of DWASA Customers at the End of June 2011

	Residential	Commercial	Industrial	Social	Office	Non-Recorded	Total
Zone 1	34,046	1,745	23	415	0	0	36,229
Zone 2	26,694	1,680	0	202	0	0	28,576
Zone 3	25,534	3,173	1	160	0	0	28,868
Zone 4	59,517	2,286	344	315	59	15	62,536
Zone 5	55,851	6,036	686	401	0	0	62,974
Zone 6	28,863	1,877	106	94	0	0	30,940
Zone 7	28,261	799	1	22	0	0	29,083
Narayanganj	14,748	450	3	112	8	0	15,321
Central Function	303	226	0	375	85	0	989
Total	273,817	18,272	1,164	2,096	152	15	295,516

Source: Dhaka Water Supply and Sewerage Authority, 2011, 44.

hours per day, and the situation becomes much worse in the summer, when customers sometimes receive water only 1–2 hours per day. Like marginalized women, customers in poor neighborhoods sometimes have to rely on standpipes for water, especially during summer.

Power-cuts are one of the reasons for not supplying water regularly to middle class or poor neighborhoods. While there are frequent power cuts in these areas, especially in summer, there are fewer or no power-cuts in the upper class areas. In addition to the power cuts, lower voltage of electricity is also responsible for not being able to operate the water pumps whenever necessary, particularly during summer. To operate a pump, 420 volts of electricity is needed. In many places, the electricity supply drops to 380 volts during most of the summer.[51]

A DWASA engineer, who also did not want his name to be revealed, informed me that theoretically there is 24 hours of water available in every neighborhood in Dhaka; the problem is not the water supply—it is the water pressure. As a result of high water demand, the pressure becomes very low and it is therefore difficult to draw water from a pipe. None of the water consumers I interviewed in Dhaka were satisfied with either the supply or the pressure of water. They informed me that they obtained a maximum of 6–7 hours of water per day and the water pressure is not sufficient to lift water to the second or upper floors. Hence, most of the middle and upper class customers had built underground reservoirs to collect water from the DWASA pipes.[52] Later, they lift this water to the second or upper floor reservoirs with electric pumps.

To put water into their underground reservoirs, middle and upper class customers usually use illegal pumps.[53] Some middle class water users informed me that they were aware that connecting water pumps with the main pipe lines is illegal, but they also informed me that there are hardly any middle or upper class households in the city that do not have water pumps connected to the main water lines. They use these pumps to collect water for their reservoirs during times of high pressure, usually at night or in the early morning.

Middle and some lower class water users informed me that usually late at night or early in the morning there had been sufficient pressure to collect water for their reservoirs, but as a result of the water pumps being used by a good number of households, it has now become difficult to obtain water without the pumps. As a result, there is sometimes no water supply to the lower-middle class or poor households in the neighborhoods, who cannot afford such pumps. As a result, women from lower to middle class backgrounds and sometimes men also need to collect water from the nearby public standpipes. Besides this, especially in summer, they can collect water from DWASA's water tankers, which are sometimes free of charge and provide for the acute water shortage neighborhoods, sometimes under the supervision of law enforcement authorities.[54]

Some marginalized women, especially those who live in old Dhaka, rely solely upon public standpipes for everyday water. Although standpipes had been available almost everywhere in Dhaka, nowadays they are mainly available in the old parts of the city and in the Narayanganj district. There are only 1,727 standpipes and 38 hydrants in the entire city of Dhaka.[55] To collect water from the standpipes, women in slum areas have to walk a 1 or 2 miles every day because none of the standpipes are located inside the slum areas. Usually, they are placed at the corners of the main roads in the old parts of the city, which are far way from the shanty areas. Most of the slum clusters are in new Dhaka.

DWASA supplies 1,136 liters of water per day to every standpipe. The DCC pays for these standpipes; that is, the DCC is paying for 1,058,752 liters of water per day.[56] In addition, the Bangladesh government has a policy of providing 92,440 liters of water per day to every religious institution, such as mosques, temples, churches, and pagodas. If any religious institution uses more water than the quota, they have to pay for the extra water. By June 2011, 1,898 religious institutions were receiving this benefit from the DCC.[57] Madrasas are not included in this program. So although the government has a program of supplying water to religious institutions, they have no policy for providing water to the low-income people or "illegal" residents in the city.

To sum up, under the state-led governance of DWASA, marginalized women are not capable of accessing sufficient, or in most cases, even minimal quantities of water for meeting their daily needs. DWASA is not able to or willing to provide the minimum requirement of water to their households. Hence, it is clear that their capability to access water has not increased in terms of quantity under the state-led governance in Dhaka. The following section analyzes whether they have the capability to access water under the price structure set up by DWASA.

Price of Water

Domestic water is cheap in Dhaka; DWASA provides 1,000 liters of water for only 5.50 taka (roughly 6 cents) to its domestic customers. Obtaining water for commercial or industrial purposes is a little more expensive (roughly 22 cents) than for domestic purposes.[58] Besides metered water, there are also non-metered water connections, whose tariffs are determined by the percentage "of valuation of holdings per annum," that is, DWASA measures the size of the holdings of the customers to set up the bills for the households.[59] In addition, DWASA vehicles sell water for relatively cheaper prices, especially during summer or in a time of water crisis in a particular area (Table 3.11).[60] However, the issue is not the price; the issue is obtaining a water connection.

TABLE 3.11.
DWASA's Water Selling Rates for Vehicle Delivery

Quantity	Rate
2200 gallons	$3.67
1800 gallons	$3.06
1200 gallons	$2.44
800 gallons	$1.83
500 gallons	$1.53
250 gallons	$0.91

Source: Dhaka Water Supply and Sewerage Authority, 2011, 57.

Obtaining a connection is both a complicated process and an expensive one. Besides high connection fees, bureaucratic complexity and corruption are also associated with obtaining a connection.[61] Even DWASA officials and workers acknowledge these complexities.[62] Besides paying the regular fees, a household owner needs to pay extra money to the DWASA staff and workers as well as the representatives (ward commissioners) of the local electoral bodies.[63] It is almost impossible to obtain a connection without bribing the DWASA staff and ward commissioners. A household owner needs to give at least $15 to the meter mechanic, often followed by the same or larger amount to other DWASA staff. Moreover, the owner needs to give about $9–15 to the local ward commissioner. There is no written provision anywhere that a city dweller has to pay the commissioner for the connection; the councilors extort this money illegally.[64]

Besides bribing several persons, a household owner also needs to pay several connection fees—an application fee, a deposit for temporary connection, pipe connection and permission fees (Table 3.12), a meter fee (Table 3.13), and a road-cutting fee, as well as the value added tax (vat). Connection and meter fees depend on the diameter of the pipes. Road-cutting fees also vary, depending on the type of road (the materials used in constructing the road). The distance of a household from the main pipeline also determines the connection fees. A long distance means a high connection fee and vice versa. Obtaining a connection for a high-rise apartment needs special permission from DWASA and the DCC, and the owner of course needs to pay fees to DWASA (Table 3.14). Instead of obtaining water connections, household owners may set up their own deep tube wells with the permission from DWASA, and then the deep tube well fees also vary, depending on the diameter of the wells (Table 3.15).

It is obvious that although water is cheap in Dhaka, pipeline connection fees are very high, especially for those who live below the poverty line. Hence, it is clear that marginalized women in the city do not have the capability to

TABLE 3.12.
Fees for Temporary Connection and Permission
for Pipe Connection (August 2004–June 2006)

Pipe Diameter	Temporary Connection Fee	Pipe Connection Fee
0.75 inch	$71	$7
1 inch	$143	$21
1.5 inch	$214	$142
2 inch	$286	$214

Source: Dhaka Water Supply and Sewerage Authority, 2006, 26/1–26/2.

TABLE 3.13.
Meter Connection, Installation, and Testing Fees (August 2004–June 2006)

Meter Size	Connection	Installation	Testing
0.75 inch	$14	$7	$3
1 inch	$31	$14	$7
1.5 inch	$91	$36	$11
2 inch	$91	$43	$14

Source: Dhaka Water Supply and Sewerage Authority, 2006, 26/2.

TABLE 3.14.
Permission for Connecting Pipe Lines in
Multistoried Building (February 2004–June 2006)

Cost of Clearance Form	$7
Floor Construction Approval Fee:	
Up to 9th floor	$29
10–15th floor	$43
Above 16th floor	$71

Source: Dhaka Water Supply and Sewerage Authority, 2006, 26/2.

obtain connections under the current price structure and with the widespread corruption in the system. Moreover, it was mentioned earlier that they are also not entitled to obtain connections inside their households because of DWASA's policy of not providing connections to households without DCC holding numbers. Such people can obtain a very limited quantity of water from DWASA when they provide free water to poor city dwellers during times of severe water crisis.

In addition, in times of dire necessity, marginalized women have no choice but to buy a very limited quantity of water from vendors at an inflated price.[65]

TABLE 3.15.
Deep Tube Well Installation and Permission Fee

	Up to 3 inch	4 inch	6 inch*
Domestic and community	$981	$1,717	$2,699
Commercial	$1,840	$3,680	$4,294
Industrial	$2,147	$3,987	$4,601
Yearly renewal fee			
Domestic and community	$613	$1,227	$1,472
Commercial	$920	$1,840	$2,698
Industrial	$1,227	$2,147	$ 2,944

* 8 inch not permissible.
Source: Dhaka Water Supply and Sewerage Authority, 2011, 55.

It is impossible for marginalized women to buy water from vendors on a regular basis when they earn less than a dollar per day. However, the issue is not obtaining water from the vendors or from non-DWASA sources. Obtaining water from both sources is not only difficult, but also time consuming and expensive. The real issue is whether they have the capability to access water resources under DWASA's price structure and distribution policy. Unlike the water companies in Metropolitan Manila (discussed in the fourth chapter), this state-led water company did not adopt a policy of providing connections to slum areas. Marginalized women are denied connections inside of or near their households by the state-led governance system. Moreover, under the current price structure, they are not capable of having connections inside their households. Therefore, despite the cheap price, marginalized women have very limited capability to access supplied water resources in Dhaka.

Quality of Water

The quality of water supplied by DWASA is too poor for drinking without boiling. In some cases, it is not possible to drink even after boiling. At present, DWASA is supplying odiferous and contaminated dirty water to 40 percent of the city.[66] City dwellers have even found worms in the water. I personally found odiferous water supplied to middle and lower class households in various parts of Dhaka.[67] A good number of DWASA consumers informed me that even after boiling, it is sometimes difficult to use this water for cooking and drinking because of the odor and sediments in the water.

Water supplied to various slum areas was also not up to the level of drinking. Marginalized women in slums complained that sometimes the water was odiferous; however, they informed me that they were used to drinking water without boiling. NGOs working in the slums sometimes supplied water purifier chemicals or tablets, which they put in the community water reservoirs. But for the marginalized women, the main issue is not the contaminated water but the lack of water connections in their households and their neighborhoods.

According to Nazrul Islam, a Bangladeshi researcher on urban planning, the level of contamination is currently very high in Dhaka. Despite treating water in various treatment plants, it becomes contaminated again because the pipelines used for supplying the water are very old, and have not been repaired or replaced for a long time.[68] Most of the DWASA pipelines were set up in the city 30 years ago.

There are also leaks in the pipelines, which not only cause system loss but also contaminate the water. Cracks in the sewer lines result in the mixture of human waste with water. The sewer lines in Dhaka are also very old and have not been replaced for a long time. Polluted rivers around Dhaka also contribute to the contamination of networked water.

Islam mentions that the quality of surface water in the Buriganga, Shitolokkha, Turag, and Balu rivers is not sufficient for drinking, even after boiling or treatment in the water plants. The pollution is so severe that the chemicals that DWASA uses to treat the water are not able to remove all the waste and pollutants.[69]

The Buriganga River is used to dump waste materials from nearby industries, including chemicals from the tanneries. There are 243 tanneries located within 2 miles on both sides of the river bank, which "pour 7.7 million liters of untreated, highly toxic liquid waste into the river every day."[70] There are more than 7,000 industries just in the metropolitan areas of the city. In addition, there are thousands of big and small industries situated around Dhaka. All of the industries use these rivers to dump their wastes.[71]

Moreover, the rivers, especially the Buriganga, are the main outlets for untreated sewage. Eighty percent of the sewage is untreated in Dhaka and dumped into this river. There are chemical elements such as aluminum, ammonium, chromium, cadmium, lead, and others that are present in the rivers around Dhaka, which are very dangerous for the human body.[72] The levels of ammonium, chromium, and cadmium in the ground and surface waters are higher than the acceptable limit for humans.[73] In the Buriganga and Shitolokkha, experts found hydrogen sulfide, chromium, oil, grease, leather cutting, lime, and poisonous lead, all of which are extremely dangerous for human health.[74]

The presence of coliforms is also very high in Dhaka's water. It is much higher than that found in the water supplied in Metropolitan Manila by the two companies discussed in the next chapter. Although 10 coliforms per 100 ml is the acceptable level for drinking, tests showed that in some places in Dhaka, there were 500 coliforms per 100 ml water.[75] DWASA has to use excessive chemicals to get rid of the bacteria; as a result, the water becomes smelly and blackish, and is harmful for human consumption. City dwellers frequently face the problems of diarrhea and dysentery as a result of consuming this polluted water. Moreover, using polluted water for a long time may cause, for example, kidney problems, ulcers, high blood pressure, rheumatic fever, asthma, and tuberculosis. Further, the excessive presence of lead in the Buriganga puts city dwellers at risk for cancer. The presence of tannery-related chemicals in the river is also very dangerous for human health.[76]

DWASA regularly tests the water they collect from surface water sources; almost 50 percent of their surface water samples fail.[77] It is interesting that their report does not mention the samples collected from the Saidabad Surface Water Treatment Plant, which is the largest among all the DWASA plants. This plant mainly treats water collected from the Buriganga River. An engineer from DWASA informed me that they sent samples of water collected from all the water plants to the laboratories, but since the Buriganga is the most polluted river in the country, there is a high possibility that the sample from this plant sent to the laboratory would fail the test. Hence, the DWASA internal report probably purposefully avoids mentioning that test result.[78] Engineers and technicians working with water NGOs in Dhaka informed me that the DWASA test results were not up to the proper level and were biased. Their own test results varied from those of DWASA (conducted in private laboratories and in the National Science Laboratory). Most of their samples failed to meet the WHO standard.[79]

It is clear from the above discussion that the capability of marginalized women to have good-quality water was not enhanced under DWASA's state-led governance. There might be several reasons behind marginalized women not having the capability to access the proper quality of water in Dhaka, however the focus of this study is to find out whether they have capability over water quality under the state-led governance, and this research concludes that marginalized women have very limited capability over the quality of water (i.e., the capability to obtain good-quality water).

To sum up, in DWASA's water distribution policy, the need or the recognition of the marginalized women as customers is ignored. There is no space in this state-led governance mechanism for marginalized women to participate in the decision-making process. It also does not have any mechanism to integrate their inputs into its governance system. Neither is DWASA interested in enhancing their political capability (or freedom), nor is it interested in the well-being aspect of marginalized women's capabilities.

All distribution decisions are made based on a paternalistic principle, where there is no room for marginalized women or citizens to decide for themselves. A group of powerful individuals make all the decisions in a closed space using a hidden power structure. Therefore, the state-led governance could not establish equitability of capability in terms of participation. Hence, this study concludes that the political capability or freedom of the marginalized women did not increase under the state-led governance of DWASA.

DWASA could also not ensure basic water rights or vital physical needs for most of the city dwellers. It was also not able to supply minimal requirements of water to the marginalized women as well as most of the slum dwellers and the poor living in the city. DWASA is not even successful in regularly supplying adequate quantities of potable water to their customers. DWASA unofficially follows an uneven policy of water distribution, and hence the consumers living in rich neighborhoods are the chief beneficiaries of their policy. Despite paying the same amount of money for water and pipeline connection, consumers living in the middle and lower middle class areas do not receive the same level of service as the rich consumers. Moreover, DWASA is also not successful at supplying drinkable water. It is therefore obvious that the marginalized women have very limited access to supplied water resources in terms of quantity, price, and the quality. The well-being aspect of capability—that is, their basic material capability to access the minimum requirement of supplied water resources—also has not increased under the state-led governance of DWASA. Therefore it is clear that the state-led governance could not establish social justice in water distribution in Dhaka.

This study compares two water governance systems by focusing on the intended and unintended effects of the systems for attaining political and basic material capabilities—that is, capabilities to participate and to access supplied water resources—from the perspective of economically marginalized women. The next chapter examines whether marginalized women's capabilities are being increased under the PPP governance in Metropolitan Manila.

Notes

1. Ministry of Local Government, Rural Development and Cooperatives, *National Policy for Safe Water Supply and Sanitation 1998* (Bangladesh: Government of the People's Republic of Bangladesh, Ministry of Local Government, Rural Development and Cooperatives, 1998) 1, 7.

2. Mehedi Hasan, "Rajdhanir 60 Bhag Elaka Panir Jonno Hahakar: Dirghomeyadi Ebong Somonnito Porikolponar Tagid, Dainik Ghattir Poriman Der Koti Liter" (Sixty Percent of the City Experiences Water Shortage: Daily Water Shortage of 15 million Liters in the City, Long Term Coordinated Efforts Are Needed to Solve the Crisis). 19 Apr., 2007. *The Daily Ajker Kagoj,* 19 Apr. 2007 <http://www.ajkerkagoj.com/2007/April19/1st_page.html#16>.

3. Dhaka Water Supply and Sewerage Authority, *Annual Report 2010-2011.* (Dhaka: Dhaka WASA, 2011) 41.

4. Nazrul Islam, A. Q. M. Mahbub, Nurul Islam Nazem, Gustavo Angeles, and Peter Lance, *Slums of Urban Bangladesh: Mapping and Census, 2005* (Dhaka: Center for Urban Studies, National Institute of Population Research and Training, MEA-SURE Evaluation, 2005) 15.

5. A slum cluster or settlement consists of "10 households or mess unit with a minimum of 25 members" (Islam et al. 14). In 2005, the estimated population of Dhaka City Corporation (DCC) was 7.2 million and an estimated 9.1 million people lived in Dhaka Metropolitan Areas (DMA). There are 90 administrative wards and 2 unions in DMA. The areas of DCC and DMA are 90 and 190 square miles respectively. Of the 4,966 slum clusters, 4,342 are in DCC areas. Among the slum population, 2.5 million live in DCC areas. See Islam et al. 20–21.

6. Anu Muhammad, "Biplober Sopno Bhumi Cuba: Dhaka aar Havana" (Cuba: Revolutionaries' Dreamland: A Comparison between Dhaka and Havana), *Saptahik 2000* (Weekly 2000), Sept. 2007:9, 36. However, other studies have different estimations regarding the number of slum dwellers in the city. One study estimates that there are 10 million people living in the burgeoning mega city of Dhaka. Among them 30 percent live in slums or in informal settlements and are classified as urban poor. (K. Iftekhar Ahmed, "Urban Poor Housing in Bangladesh and Potential Role of ACHR," the Asian Coalition for Housing Rights [ACHR], May 2007, 3). Dustha Shaystha Kendra (DSK, Health Center for the Destitute), a Bangladeshi NGO, categorizes slum populations as A, B, C, and D for the purpose of supplying water: A = not poor, B = poor, C = very poor, and D = vulnerable groups. Based on my conversation with Zakir Hossain, senior project coordinator, Water and Sanitation Project, DSK, Dhaka, Aug. 2007.

7. Islam et al. 12. A mess unit or mess housing refers to a household where a group of single individuals live in a hostel type of arrangement.

8. Islam et al. 12. See also Tanvir Sohel, "Dhaka-er Jonosonkhar 37 Bhag Bostibasi, 6 Mohanogore 54 Lakh: Ucheder Por Ghor-Kaj Dutoyi Harachhen Tara" (37 percent Population Live in the Slums in Dhaka and 5.4 million in Six Mega Cities: They Lost Both their Households and Livelihoods When They Were Evicted From Their Slums). 29 Jan, 2007. *Prothom Alo,* 29 Jan. 2007 <http://www.prothom-alo.org/index.news.details.php?mid=MzM4MQ==>. OSK is one of the Bangladeshi NGOs working as an agent for the slum dwellers to bring water connections from DWASA to the slum areas. They are now working in approximately 100 slum clusters. DSK estimation regarding the number of slum clusters varies slightly from the study report mentioned above. Zakir Hossain, a senior DSK project coordinator (water and sanitation project), informed me that according to their estimation, there are at least 4,572 slum clusters in Dhaka. According to Prof. Nazrul Islam, despite the 5 percent economic growth, the gap between the rich and the poor has widened in the last 5 years, which pushed more people into the slum areas. Quoted in Afroza Naznin, "Kal Rajdhanibasike Grihobondo Korechilo Shittoprobah" (Yesterday City Dwellers Stayed in Their Houses Due to the Cold Wave). 5 Jan., 2007. *Ajker Kagoj,* 5 Jan. 2007 <http://www.ajkerkagoj.com/2007/Jan05/1st_page.html#7>.

9. Islam et al. 39.

10. Population density in the city is 29,857 per square km, whereas in the slum areas it is 220,246. See Islam et al. 40.

11. In 1974, the estimated slum population was 275,000 in Dhaka city. In 1991, there were 718,143 people living in 2,156 slum clusters. In 1996, 1.5 million lived in 3,007 clusters. See 20.

12. Islam et al. 21.

13. Islam et al. 15, 42.

14. Islam et al. 40.

15. The owners of the slums provide electricity connections to the households by bringing power lines illegally from the main line. For offering this service, they charge a much higher rate than the power supply authority. The renters of these households have no other choice except to obtain service from their landlords because the Dhaka Electricity Supply authorities do not set up connections to the households that do not have legal holding numbers. One study mentions that 96 percent of the households in slum areas have electricity connections; see Islam et al. 12. Besides paying for electricity, slum dwellers also need to pay the owners of the slums for facilities such as toilets, drinking water, bathing water, and gas. Usually the slum owners illegally occupy government land, and sometimes private land, and build makeshift or low-quality houses for rent. They do not pay taxes and are not accountable for the condition or safety of the slum dwellers. Evictions are common in slums. As a result of constructing houses on illegal land, residents in slums often face eviction by the various authorities of the government, although there are policies against eviction without resettlement. Ahmed 3.

16. Islam et al. 37.

17. Islam et al. 36.

18. Islam et al. 21.

19. Based on my interview with slum dwellers in various clusters.

20. Islam et al. 15. Estimations from other studies vary slightly. The slum dwellers' monthly incomes reported in the various studies fall in the range of $60 to $82. It is necessary to mention that children in slums also work 10–14 hours per day in Dhaka. See Tiina Podymow et al., "Health and Social Conditions in the Dhaka Slums," *International Society for Urban Health*, 21 March <http://www.isuh.org/download/Dhaka. pdf>.

21. The municipal government of Dhaka was established in 1864. Later through various changes, the Dhaka City Corporation (DCC) was established in 1993 under the Dhaka City Corporation (Amendment) Act, 1993. Before the DCC, the municipal government in Dhaka was in charge of solid waste management. A. K. M. Jafar Ullah, "Country Report of Bangladesh: Management of Urban Water Environment," JICA Executive Seminar on Public Works and Management JFY 2004, National Institute for Land and Infrastructure Management, 27 Oct. 2006 < http://www.nilim.go.jp/english/conference/04.13th/7/13-7-2.pdf>.

22. Jafar Ullah, *Country Report.*

23. Jafar Ullah, *Country Report.*

24. Dhaka Water Supply and Sewerage Authority, 2011, 18.

25. Jafar Ullah, *Country Report.*

26. As of June 2011, the names and the designations of the twelve DWASA Board members are as follows: 1. Dr. Engineer Gholam Mostofa, Chairman, DWASA; 2. Zuana Aziz, Joint Secretary, Local Government Division; 3. Shudhansu Shekhar Biswas, Joint Secretary, Finance Department; 4. Abul Kashem Khan, President, Dhaka Chamber of Commerce and Industry; 5. Jamal Uddin Ahmed, Ph.D., FCA, Chairman, Institute of Chartered Accountants of Bangladesh; 6. Engineer Md. Nuruzzaman, Chief Engineer, Department of Public Health and Engineering; 7. Shirin Jahan, Councilor, Reserved Seat-12, Dhaka City Corporation; 8. Liakat Ali, Councilor, General Ward-77, Dhaka City Corporation; 9. Alhaj Mohammad Israfil, Advocate, Bangladesh Bar Council; 10. Altaf Mahmud, Secretary General, Bangladesh Federal Union of Journalists; 11. Professor Dr. Md Sharfuddin Ahmed, Secretary General, Bangladesh Medical association (BMA); 12. S.M. Azharul Islam, Social Welfare Secretary, Institute of Diploma Engineers, Dhaka; 13. Engineer Taqsem A. Khan, Managing Director, Dhaka WASA.

27. It is probably due to the same socio-economic background of the non-DWASA and DAWASA elites. Based on my conversation with a senior DWASA staff, who preferred to be anonymous.

28. Based on my conversation with DWASA staff and workers.

29. Personal interview, Mohammadpur, Dhaka, October 2006.

30. Personal interview, Gopibag, Dhaka, October 2006.

31. Personal interview, Khilkhet, Dhaka, September 2006.

32. Personal interview, Mohammadpur, Dhaka, September 2006.

33. Islam et al. 12.

34. Islam et al. 46.

35. Islam et al.15, 40.

36. Islam et al. 12.

37. None of the slum households that I visited during my field work in Dhaka had water connections.

38. DWASA sends bills to the NGOs and they collect money from the slum dwellers to pay the bills. Marginalized women in slum clusters play leading roles in collecting bills and distributing water among the slum dwellers under NGO supervision. NGOs have formed many groups in slums and women are the leaders of almost all of these groups. Besides collecting monthly bills, women supervise to make certain that the members of these groups collect water from the designated water sources and that no one wastes water from these sources. Women group members take turns continuously guarding these water sources. Based on my conversation with slum dwellers in Mohammadpur, Sept 2006.

39. Nikhil Bhodro, "Rajdhanite Tibro Hocchhe pani Sonkot: Poristhiti Mokabelay Sorkarer Karjokor Uddok Neyi" (Water Crisis Worsens in the Capital: Government Does not have any Efficient Initiative to Tackle the Problem), 29 May, 2005. *Weekly Ekota*, 30 May 2005 <http://www.cpbdhaka.org/Ekota83.pdf>.

40. Dhaka Water Supply and Sewerage Authority, 2011, 41.

41. Mithun Kamal, "Pani Ghattir Poriman 100 Koti Liters: Rajhdhanite Pani Somossa Prokot" (Severe Water Crisis in the Capital: Water Shortage Is 1,000 mld per Day), 11 April 2006. *The Daily Inquilab*, 18 May 2006 <http://www.dailyinquilab

.com/april1/index.htm>. See also Mizanur Khan, "Water Crisis: WASA Blames Power Cuts, Depletion of Groundwater," 8 June 2005. *The Daily Star*, 8 Jul. 2005 <http://www.thedailystar.net/2005/06/08/d506082501121.htm>.

42. Hasan, *Daily Water Shortage*; see also Imam, *Crying for Water*.

43. Atiur Rahman, M. Ashraf Ali, and Farooque Chowdhury, *People's Report on Bangladesh Environment 2001: Main Report, Vol. 1* (Dhaka: Unnayan Shamannay, University Press Limited, 2001) 110.

44. Dhaka Water Supply and Sewerage Authority, 2011, 34, Mehedi Hasan, "Dhaka-ke Paritakto Sohor Ghosona Kora Hote Pare: Ek Dosaoker Moddhe Bhu-Gorbhosto Panir Stor 40 Meter Niche Nemeche" (Dhaka Might Be Declared as a Deserted City: Underground Water Level Went Down 40 Meters in a Decade), 19 Jan. 2007. *The Daily Ajker Kagoj*, 22 Jan. 2007. < http://www.ajkerkagoj.com/2007/Jan19/1st_page.html#21>. For lifting water, in 2008 DWASA set up 21 new tube wells, 3,000 feet in depth, in some parts of Dhaka. Moreover, they have also replaced 45 old tube wells. As a result, the production of water has been increased by 200 million liters. See Arup Saha, "Susko Mousume Pani Sankat Erate WASA Totpor" (WASA Taking Adequate Measures to Avoid Water Crisis During the Dry Season), 1 March 2008. *The Daily Jaijaidin*, 1 March 2008 <http://www.jaijaidin.com/details.php?nid=57426>.

45. Dhaka Water Supply and Sewerage Authority, 2011, 34. Besides DWASA, some middle and upper class households as well as some private corporations and offices (both public and private) use deep tube-well in their premises. By June 2006, there were 1,179 deep tube wells used by "other agencies" in Dhaka; see Dhaka Water Supply and Sewerage Authority, *Management Information Report* (Dhaka: Dhaka WASA, 2006) ii. However, interviewed DWASA officials and workers said that unofficial estimation would be much higher than that. Use of a private deep tube well is legal in Dhaka; yet, a deep tube well should not be more than 600 feet deep and is not allowed within 600 feet of a DWASA tube well location. DWASA does not have enough manpower to monitor whether this rule is properly followed.

46. Dhaka Water Supply and Sewerage Authority, 2011, 34.

47. Mehedi Hasan, "Grismo Suru Na Hoteyi WASA-er Dainik Pani Ghati 55 Koti Liters, Dhaka-Basike Bachate Ekhoni 12 sh Koti Takar Prokolpo Hate Nite Hobe Sorkar-ke: Bhu-Gorbhosto Panir Stor Proti Bochor 10 Meter Kore Neme Jayoyar Asonka" (Even Before the Summer Season Begins, the Daily Water Crisis in the City Reached to 550 millions Liters per Day; Government should Immediately Take a Project of $172 m: It Is Apprehended that the Water Layer Will Go Down at the Rate of 10 Meter Per Year), 4 Apr. 2007. *The Daily Ajker Kagoj*, 7 Apr. 2007 <http://www.ajkerkagoj.com/2007April04/last_page.html#2>.

48. Imam, *Crying for Water*.

49. Pipeline leakages are one of the major causes for system loss in Dhaka. Pipelines used for supplying water are very old and they need to be replaced immediately. Under-billing, stolen water, and illegal connections are the other reasons for system loss. Usually, middle and upper class customers steal water from the main pipelines by connecting electric pumps with the pipelines inside their residents.

50. DWASA supplies 24 hours of water to only 39 and 44 percent of domestic and non-domestic connections respectively; see Asian Development Bank. "Diagnostic Water

Market Assessment for Dhaka Water Supply and Sewerage Authority," *Asian Development Bank*, 2 Jun. 2007 <http://www.adb.org/Water/Tools/DWASA-TOR-digest.asp>.

51. Among the 599 deep tube wells, 493 have diesel driven generators to operate during power cuts (Dhaka Water Supply and Sewerage Authority, 2011, 34). In addition, DWASA had 31 movable generators to be used with the tube wells that did not have generators. During summer, due to acute power crises (low voltage and power cuts), instead of using these generators as mobile generators, DWASA had to use these as immobile generators to fix these particular tube wells. A generator should run for only 2 hours per day (that is 60 hours per month), but due to acute power crises, DWASA had to run every generator 60 hours per week. In February, only a few tube wells were operated by the generators, but in summer most of the tube wells need generators. Moreover, DWASA had to spend $1,429 per month for each generator (Imam, *Crying for Water*). In an interview with the newspaper, the DWASA MD Rayhanul Abedin said that due to the problem of power cuts, DWASA produced 200 mld less water in summer 2008. See Arup Dutt and Anis Rahman, "Loadsheding, Prochondo Gorom, Panir Tibro Sonkot" (Power Cut, Severe Heat and Acute Water Crisis), 27 April 2008. *Prothom Alo*, 30 Aug. 2008 < http://www.prothom-alo.com/archive/news_details_home.php?dt=2008-04-27&issue_id=906&nid=MTU2NDA=>.

52. According to one estimation for 2012, in Bangladesh there are 47 million people (31.3 percent) in the middle class and 4.1 million (2.7 percent) in the affluent or rich class. UNB, "66 pc population still poor: Study," 21 July 2012. *The Daily Star*. 21 July 2012 <http://www.thedailystar.net/newDesign/news-details.php?nid=242961>.

53. Several DWASA staff members and engineers informed me that they were aware of the use of illegal water pumps in the city. However, they could not take any action against it because there are no clear guidelines regarding the use of pumps by the city dwellers, and also because there is a lack of staff. Therefore, despite their knowledge, they completely overlook the presence of illegal pumps in the city. DWASA staff and the water users told me that they never heard that DCC or any other legal enforcement authority took any legal action against the illegal users. DCC also does not have any guidelines regarding the use of water pumps.

54. Each DWASA truck can carry 250–300 gallons or 1155–1386 liters of water. A deputy revenue collector of DWASA informed me that they supply water to the households free of charge if the supply is disrupted due to the mechanical failure of DWASA. In this case, a household owner needs to report the problem to the DWASA authority. Yet, in reality, most of the water users I interviewed told me that they were unaware of the service. Only a handful of water users were aware of this service, although after calling the DWASA, most of the time they did not receive any cooperation from them.

55. Dhaka Water Supply and Sewerage Authority, 2011, 1.

56. Based on my conversation with a DWASA deputy revenue collector, who wanted to remain anonymous. It is interesting to note that the officers and the engineers whom I interviewed in DWASA preferred to remain anonymous because they were government officials, and as a result they did not feel comfortable being quoted in my dissertation or any other type of publication. On the contrary, workers and union leaders did not have any hesitation in disclosing their names in any publication.

57. Dhaka Water Supply and Sewerage Authority, 2011, 19.
58. Dhaka Water Supply and Sewerage Authority, 2011, 56.
59. Dhaka Water Supply and Sewerage Authority, 2011,56.
60. DWASA has 22 vehicles; each can carry 5,400 liters of water. It also has 14 trolleys, which can each carry 2,300 liters of water; see Hasan, *Daily Water Crisis.*
61. Zaber Hossain, DWAS revenue collector, and other officials and mechanics working for the DWASA acknowledged the presence of bureaucratic complexity and corruption in obtaining a water connection. In addition, middle and lower-middle class city dwellers with whom I conducted interviews also informed me about the complexities and corruption associated with the connection.
62. Besides several DWASA staff members, Zaber Hossain informed me that there is widespread corruption associated with water connections and as a result, it is very difficult and expensive to obtain a connection.
63. Ward is the lowest local administrative level in Dhaka under the DCC. There are 90 wards in the city and 90 commissioners, directly elected by adult citizens who reside and vote in the wards. Further, there are thirty reserved seats for women, who are also elected by direct votes, by both males and females. For details, see Dhaka City Corporation. *Dhaka City Corporation*, 14 Jan. 2007 <http://www.dhakacity.org/profile.html>. Among the elected commissioners, mainly those who are elected from the general seats are more powerful than the women commissioners. Out of 90 elected ward commissioners, only 7 are female. There are 8 wards in the Narayanganj district, and therefore there are eight elected commissioners in this district. There are also four seats reserved for the female commissioners in Narayanganj.
64. Based on my conversation with several customers in various parts of the city.
65. As of April 2008, vendors sold a 5-liter can for 10 taka (14 cents) and a 10-liter can for 15–18 taka (22–26 cents). Keraniganj (Dhaka) Correspondent, "Keraniganj Theke Protidin 50 Hazar Liter Pani Dhakay Asche" (Every Day 50 Thousand Liters of Water Supplied to Dhaka from Keraniganj), 27 April 2008. *Prothom Alo*, 30 Aug. 2008 <http://www.prothom-alo.com/archive/news_details_home.php?dt=2008-04-27&issue_id=906&nid=MTU2NDE=>.
66. Mehedi Hasan, "Nogorir 40 Bhag Elakay Sorboraho Kora Hocchhe Moyla O Durgondhojukto Pani: WASA-er Panite Payoya Geche Moricher Bichi, Balu and Chera Polythene." (DWASA Supplying Dirty and Odiferous Water to 40 percent of the City: Pepper Seeds, Sand Particles and Torn Polythene Found in the Supplied Water), 20 Apr. 2007. *The Daily Ajker Kagoj*, 20 Apr. 2007 < http://www.ajkerkagoj.com/2007/April20/1st_page.html#13>.
67. The areas where I found odiferous water were Gopibagh, Tikatuli, Hatkhola, Jatrabari, and Moahammadpur.
68. Quoted in Hasan, *DWASA Supplying Dirty Water.*
69. Mansur Helal, Susko Mousumer Ageyi Rajdhanite Panir Sankot: Stor Neme Geche 46 Meter Niche, Barche Nogorir Tapmatra." (Capital's Water Level went Down 46 meters before the Dry Season Starts: the Average Temperature of the City Increasing). Jan. 24., 2007. *The Daily Ajker Kagoj*. 24 Jan. 2007. < http://www.ajkerkagoj.com/2007/Jan24/1st_page.html#17>.

70. The length of the Buriganga is roughly 10.5 miles. Morshed Ali Khan, "Tanneries 'Kill' the Buriganga River," 11 Sep. 2006. *Asia Water Wire*, 24 Jan. 2007 <http://www.asiawaterwire.net/node/428>.

71. Ahmed Nure Alam, "Pani Noy Bish Pan Korchi: Rajdhani-soho Drihottoro Dhaka-er 1500 Borgo Km Elakar Pani Bisakto, Charpaser Nodigulo Bhoyaboho Dusone Aakranto" (We Are Drinking Poison Not Water: Including Greater Dhaka, Water Has Been Poisoned in 1,500 sq km of Area: The Level of River Pollution Around the City Is Very High), 15 Mar. 2007. *The Daily Janakantha*, 16 Mar. 2007 <http://www.dailyjanakantha.com/p1/html1>.

72. Mansur Helal, *Capital's Water Level.*

73. As far as pH value is concerned, during May–June 2006, a study team in Dhaka collected ground water from 18 points in the city. In their test, they found the pH value of water was below 7 in all the samples they collected. Quoted in Alam, *We Are Drinking Poison.* In any solution, if pH value is less than 7, it is considered acidic; greater than 7 is basic (alkaline). The acceptable level of pH for pure water at 25°C is 7, although in absolutely pure water, the pH value is 0.

74. Quoted in Hasan, *Daily Water Crisis.* See also Alam, *We Are Drinking Poison.*

75. This test was conducted by the Environment Ministry of Bangladesh in Elephant Road, Mohammedpur, Shamoli, and Framgate at the beginning of 2008. Wasek Billah and Niaz Morshed. "Rajdhanite Pani Pan Kotoa Nirapod" (Drinking Water in Dhaka Is Not Safe), 24 Aug. 2008. *Prothom Alo*, 2 Sep. 2008 <http://www.prothom-alo.com/archive/news_details_home.php?dt=2008-08-24&issue_id=1023&nid=MTgzMzY=>.

76. Anwar Aladin and Mohhamad Abu Taleb, "Eyi Pocha Pani-I Khacchhi" (We Are Drinking Polluted Water), 21 April 2009. *The Daily Ittefaq*, 22 April 2009 <http://www.ittefaq.com/content/2009/04/21/news0580.htm>.

77. Dhaka Water Supply and Sewerage Authority, 2006,4.

78. There are 615 mg of alkali in one liter of water in the river Buriganga, whereas the WHO standard is 400 mg per liter. While the acceptable level of turbidity is 10, in the Buriganaga it is 98.7; the amount of ammonia is 2.5 mg in the river, whereas the acceptable level is 0.5 mg. In addition, the level of calcium is 36 mg in the river, while 75–200 mg per liter is the acceptable level. The amount of oxygen is only 1.2 mg, which is much lower than the acceptable level; see Masudujjaman Rabin, "Buriganga Ekhon Biser Adhar, Pani Sodhon Kore Pan Korche Dhaka-basi: Bisakto Shilpo-Borje Dushito Hocchhe Nodi" (Buriganaga Becoming a Poisonous River, the City Dwellers Are Purifying Water Before Drinking: Poisonous Industrial Waste Is the Main Cause of River Pollution), 16 Mar. 2007. *The Daily Inqilab*, 2 Apr. 2007 <http://www.dailyinqilab.com>.

79. Mobassor Hossain Ripon, an engineer in ARBAN, informed me that he collected water from different locations and took it to the various laboratories in Dhaka; however, none of the test results met the WHO standard.

4

Public-Private Participation (PPP) Water Governance and Marginalized Women's Capabilities: The Experience of Metropolitan Manila

From a national agency, attending to the water needs of the entire Philippines, the MWSS by virtue of its Charter was tasked to provide water to Metro Manila and environs.

MWSS Regulatory Office: Information Kit

Metropolitan Manila was the first South East Asian city to allow private companies in its water sector through Public-Private Participation (PPP) governance. In 1997, the state-led governance of the Metropolitan Waterworks and Sewerage System (MWSS), responsible for supplying water to roughly 12 million residents in the city, was replaced by PPP governance. The government's decision to transform the state-led governance to PPP was implemented under two separate 25-year concession agreements.[1] The agreements awarded responsibility to the winning bidders for handling water treatment, distribution, tariff collection, facility improvement, and "overall management" of the MWSS.[2] The 25-year lease agreement formed the basis for transferring the rights to operate the water and sewage systems from MWSS to two consortia: The Manila Water Company, Inc. (MWCI) and Maynilad Water Services, Inc. (MWSI). In turn, the government repeatedly guaranteed the city residents that the new governance system would decrease the tariffs and ensure efficiency as well as improving the service delivery.[3]

Like in Dhaka, a good number of marginalized women residing in informal settlements in Metropolitan Manila did not have sufficient access to water resources under the state-led governance of the MWSS. They also did not have the capability to participate in MWSS's decision-making process. Did their capability to access supplied water and to participate in decision-making spaces increase after the introduction of PPP governance?

   This chapter discusses the effects of PPP governance on the political and material capabilities of the marginalized women—that is, their capabilities to participate in decision-making spaces and to access the supplied water resources. As mentioned in the previous chapter, women's capability to participate is measured through the lens of the participatory typology. John Gaventa's "power cube" theory is also used to understand the spaces and patterns of power in the participatory process. However, participation does not mean direct participation of all women; instead, it means the capability of those women to send representatives to the formal spaces to represent their interests. Two formal spaces—the company board and the governmental regulatory oversight—are presented here to comprehend the political capability of the marginalized women, i.e. their ability to contribute to the final decision through participation in these spaces. Women's capability to access water is measured in terms of the quantity of water they receive, its quality, and its price. A brief discussion of the conditions of the marginalized women in Metropolitan Manila serves as an introduction to a discussion of their capabilities.

Marginalized Women in Metropolitan Manila

This study classifies marginalized women as those whose per capita incomes are below the poverty threshold; they are unable to meet their basic needs. In Metropolitan Manila, the majority of these marginalized women reside in slum areas (Table 4.1). The Philippines government uses the World Bank's standard for measuring poverty, that is, less than $1 per person per day. The national annual per capita poverty threshold of the country is $278. Besides per capita income, the government also uses the ability to procure and consume at least 2,000 calories per person per day as an indicator to measure poverty.[4] Therefore, marginalized women are those who earn less than $1 per day ($278 per year) and who consume less than 2,000 calories per day. As a result of low income, they are not able to meet the food subsistence threshold, hygienic sanitation standards, housing with proper facilities such as water pipe connections, medical care, education, and the other basic amenities of life.

   More than a third of the Metropolitan Manila population resides in slums or poor quality households, and 35 percent of urban poor households are located solely in two areas of Metropolitan Manila: Quezon City and Manila. Also, seventy percent of the population of Pasay City (in Metropolitan Manila) resides

TABLE 4.1.
Percent of Informal Households in Metro Manila by City and Municipality, 2002

City/Municipality	Total Households	Informal Households	Percent of Total
City of Manila	333,547	99,549	29.8
Mandaluyong	59,682	25,383	42.5
Marikina City	80,160	28,580	35.6
Pasig City	107, 835	27,328	25.2
Quezon City	480,624	169,490	35.2
Kalookan City	249,567	67,292	26.9
Malabon	74,137	12,461	16.8
Navotas	49,450	19,030	38.4
Valenzuela City	106,382	36,404	34.2
Las Pinas City	97,962	36,107	36.8
Makati City	98,225	27,024	27.5
Muntinlupa City	78,016	40,457	51.8
Paranaque City	94,106	29,790	31.6
Pasay City	78,180	57,436	73.4
Pateros	12,029	3,502	29.1
Taguig	102,723	21,931	21.3

Source: The Housing and Urban Development Coordinating Council (HUDCC) Unpublished Report, 2002. Published in Junio M. Ragaragio. "The Case of Metro Manila, Philippines." Massachusetts Institute of Technology (MIT). 22 Mar. 2008 <http://web.mit.edu/sigus/www/NEW/challengecourse/pdfs/pdfscities/Manila.pdf>.

in slums or very poor households.[5] Most of these slum households have been residing more than two decades in these localities.[6]

Most of the slum residents live below the poverty level; in fact, 34.2 percent of the total household population, or 5.2 million families, live below the poverty line in the country. In Metropolitan Manila, nearly half of the families have a monthly income of roughly $400, whereas individuals or families combined in the slums have an income below the poverty threshold.[7] A family with five members living in the city is thought to need at least $300 per month to meet basic needs.[8] A survey conducted by the Asian Development Bank (ADB) revealed that the monthly income of a typical poor household with five members in Metro Manila was roughly $261.[9] The poorest urban households there could thus spend roughly 3.7 percent of their income per month—just 8 cents—for water.[10]

Marginalized women's (and men's) households in slums are characterized as "deteriorated, hazardous, unsanitary or lacking in standard in convenience. They [are] also defined as the squalid, crowded, or unsanitary conditions under which [marginalized women] live, irrespective of the physical state of the building or area."[11] Moreover, what I saw in various localities was that there were no water pipeline connections at all inside their homes. We can distinguish marginalized women's households from those not in this category by the household water connections. In Metropolitan Manila, marginalized women have no connections inside their households.

Like in Dhaka, marginalized residents also live "by the riverbanks, along the walls of Manila Bay, under and over bridges, in public parks and along railroad tracks."[12] They are not concentrated in a particular city or municipality; they are found all over the twelve cities and five municipalities of Metropolitan Manila.[13] They are generally dispersed, although as mentioned a large number of them reside in slum areas. These slums are scattered over 526 communities in all the cities and municipalities of Metropolitan Manila.[14] They are mainly located on "vacant private or public lands, usually along rivers, near garbage dumps, along railroad tracks, under bridges and beside industrial establishments."[15] It is not uncommon in the city that slums are located right next to the rich neighborhoods or mansions. They have developed in any places where there was an opportunity and a space to build some form of household. It is thus not possible to segregate the slum localities in Metropolitan Manila like the ghettos in some countries.

Moreover, a significant number of marginalized women reside in various slums located in the dangerous zones of the city. When it comes to the issue of providing basic services such as water, electricity, gas, and sanitation, the people living in these zones are the most neglected by both the government authorities and private companies. Steep riverbanks, areas along canals and streams, floodplains, hillsides, garbage dumps, and areas along railroad tracks are all considered dangerous living zones. Besides the inaccessibility of these locations, authorities believe that it is futile to provide services to those places, which are frequent targets for demolition by both the municipal and local authorities.[16]

There are no accurate statistics regarding the number of people living in slums and informal settlements in Metropolitan Manila, though some estimates put the figure between a quarter and a third of the city population.[17] The total population of the city in 2010 was about 11.85 million.[18] We can therefore assume that at least 2.96 to 3.95 million people resided in informal settlements, which was nearly a third of the city population. UN-Habitat statistics (2003) show that at least 2.5 million people resided in various slums in Metropolitan Manila. Thus about the same percentage of the population in both Metropolitan Manila and Dhaka resides in either slums or various forms of informal urban settlements.[19]

The national average household size is five members in the Philippines, but more than half of families in slums or depressed areas comprise extended families, with up to nine members.[20] According to the Metropolitan Manila

Development Authority (MMDA), at least 85,000 families live in various slums.[21] Therefore, we can assume that a good number of people live there without families; I personally met some slum dwellers who lived there without their families.

Like in Dhaka, slum dwellers in Metropolitan Manila are also regarded as illegal inhabitants in the conurbation. Eighty percent of the low-income households have no legal property rights in Metropolitan Manila.[22] One major difference between Dhaka and Metropolitan Manila lies in the perception regarding the slum dwellers. In Dhaka, slum dwellers are officially illegal residents, but government officials, NGO workers, and city residents do not perceive them as "squatters" or illegal residents. On the contrary, I observed that in Metropolitan Manila not only the government officials and NGO activists, but also the legal inhabitants there perceived the slum population as squatters or illegal residents. Government and corporate publications as well as newspapers there also addressed them as squatters or illegal residents.

Like in Dhaka, slum dwellers in Metropolitan Manila often face eviction by both the government and the owners of the land. Presidential Decree 772, promulgated in 1975 during the regime of Ferdinand Marcos, criminalized illegal occupancy and squatting in the city, thus creating a legal basis for treating the squatters and slum dwellers as criminals. This decree "effectively condemned an estimated 10 million urban poor Filipinos who cannot afford legal housing."[23] Sometimes it was also used against the slum dwellers as the basis for bringing criminal charges against them. The continual implementation of this decree resulted in the eviction of 100,000 families just in Metropolitan Manila during the years 1986 to 1991.[24] During my stay in Metropolitan Manila, some women residing in slums and informal settlements informed me that they considered themselves to be legal residents of the city, and they further stressed that the government should come forward with appropriate measures to solve the housing crisis of the poor instead of evicting them or treating them as illegal residents.

Poverty in the villages and massive unemployment are the major reasons for internal migration into the urban areas in the Philippines. Drought and reduced farm activities are also driving factors behind this migration.[25] Most of the marginalized women are unemployed, underemployed, or irregularly employed. During my visit to slums, women residing there informed me that they were mainly housemaids, vendors, factory workers, day laborers, housewives, or self-employed (mainly as handicrafts makers). Males worked as tricycle drivers, construction laborers, factory laborers, day laborers, vendors, domestic helpers, carpenters, or self-employed handicraft makers. More women than men work as domestic helpers. In Metropolitan Manila, 50.2 percent of people in the labor force have no job, and only 49.8 percent have full or part-time employment. This statistics indicates that with the average family size of 5–7 members, 2–3 members have no employment.[26]

Under the previous state-led governance, the marginalized women and informal settlers of the city did not have necessary access to water resources.[27] The political capabilities of marginalized women to participate in the decision-making space also did not develop. This chapter examines the capability of marginalized women to participate in PPP governance and analyzes their capability to access supplied water resources under that governance system. A brief discussion of the background of the PPP governance in the water sector in Metropolitan Manila will aid in the analysis of these issues.

Adoption of PPP Governance in the Water Sector of Metropolitan Manila: Background History

Founded in 1878, the MWSS was one of the oldest water governance systems in Asia, and it was a classic example of state-led governance. Its genesis was "traced to the first water system laid out in old Manila … from funds donated by Spanish philanthropist Francisco Carriedo y Peredo."[28] This state-led system (colonial government organization) was introduced by the then-colonial state of the Philippines. In 1878, this water system delivered 16 million liters of water per day (mld) to the 300,000 residents of the city. The major objective of the system was "to improve the people's health and living conditions through clean drinking water."[29]

The Carriedo system was changed from the Manila Water Supply System to the Metropolitan Water District in 1919; this nomenclature was again changed to the National Waterworks and Sewerage Authority in 1954. The government renamed the water supply system again in 1972, to the Metropolitan Waterworks and Sewerage System; since then to this date, it has been known as the MWSS. It was the failure of the MWSS to meet the needs of the city dwellers that set the stage for PPP governance in the water sector.

After the fall of Ferdinand Marcos's regime in 1986, the succeeding administration of Corazon Aquino commenced significant reforms for transforming state-led governance into market-led governance, through partial or full transferring of the hundreds of state enterprises into the hands of private companies. To attract private investments, in 1990 her administration endorsed a law that granted the legal basis for Build-Operate-Transfer (BOT) agreements. Fidel Ramos's victory in the 1992 election further accelerated this process of adopting market-led governance. Privatization and deregulation were "the cornerstones of the economic policies" of his administration.[30]

Ramos's administration decided to open the country for large-scale foreign investments through promoting private sector participation, at a time when his country was suffering from an acute scarcity of electricity. To combat the electricity crisis, the Ramos administration used the BOT law to involve the private sectors in constructing the power capacity that laid the basis for continual economic growth during his regime (from 1992 to 1998).

By the mid 1990s, the Ramos administration faced severe problems with supplying sufficient water to Metropolitan Manila and adjacent areas, which adversely affected the lives of 10.6 million people. Among the major Asian cities, the Metropolitan Manila water service coverage was one of the worst. For example, in 1996, while the water authorities in Singapore, Hong Kong, Seoul, and Kuala Lumpur ensured 100 percent water coverage, the MWSS served only 67 percent of city residents, which was 33 percent less than the other major South East Asian (SEA) cities (Table 4.2).[31] Even this service was not regular; the city residents had only intermittent, low-pressure connections. The MWSS was able to supply water only 16–17 hours per day, while other cities in the region provided a 24-hour supply.

Compared to other SEA cities (on average 30%), the MWSS had the "highest rate" (58%) of non-revenue water (Tables 4.2 and 4.3).[32] Fifty-eight percent of non-revenue water consisted of leakages, defective meters, unauthorized connections, and an inefficient billing system.[33] This was even higher than in Dhaka (51%). The Philippines government was unable to invest in the water sector to improve the supply system, and by 1997, the MWSS had incurred $1 billion in debt. It often asked for and received financial subsidies from the government to "service its debt."[34]

As mentioned, the inability of MWSS to provide "universal access and effective service," the lack of funding for the improvement of the waterworks

TABLE 4.2.
Water Coverage in Selected South East Asian Cities and Dhaka in 1996

City	Population (million) (hours/day)	Water Availability	Water Coverage (% of population)	Non-Revenue Water (% of water production)
Manila	10.6	16	67	58
Dhaka	9.0	17	42	51
Singapore	3.0	24	100	7
Hong Kong	6.3	24	100	36
Seoul	10.6	24	100	35
Kuala Lumpur	1.4	24	100	36
Bangkok	7.3	24	82	38

Compiled by McIntosh and Yniguez in Arthur C. McIntosh and Cesar E.Yniguez (ed.). *Second Water Utilities Data Book: Asian and Pacific Region*. Philippines. Asian Development Bank. 1997.

Table 4.3.
Water Supply Condition in Metro Manila under the MWSS State-led
Governance in 1997 (Before the Introduction of PPP Governance)

Service population	11 million
Population served	7.5 million
Total no. of connections	825,000
Average daily water production	3,000 million liters
No. of treatment plants	3
Total length of pipeline	12,000km (7,456 miles)
Average daily water availability	16 hours
Average daily non-revenue	58 percent
Water losses (May, 1996)Per-capita daily	133 liters
Consumption billing efficiency	42.8 percent

Source: Raj Chotrani, "Lessons from Philippines Water Privatization" (Asian Water, July 1999). Posted in Metropolitan Waterworks and Sewerage System (MWSS). 5 Aug. 2008. <http://www.mwss.gov.ph/news/default.asp?action=article&ID=66 >. See also Jocelyn C. Cuaresma, "Pro-Poor Water Services in Metro Manila: In Search for Greater Equity." Regulatory Governance in Developing Countries, Eds. Minogue, Martin, and Ledivina Carino (UK and USA: Edward Elgar Publishing) 2007, and McIntosh and Yniguez (ed.).

system, and the significant decline of its financial performance eventually encouraged the government to adopt PPP governance as a "promising alternative."[35] In 1995, the Philippines Congress enacted the National Water Crisis Act (R.A. No. 8041), which provided the legal framework for "the biggest (partial) water privatization in the world" in terms of the population it covered.[36] This Act states that it is crucial for the government to implement immediate and useful tasks that address the widespread water crisis, "which adversely affects the health and well-being of the population, food production and industrialization process."[37]

The goals of introducing PPP governance were to develop quality and efficiency, expand services, decrease water tariffs, and stop providing subsidies.[38] The International Finance Corporation (IFC, the World Bank Group) assisted the government to set up a plan for privatization contracts, to provide technical assistance in developing the transformation process, to organize relevant data, and to ensure transparency in the tender procedure.[39] An interdisciplinary team at the IFC suggested dividing the Metro Manila into two service zones (the East and the West) for "promoting competition, providing scope for performance benchmarking, and allowing one concessionaire to take over (temporarily)" if the other were not successful in meeting the requirements of the agreement.[40] The West Zone is much bigger than the East in terms of both population and area. Sixty percent of the city population, including the vast majority of the low-income people, resides in the West Zone. Relatively wealthy people live in the East Zone. In comparison to the East, the West

Zone was known for "a higher rate of non-revenue water" (60–70 percent in the West Zone vs. 50–55 percent in the East Zone).[41]

In accordance with the IFC's recommendation, the MWSS adopted a concession model for the bidding process. It arranged a competitive bid to auction off two 25-year concessions to hand over the responsibilities of water treatment, allocation, tariff collection, infrastructure development, and overall management to the private companies. The two Concession Agreements between MWSS and its concessionaires leased the public water facilities and real estate assets to the private companies. The agreements authorized the MWSS's Regulatory Office (RO) to regulate the rates. The concessionaires need to pay about $1.2 billion as concession fees over the 25-year concession period, and concession fees were requested to mitigate MWSS's existing foreign debt obligation. These are also viewed as rental or lease fees for employing the MWSS amenities.[42]

Fifty local and foreign companies expressed interest in participating in the bidding process. To narrow down the competition, the government decided to enforce "a strict set of criteria," that is, an interested bidder should have a local sponsor and a foreign operator.[43] Further, no single bidder should win both the concessions. The MWSS imposed a regulation that one winner could win only one zone rather than two; they probably thought it would prevent monopoly as well as encouraging competition and efficiency. Further, it would ensure better and widespread service coverage. The criteria helped eliminate all but seven of the 50 prospective companies from the bidding process, eventually reducing the number to only four (Table 4.4). These four consortia participated in the bidding process on January 23, 1997.

The Manila Water Company, Inc. (MWCI) and Maynilad Water Services, Inc. (MWSI) won the East and the West Zones respectively. On August 1, 1997, according to the agreement, the management and operation of the MWSS was handed over to the MWCI and MWSI for twenty-five years, until 1922.[44] Thus, on its 120th year of continued service, the MWSS was partially privatized to adopt the distributed or hybrid model of governance, which is also known as a public-private partnership (PPP) system. In 2009 the MWCI and in 2010 the MWSI received a fifteen-year extension of the concession; they will thus be in charge of managing these two zones until 1937.

As mentioned, PPP governance is the empirical manifestation of state management of the external affairs of private companies or corporations. It is a state-private joint management system wherein the state and private companies reorganize distribution for the benefit of the customers or citizens depending on the context. Often, the state manages the external affairs of the company through an appointed regulatory body. The concession accord transformed the MWSS to "an oversight body via a regulatory office," whose

TABLE 4.4.
Pre-Qualified Four MWSS Bidding Consortia

Pre-Qualified Consortium	Business Interests
1) Filipino Sponsor: Metro Pacific Corporation	Property development, telecom etc.
Foreign Partner: Anglican Water International (UK)	UK based water and sewerage management
2) Filipino Sponsor: Ayala Corporation	Real estate, telecom, electronics, banking and financial services, electronics and IT etc.
Foreign Partner: North West Water (UK) (a division of United Utilities Ltd.)	Operation in Manchester area
3) Filipino Sponsor: Benpers Holdings Corporations	Property development, telecom, electronics, banking and financial services, power generation and distribution
Foreign Partner: Lyonnaise des Eaux (later Onedo)	A global player in the field of environmental services
4) Filipino Sponsor: Aboitz Holdings Corporation	Power generation and distribution, financial services etc.
Foreign Partner: Campagnie Generale des Eaux (later Vivendi)	Telecom, media, entertainment etc.

Source : Rivera, Virgilio C. Jr. "The Experience of Manila Water Company under the MWSS Privatization." Presented in Regional Conference on Universality of Infrastructure Services: Financing, Delivery and Regulatory Issues. The India Habitat Center, New Delhi, India. 2006. 12; see also Ayala Corporation, 12 July 2007 <http://www.ayala.com.ph/>; Vivendi, 12 July 2007 <http://www.vivendi.com/corp/en/home/index.php,>; Lyonnaise des Eaux, 12 July 2007 <http://www.lyonnaise-des-eaux.fr/sommaire.php>

responsibility was to monitor the concessionaires regarding the implementation of the concession contracts.[45] Based on the agreement, the MWSS Regulatory Office (RO) was created in August 1997.

According to the concessions, the government transferred operational and managerial responsibilities, including servicing the debt of the water companies without shifting the ownership of assets. The concession agreements mention some of the following objectives for PPP governance:

1. Augment investment and operational efficiencies to ensure full service coverage.
2. Ensure 24-hour per day water supplies by June 2000. Nowhere in the agreement was it written that ensuring 24 hours of water would depend on the ability of the customers to buy it; it was just vaguely stated that the goal of the companies was to ensure 24-hour per day water in its coverage areas. Ensuring a 24-hour per day supply to a particular house or locality nevertheless does depend on the ability of the household owner or the local community to pay for the water because the water

distribution system was completely transferred to the hands of the private companies. How the marginalized women or the most economically vulnerable citizens of the city would pay the bills was completely overlooked in the agreements. The water companies and the MWSS authority thus paid insufficient attention to the needs of the poor or their capability to pay for water.

3. Assure that water quality conforms to the National Standard for Drinking Water (which was based on WHO water quality guidelines).
4. Decrease non-revenue water to a satisfactory level.
5. Ensure that the companies bear the financial burden of improving MWSS facilities.
6. Achieve standard water pressure and flow (16 pounds per square inch, or psi).
7. Renegotiate tariff patterns every 5 years.
8. Ensure a maximum fee of $106 for water connection.

There are no "specific incentives" or clauses in the concessions regarding reaching out to the poor or the marginalized women, except in setting up public standpipes.[46] There are also no provisions for marginalized women to increase what Sen mentions as their political capabilities through participating in any of the decision-making or policy spaces, or by creating a separate space for their participation. It appears that the arrangement was set up so that the concessionaires would rely on administrative and technical procedures to allocate water to the customers. The concession agreements did not provide for the concessionaires to consider feedback from the marginalized women or other economically vulnerable groups to meet their demands. Therefore, this study investigates the political capabilities of the marginalized women under the PPP governance system in Metropolitan Manila in terms of their ability to participate in any level of the decision-making processes or spaces (directly or indirectly) in the governance mechanism. Moreover, the role of the RO is also analyzed because the "issue in water regulation is where the ultimate decision-making power [is] lodged."[47]

Public-Private Participation (PPP) Governance System and Marginalized Women's Capabilities to Participate in the Formal Decision-Making Spaces

The MWCI and MWSI both follow market-led corporate governance. However, both have signed agreements with the MWSS to become partners with this state institution, and have adopted the PPP governance mechanism. The board of directors is the highest body in both corporations; management is ultimately responsible to the boards. Hiring, selecting, or nominating anyone to any position is subject to final approval by the boards, which constitute a group of powerful citizens who make decisions behind closed doors. These places are exclusively reserved for the economically powerful elites; marginalized women, vulnerable groups, "common" citizens, or customers' representatives have no access to these exclusive spaces. Since both companies follow almost the same pattern of hierarchical, centralized governance, the comparatively more successful MWCI is used here to illustrate the exclusionary pattern of participation that is practiced by both companies.

The MWCI's Governance Mechanism

The MWCI, a private utility company, was incorporated on January 6, 1997, and it launched its commercial operation on January 1, 2000. As mentioned, it is a joint venture company, comprising various corporations (Table 4.5; see Table 4.6 for MWSI).[48] The board of directors (the board) is the highest body of the company; it "oversees the management" and "provides direction towards the formulation of a sound corporate strategy."[49] In theory, this is what Gaventa refers as an "invited (policy) space." According to him, in this type of space, people or citizens are invited to participate by the elites as well as by government authorities, transnational agencies, and non-governmental organizations. In this sense, the board is also an invited space, where any citizen with ownership of at least one share of stock in the company is eligible to participate (Article I, 1.2 a).[50]

However, the reality tells us a different story. The board comprises 12 directors, among whom no one holds only one share. All are at the same time

TABLE 4.5.
MWCI's Shareholding Structure in 1997

Shareholders	Percent Ownership
Ayala Corporation	51.1
United Utilities B.V.	19.9
BPI Capital	11.4
Mitsubishi Corp.	11.4
Employees	6.3
Total	100.0

Source: Buenaventura, Mae and Bubut Palattao. "Taking Stock of Water Privatization in the Philippines: The Case of the Metropolitan Waterworks and Sewerage System (MWSS)." PAID (Official Publication of the Freedom from the Debt Coalition). 14. (2004): 21.

TABLE 4.6.
MWSI's Shareholding Structure in 1997

Shareholders	Percent Ownership
Benpers Holdings Corp.	59
Suez Lyonnaise: Onedo	20
Lyonnaise Asia Water	20
Metropolitan Bank & Trust Company	1
Total	100

Source: Mae Buenaventura and Bubut Palattao, "Taking Stock of Water Privatization in the Philippines: The Case of the Metropolitan Waterworks and Sewerage System (MWSS)" PAID (Official Publication of the Freedom from the Debt Coalition) 14 (2004) 21.

serving as directors, CEOs, or high-ranking officials of the corporations or companies affiliated with the MWCI, as well as other companies and corporations. For example, Frenando Zobel De Ayala has been serving as the chair of the board and the Executive Committee as well as the Filipino director of the company since May 15, 1997. His brother James Augusto Zobel De Ayala has been serving as the vice-chair and the Filipino director also since the time mentioned above. Both of them are also serving in a good number of other companies, some associated with the MWCI and some not. They are also associated with some philanthropic foundations.[51] The probable reason that they have been serving in the same positions for a long time is that they own the largest share of the company. Their long-term service in the same positions reveals how this "invited space" is in practice controlled by economically powerful elites, and in practice it is a "closed space," where a group of actors make decisions behind closed doors. As mentioned earlier, in this type of space the elites (in the case of the Boards, it is the economic elite) make and implement decisions for the people without the requirement for discussion or any kind of involvement of the people.

The other eight directors also serve in various corporations besides MWCI.[52] In addition, there are two "independent" directors serving on the board; one of these, in accordance with the corporate governance manual, has to serve as the chair in the Audit Committee. The persons working as independent directors are also related to other corporations not affiliated with MWCI.[53] "Independent" directors are those who are not in any way related to the company and are expected not to hold any interest with the company that may hinder exercising their "independent judgment."[54]

It is not uncommon in any corporation that the largest shareholders monopolize the decision-making spaces; in fact, it is the norm. In these situations, poor women are not the only people who are not invited, but also virtually anyone else who does not have enough shares to participate in these spaces. The aim of this study is not to argue that this system itself is evil but to highlight that the marginalized women's political capability to participate in the decision-making spaces did not develop under the corporate structure of the MWCI. In other words, they could not participate in any form of decision-making process in the formal spaces through their representatives. Like other corporations, the economic elites monopolize the formal spaces of the MWCI board and make decisions regarding water distribution to the East Zone. The representatives of the marginalized women or low-income citizens are never asked by the board to become members or observers of this invited space.

The board is a good example of a combination of what Gaventa calls "visible" and "hidden" power structures, where a certain group of influential people maintain their authority through visible institutions but also "who gets to the decision-making table and what gets on the agenda" are controlled by these influential people. Less-powerful people's agendas and participation (here marginalized women's representatives) are "excluded" and "devalued" in this power dimension. The governance mechanism of the company developed in such a way that it provides "opportunities" and "freedoms" to only a certain group of powerful persons to maintain their influence and authority, while excluding not only marginalized women's representatives but also small shareholders and company staff. Within the company, there is virtually no mechanism for making the board accountable to anybody or any branch. Moreover, there is no deliberative, reflexive network there to hear the voices of the marginalized people for estimating their needs. In theory, the board is a de juror "invited space," but in practice it is a de facto "closed space," restricted to just the economic elites, who control the space and the decision-making agendas through visible power structures.

Several committees were created by the board to support "the performance of its functions" (Article I, 2): the Executive Committee, Audit Committee, Nomination Committee, and Proxy Validation Committee. In addition, there is a position of Compliance Officer. Marginalized women's representatives cannot participate in these other committees either, including the Executive Committee. According to the company's manual, "The Board shall appoint from among its members an Executive Committee composed of not less that five (5) members" (Article I, 2.1 a). Therefore, this space is also restricted for a set of powerful actors who are monopolizing the implementation process of water distribution. The Audit Committee comprises three members, one of whom came from a pool of independent directors and would be the chair of the committee. The other two members, who are chosen by the company, must have "an adequate understanding of accounting and auditing principles in general and of the company's financial management systems and environment in particular" (Article I, 2.2 a).

The Nomination Committee also comprises three members, one of whom has to come from the independent directors. The major functions of this committee are to ensure that the persons who want to be nominated to the board at the annual general stockholders' meeting have "due qualifications" to compete for these positions (Article I, 2.3 a). In addition, it also reviews and evaluates the credentials of other persons who want to be nominated for other positions in the company. However, all nominations must be approved by the Board (Article I, 2.3 c).

Marginalized women cannot be considered for nomination because they do not have the capability to purchase shares equal to the economically powerful persons. The board, which is the final authority for nominations, has the absolute power to exclude somebody who lacks sufficient shares. It also appears that in the last fifteen years they have not been willing to allow anyone into their space who does not share their economic background. Hence, marginalized women are not capable of organizing their demand to be nominated there.

There are three members in the Proxy Validation Committee; one serves as the chair of the committee. The board appoints the three members. There is no restriction regarding committee members being stockholders of the company (Article I, 2.4). Management is the center of day-to-day decision making (Article II, 1 a). It comprises a techno-bureaucratic staff that is primarily accountable to the Board (Article II, 1 b). They make decisions based on the directions and guidelines set up by the Board.

It is clear that in MWCI's internal governance system, there is no provision for the representatives of the customers or citizens to participate in any form at any level of decision making regarding water distribution in the East Zone. Therefore it can be argued that like the state-led governance of DWASA, under the MWCI's governance system, marginalized women's political capability to participate in the decision-making spaces did not develop. From the lower to the upper level, their representatives cannot participate in any space as a group or as an individual. They are not even capable of "light interaction" through "minimal participation," where, as mentioned earlier, the participant's role is only to provide information, which would not lead to what Sen refers to as "agency achievements" through contributing to the final decision.

The board is thus a very powerful body and this space is exclusively restricted to the wealthy and powerful citizenry. They have absolute authority to set up their own agendas and make decisions about who in the East Zone should receive what amount of water. These powerful actors created the space of the board, and as a result, they can decide who should be invited into their own space and on what basis. They keep their space "closed" to the "outside" participants; hence, it is almost impossible for a representative of a less powerful person or marginalized woman to participate in the governance mechanism of the company. Moreover, the technical expertise of the members of various committees also deprives others of opportunities to participate. There is no space in these committees for the representatives of the customers or women to influence their decisions through participation.

There are some astounding similarities between the state-led governance system in DWASA and the PPP system in MWCI. Both are highly exclusionary; the representatives of marginalized women and low-income city dwellers could not participate in the policy spaces in both governance mechanisms. In both organizations, a group of selected economically powerful elites and technical know-how actors are in charge of making and implementing decisions; in DWASA, it is government-appointed technological and bureaucratic elites, and in the MWCI, it is technological and corporate elites. Like DWASA, the MWCI's governance mechanism is also hierarchical and centralized and the decisions are made at the top of the organization (Figure 4.1). Also like DWASA, under the MWCI's governance system, the political capabilities of the marginalized women did not increase through participation in the governance mechanism and they cannot attain "agency freedom" that would lead to "agency achievements" under this governance system. Therefore, based on these findings, this study concludes that political capabilities of marginalized women regarding participation in the decision-making spaces about allocating water failed to develop under the MWCI's governance mechanism in Metropolitan Manila.

The Regulatory Office

It is important to regulate these two water companies, "not only from the point of view of tariff increase but also with respect to all their obligations under the Concession Agreement, since many of those obligations had a direct impact" on the capabilities of the marginalized women residing in the concession zones.[55] Moreover, in the case of a natural monopoly (provision of water), regulation is needed because users of water cannot exercise enough bargaining power within the administrative/technical structures.[56]

Regulation is necessary in Metropolitan Manila because common customers and marginalized women do not have the capabilities to influence the decision-making process regarding either the allocation of water or the tariff system. In such a context, a powerful pro-people regulatory body might preserve the interests of the economic marginalized people in the city. In addition, the "regu-

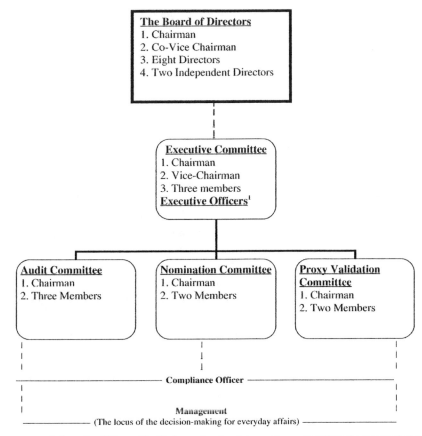

The Board of Directors
1. Chairman
2. Co-Vice Chairman
3. Eight Directors
4. Two Independent Directors

Executive Committee
1. Chairman
2. Vice-Chairman
3. Three members
Executive Officers[1]

Audit Committee
1. Chairman
2. Three Members

Nomination Committee
1. Chairman
2. Two Members

Proxy Validation Committee
1. Chairman
2. Two Members

──── **Compliance Officer** ────

Management
(The locus of the decision-making for everyday affairs)

1. Executive Officers: The Chairman, the vice-chairman, the president/CEO, the Treasurer/and or Chief Finance Officer, and the Corporate Secretary

Figure 4.1. MWCI's Governance Mechanism

latory framework is also crucial to making service providers accountable to consumers."[57] Whether managed under the state-led, market-led, or PPP governance systems, the water supply is subject to a monopolistic market. Hence, the proper regulation is important to protect the interests of the customers as well as the most economically disadvantaged sections of society, including the marginalized women, in terms of controlling price and quality.[58]

Regulation of water is not an easy task; it requires expertise and experience. Besides technical know-how, the issue of power is associated with the regulation. The major issue of regulating supplied water is that it is deeply related to the locus, "where the ultimate decision-making power [is] lodged."[59] Therefore, the following questions arise: Is the Regulatory Office (RO) the central locus for regulating water or are there other bodies that influence or alter the decisions taken by the RO? If there are other bodies, who is in charge of these bodies for regulating water? Who is in charge of regulating water at the RO? Did the RO monitor whether marginalized women's or other low-income groups' demands were met by these two water companies?

In August 1997, the MWSS's RO was created on the basis of the Concession Agreement signed between the MWSS and the two concessionaires: MWCI and MWSI. It is a government organization whose main responsibility is to monitor whether the companies follow the agreements properly. It works as a "collegial body," which is composed of five members headed by the director or chief regulator, who is in charge of overall supervision of the agency's functions. The RO has four divisions: Technical Regulation, Customer Service Regulation, Financial Regulation, and Administration and Legal Affairs. Four members are in charge of these four divisions.[60] Each member can serve a fixed 5-year term. They must not have present or prior affiliation with MWSS or the two concessionaire companies.

The RO is mandated to implement the Concession Agreement provisions. At least three votes are required to adopt a resolution on substantive matters. The chief regulator is the principal spokesperson for the office. S/he also presides over the meetings of the Regulatory Office and has the final authority regarding hiring and dismissal of the professional staff for the office. The Concession Agreement gives the RO the authority to (1) appraise, decide, and enforce rates and service standards, (2) prepare regular independent audit reports regarding the performance of the concessionaires, and (3) monitor the maintenance of the infrastructures. Its functions may change over time to ensure effective regulation.

The primary tasks of the RO are to determine water tariff rates and to implement service standards. In reality, however, the regulation process goes beyond the RO,[61] which was set up by the MWSS's Board of Trustees (BT).[62] Trustee members are appointed by the president of the Philippines.[63] The funds for the RO come from the concession fees paid by MWSI and MWCI. The BT is authorized to make changes in the RO, if necessary, and they can veto any decisions taken by the RO. Therefore, it appears that the BT is the ultimate decision-making authority for regulating water. In addition, the RO also needs the assistance of the Department of Environment & Natural Resources (DENR) and the Department of Health (DOH) to monitor the standards of pollution control and the quality of potable water. Figure 4.2 shows the regulatory mechanism of MWSS's Regulatory Office.

The BT is a closed space. Marginalized women or anybody who is not favored by the president of the country is not able to participate in this space. The president appoints high officials who make the ultimate decisions regarding water regulation. In this regulatory process, any form of involvement by the customers—low-income citizens or women—is denied. As mentioned, the BT is an example of a "visible power" structure, although only partially, so the influential people make decisions openly there through an observable structure of political power. However, the other aspects of a visible power structure—such as a relatively democratic system of decision making and accountability to the common people—are missing. The BT is also not altering the "who, how and what" aspects of policymaking, an important character of a visible power structure. There is no special clause or mechanism in the RO's mandate to preserve the interests of marginalized women or low-income citizens, especially for fixing prices and providing water connections. The BT has shown no interest in incorporating an agenda or policy that would preserve the interests of the marginalized women in the city. Based on the available information, I did not come across any document which shows that the BT adopted any policy in favor of the marginalized women of the city.

The RO has to work with many limitations. The World Bank reports that one weakness of the RO is its "fragmented" regulatory functions, a result of different "entities" controlling the organization.[64] The RO is dependent on the BT because the organization itself was set up by the BT. The RO is also

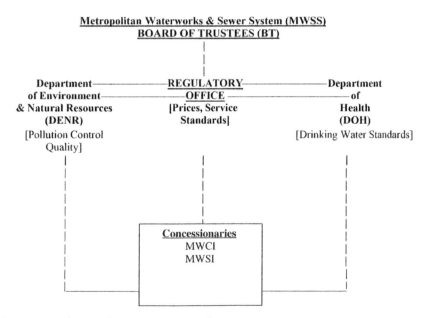

Figure 4.2. The Regulatory Mechanism of MWSS

dependent on the concessionaires for funding; financial dependence restricts the RO's authority to regulate water.

Based on the study, this research found that although in theory the RO is the central locus for regulating water, there are other bodies, such as the BT, MWCI, and MWSI, that can influence the decisions taken by the RO as it is dependent on them in many ways. Moreover, the RO is also dependent on DENR and DOH when it comes to regulating the quality of water. Political, economic, and technological elites are mainly in charge of these bodies. After all, the RO is a "public-private partnership" and there should be an opportunity for the people to participate in the regulatory process. Unfortunately, in reality, the "public" part of the RO is completely ignored. There is no provision for public representation in this formal body. There is no space in the RO for the general public to participate in the decision-making process. Moreover, due to the absence of a reflexive network in the RO's governance system, it is not possible to include inputs from the marginalized women and customers in water regulation. Marginalized women or poor people could not exercise their political capabilities in the spaces created by these bodies. It also appears that these bodies' (mentioned above) prime concern is not to monitor the interests of the marginalized women or other economically disadvantaged groups, especially when it comes to the issue of monitoring the price of water and supplying water to their households. Therefore, this study concludes that the RO is not willing to protect the interests of marginalized women.

Despite various limitations, the PPP governance model offers a regulatory authority, rather than no oversight at all. At least officially, the water companies are responsible to this body, and are obliged to maintain all the provisions signed in the concessionary agreements. This official body, despite limited capacity (funds, personnel) for oversight, would therefore work as a *de jure* monitoring authority when it comes to the issue of providing services to the residents of Metropolitan Manila in terms of quantity, quality and price as well as expanding the service networks.

The Role of the Collective Action on the Decision-Making Process

It is clear from the above discussion that marginalized women or underprivileged sections of the population have no access to the formal spaces created by the institutionalized structures mentioned above. In other words, they could not play any role in the formal decision-making process. Various grassroots organizations and NGOs are active in Metropolitan Manila for protecting the water rights of the marginalized people in the city. How much these NGOs are representing the interests of the poor or whether there is any space for marginalized people in their organizations is a subject for further research. I asked some NGO activists in Metropolitan Manila whether they wanted to create a space for marginalized women in the formal organizations. They believed that water resources should be managed by the representative of the people and women, not by the elites of the water corporations. NGOs in Metropolitan Manila regularly organized campaigns for equitable distribution of water at an affordable price for all citizens. They are also vocal against the involvement of the private corporations through PPP governance in water business. Various NGOs, especially the Freedom from Debt Coalition (FDC) are very active in the city against the high price of water as well as the private sector involvement through PPP governance in the water distribution process. They also monitor the quality of water supplied by these two companies.

Bubut D. Palattao (team coordinator, FDC) informed me that her organization is strongly opposed to any kind of private corporation involvement in water distribution. She mentioned that "I and my organization believe that water is a human right and hence, involvement of the private enterprises in water resource management is not conducive to the implementation of this right. The profit motive of the corporations would take away this public good and confine it to the hands of a few corporate elites." Palattao further stressed that "my organization and like minded NGOs are active in Metropolitan Manila against the involvement of the private enterprises in the water business. We regularly organize signature campaigns, demonstrations, awareness-raising workshops etc. against the price hikes and the involvement of the corporations in water business. Moreover, NGOs, especially FDC also published pamphlets, brochures, reports, booklets as part of the awareness raising campaign."

There is a wide range of claimed spaces in various slums and communities created by the local residents and NGOs. As discussed earlier, these spaces are created by social movements and associations where people can gather to debate, discuss, and resist the powerful elites. In these grassroots organizations, marginalized women and the poor local residents can gather to debate and discuss the pros and cons of the management of water resources under the PPP governance in the city. As my research focus is on the formal governance sector, I did not collect detailed information about the claimed spaces during the time period I stayed in Metropolitan Manila. However, after discussions with the NGO activists, slum dwellers, and poor people, it appeared to me that these grassroots organizations and the NGOs are active about the water rights of the poor people and they work as pressure groups for ensuring these rights. They are working as advocacy groups to exert pressure on the private companies as well as on the government to ensure water rights for the poor.

However, as my study's prime focus is the participation in formal spaces, I did not examine the effectiveness of these pressure groups. These activities sustain public awareness of their elected officials' role in the PPP governance system and also promote transparency.

Palattao informed me that in these claimed spaces, FDCs and other NGOs as well as various grassroots organizations promote the ideas of democratic management for water governance. She further informed me that other like-minded NGOs and civil society organizations believe that people should have the right to determine and recognize their needs instead of having elites, who are not part of this population, identifying their needs. She also discussed with me the role of power in water distribution and mentioned that due to this powerful location of the water elites, they were not accountable to the people. The major problem of managing water by private corporations is that they are not accountable in any way to the people, especially to poor people and marginalized women. Although she was not able to provide definite guidelines or an alternative water governance model, Palatto believed that people should be the managers of their resources, especially water.[65]

The NGO Forum on ADB is another leading NGO in Metropolitan Manila who are against any kind of private sector involvement in the management or distribution process of water resources. According to them, the problem of the involvement of private sectors is that the public property became private and hence, people lost control over their resources. Eventually, even the government also could lose control over the public resources. Further, because of the profit motive, the private corporations unnecessarily increase tariffs. They also believe that water is a human right and the minimum level of water should be assured to everybody. For them, when water is managed by a private corporation, the people, especially poor people, lose their rights on water resources. They are also very active in awareness-raising campaigns against PPP governance through various publications, organizing demonstrations, and other ways.[66]

After discussions with several NGO activists, I came to know that various NGOs and other grassroots organizations are active in Metropolitan Manila against the PPP governance. They are also vocal against the increased tariffs of water. According to them, although service coverage networks (discussed later) were extended after the introduction of PPP governance, the private corporations are making unnecessary profits through excessive increases of tariffs. After interviews with NGO activists and some slum dwellers, I received mixed opinions about the private enterprise involvement in the water sector. Some NGOs are against any kind of involvement of private corporations. It appeared to me that the limited number of slum dwellers I interviewed were not against the involvement of the private corporations in the water business as long as they could obtain water services at an affordable price. For example, one woman (who preferred to keep her identity anonymous) who was working as a house-maid in a comparatively rich Makati city area but was living in a slum in the Tondo district, said that "I do not care much whether the government or a private corporation is in charge of supplying water in our neighborhoods as long as they are able to supply water to all the residents living in the area. I firmly believe that obtaining water is our basic right and the government or the company who is in charge of providing water should be responsible enough to ensure this right."[67]

However, almost all of the twenty-five interviewees told me that they considered obtaining water to be their fundamental right and that their opinions should be considered regarding the distribution of it in terms of price, quantity, and quality, as well as expanding the service networks in their localities. An important difference I noticed between the NGOs and the marginalized women in terms of their position regarding the role of private corporations in distributing water was that although the NGOs in general were against any kind of corporate involvement in water distribution mechanism, the poor women were not much concerned with who was in charge of distribution; their major concern was to fulfill their water need. Yet, the women believed that the distribution authorities should open their decision-making spaces for them because it would help them to assess the water needs of the poor.

As the focus of my research is to examine how the governance systems affect women's participation in the formal spaces, this study does not examine the claimed spaces that were created outside the formal institutions. However, there might be some impacts of these collective actions (that organized in the informal spaces) on the decision-making process of the water corporations and the RO. In the informal spaces, there might be some levels of participation of the marginalized women. Moreover, during my stay in the city, I was unable to determine whether there were any organized labor movements against the private sector involvement in the water governance system. Nevertheless, the two companies—the MWCI and MWSI—have increased services in Metropolitan Manila to the underserved population, including marginalized women, as discussed below.

Water Supply Mechanisms and Capabilities of Marginalized Women to Access Supplied Water Resources

The Concession Agreement has no specific provision for improving services for the low income people living in informal settlements. The only requirement mentioned in the Concession Agreement is to supply water to low-income people through maintaining the existing public faucets. Therefore, developing marginalized-women centered or pro-poor water services delivery projects are subject to the discretion "on the part of the concessionaires."[68] The two concessionaires have adopted many variants of mechanisms to supply water since becoming MWSS's PPP governance partners. Their aim has been to expand business by including the underserved population into their service networks. The two companies—the MWCI and MWSI—supply water to the informal settlements (through which marginalized women are also benefited) under two projects: Tubig Para sa Barangay (TPSB, Water for the Poor) and Bayan Tubig (BT, Water for the Community) respectively. Under these projects, services are provided through individual water connections, public faucets, private vending, group taps, and bulk water supply. As of 2002, 6 percent of all MWCI connections were installed for low-income people, and as of 2001, 11 percent of all MWSI connections were installed for the poor in the East and West Zones, respectively.[69]

Under the state-led governance, there were only 825,000 water connections in the entire area of Metropolitan Manila, serving 7.32 million out of 11 million city residents (or 66.5% coverage). Among the population living below the poverty threshold, 80 percent did not have water connections in their households.[70] The reason was that like in Dhaka, people living in informal settlements did not have legal claims over the land. As a result, they were deprived of receiving connections from MWSS, who followed the policy of providing connections only to the legal inhabitants of the city. The MWSS produced 3,000 mld from the three treatment plants and average water availability was 16–17 hours per day. The per person water consumption was 133 liters.[71]

In comparison to MWSS, both the companies have been able to increase water production, water connections, and per capita consumptions. The number of total water connections has increased as a result of the various mechanisms adopted by the two companies. Between 1997 and 2001, both of the concessionaires installed 238,000 new water connections, of which 128,000 were in low-income communities. Under the state-led governance, the average new connections were 17,040 per year.[72] As of December 2011, the MWCI was able to establish 857,981 service connections in the East Zone. It was able to increase its water service network from 3 million people in 1997 to 6.1 million in 2011. The company was also able to considerably reduce non-revenue water, from 63 percent in 1997 to less than 11.2 percent in 2011.[73] In 2011, the company supplied 1,200 mld of water to the East Zone and hence, per capita water consumption also increased in its service area, roughly to 253.16 liters per person (much higher than the per capita water DWASA supplied in 2011). Therefore, in theory every resident living in the East Zone should have received the minimum daily requirement of water. In terms of service availability, in 2011, 99 percent of the customers had 24-hour water availability (with low pressure) in comparison to 26 percent in 1997. Metropolitan Manila residents who were used to having limited water found that they had water in their faucets 24 hours per day.

MWSI however has not been as successful as the other company in increasing its service coverage.[74] Under the state-led management, there were only 464,644 pipeline connections in the West Zone.[75] MWSI was able to provide water to only 88 percent of the West Zone residents, totaling 903,682 connections by December 2010.[76] Only 71 percent of customers had 24-hour water, and 29 percent had intermittent or no supply at all due to low pressure, like in Dhaka. The average water pressure in 86 percent of the MWSI network was only 7 psi, which was far below the contractual agreement of 16 psi,[77] which resulted in intermittent or no water supply.[78] However, this number was far below the projected target of the company.[79] Residents who were not connected with the MWSI water networks mainly relied on water vendors and deep wells for collecting their everyday water. However, in comparison to MWCI, the MWSI network was still servicing only 53 percent of the population in its service zone.[80]

The Tubig Para sa Barangay (TPSB, Water for the Poor) Project

According to the Concession Agreement, the concessionaires are obliged to set up public standpipes with no installation charge for every 475 people living in the informal settlements. The aim of this provision is to cover the areas of the low-income residents, who cannot afford individual connection fees for their households. The MWCI adopted the TPSB project to implement this provision. To implement the TPSB project, the MWCI received a "grant" from the World Bank–funded Global Partnership on Output-Based Aid and its donor, the International Finance Corporation.[81] The public standpipes are operated and managed by individuals, Barangay staff, or local community associations.[82]

The MWCI launched the TPSB project in the East Zone in 1998 to incorporate the poor areas into its service networks. The uniqueness and the positive aspect of this project were to waive the land title requirement for obtaining a water connection. This project was not part of the Concession Agreement, but was undertaken later after joint discussions between the RO and the company to extend its business network to include the informal settlements of the city.[83] Virgilio Rivera described the TPSB project as "an innovative scheme, introduced to provide legal water connections to poor communities who live in crowded, densely populated areas where it is often difficult to install conventional water pipes."[84] This project "relaxes some application require-ments," such as legal entitlement to the land, therefore enabling the company to include the informal settlements into its coverage networks.[85]

Under this project, the MWCI offers three different types of water con-nections: individual metered connections, group taps, and community taps.[86] In practice, however, the company does not offer individual con-nections to informal households; only "legal" residents, businesses, and offices are entitled to receive individual connections. The company mainly relies on group taps to deliver water to the informal settlers. Under the group tap scheme, a group of three to five households is connected with a central meter, and they can then set up their own sub-meters. Sometimes groups are composed of relatives who can obtain water connections to-gether under one central meter. Each group of households is responsible for paying the bill.[87] The informal settlers thus have to form a group under the guidance of the MWCI staff, who have a significant influence regard-ing the decision-making process of the group. One woman who was a group member and wanted to keep her identity anonymous informed me that any decision regarding water distribution in her neighborhood was taken in the group under the firm guidelines set up by the MWCI staff. She further elaborated that "the staff not only sometimes influenced the group members to select the team leader they prefer, but also 'compelled' the group to collect the bills within the deadlines that they set. We did not have much influence over the terms and conditions under which our group was organized."[88] The group needs to select a team leader or trea-surer for collecting the bills from every household. Under this project, by December 2011, the MWCI was able to provide water to more than 1.7 million low-income residents or 287,000 households in various informal settlements of the East Zone.[89]

Besides setting up new faucets, the MWCI also repaired inactive faucets established by the MWSS before it adopted the PPP governance. Under the TPSB project, the company also set up communal taps in various informal settlements, and as a result, 4,000 new households received access to potable water solely in 2007.[90] As of 2004, under this project, 43,771 new connections were set up in the East Zone, benefiting 106,737 households.[91] The biggest TPSB project, the Manggahan Floodway Water Supply Project, was inaugu-rated in September 2001 in Pasig City. The aim of the project was to supply 15 mld water to more than 200,000 informal residents—that is, to ensure on average 75 liters of water per person per day—living in the 5-mile west bank of the Manggahan Floodway along the Pasig River. Before this project, the residents mainly relied on a few vendors who collected water from deep wells and sold to them at exorbitant rates.[92]

The company's major focus now is to expand its service areas in the cities of Taguig and Antipolo, as well as in other key municipalities in Rizal Province, such as San Mateo, Montalban, Taytay, and Angono. The necessary networks for this expansion are under construction. The company aims to expand its services to 1 million people in these areas over the next few years. To achieve this goal, in addition to setting up new networks, MWCI officials are considering expanding the coverage of bulk water provision to include the informal settlers in the province of Bulacan.[93]

The major criticism of this project is that a group of households' combined water consumption subjects them to the higher tariff level compared to the individually connected households. As a result, marginalized women and informal settlers receive "a higher water bill per household" compared to the "residential" customers. Moreover, they also bear the extra cost for pipeline connections because the main water shoulder is usually 25 meters away from their households.[94] However, when considering the option of buying water from the public faucets, where they have to carry water from the taps to their households or buy water from the vendors at a much higher price, receiving supplied water through TPSB's group tap project might be a better option for low-income people and marginalized women living in the informal settlements.

The Bayan Tubig (BT, Water for the Community) Project

MWSI adopted the BT Project in February 1997 to supply safe water to the informal settlers of the West Zone at an affordable price. It was also a part of the company's strategy to expand water coverage to the "hard-to-reach households" and to reduce the amount of non-revenue water.[95] The best part of this project is that the residents can obtain individual connections without property titles. Another good part of this project is that the customers can pay the connection fees through installments for a period of 6 or 12 months, and in some cases, even 24 months. Installation fees are lumped into the regular water bills, and hence payments can start after receiving the first bill.[96] This initiative simplified the process of obtaining water, benefiting not only the informal settlers but also the concessionaire.[97] Under this project, MWSI offered three levels of services:

1. Public Faucet (Level I): The local government unit's (Barangay) endorsement was needed to set up a faucet in the community.
2. Public Faucet (Level II): The NGO or community organization's request was needed.

3. Level III: Individual household meter connection.[98]

Under the BT project, in setting up water connections in various informal settlements, the company provided pipes and other equipment and the community dwellers participated in digging the trenches for the pipes under the supervision of MWSI personnel.[99] The important part of this implementation process was the involvement of the local community-based organizations and NGOs in intermediation and network mapping. To obtain service from the company, the local community needs Barangay approval, and then the concessionaire would come forward to start the project. Moreover, the following criteria have to be met before implementing the project: (1) The area is reasonably close to the primary network, (2) beneficiaries are not located in an area liable to flooding, (3) the scheme is technically feasible, and (4) the site is on private land where questions of tenure pose no problems.[100]

However, since its launch in 1999, 216,000 poor households came under its coverage.[101] Moreover, in 2009 MWSI adopted a BT-like Samahang Tubig Maynilad (STM) project in Tondo, Manila to expand its service networks to the urban poor areas, covering 1,139 households in the North Caloocan, Malabon, Pasay, and Quezon City areas.[102] In comparison to TPSB, informal settlers in the BT project have choices regarding the patterns of connection—that is, a household can apply for an individual connection. MWSI has a greater preference for individual connections than group connections. It is also flexible regarding setting up the pipes. Because of narrow roads and alleys in informal settlements, if possible, the concessionaire laid the pipe underground, and if not, above the ground, or they attached it to the wall. In addition, the number of persons per connection is lower in the BT project than the TPSB—9.2 versus 17.8.[103]

Before the BT project, marginalized women and informal settlers in the West Zone mainly relied on vendors or gangsters who illegally operated some water sources.[104] To obtain water from the gangsters, they had to pay them on a weekly basis. In addition, they also relied on the Barangay officials who were commissioned to operate the local public faucets. Besides paying, they had to stand in line or walk some distance to collect water. After receiving the water, they had to bring it home either by carrying it by hand or by using a cart. Those who could not collect water from local faucets had to find alternative sources, which meant paying more for water as well as walking a longer distance. My conversations with the women living in informal settlements suggest that they would prefer individual connections over public faucets because these reduced not only the water charges but also physical hardships.

Water Delivery Mechanisms

Water delivery mechanisms comprise either individual water connections, public faucets, or bulk water supply. Although an individual connection is more desirable as well as being the "cheapest and most convenient" for marginalized women, the MWCI usually does not offer individual connections to the residents living in informal settlement in the East Zone. As mentioned above, MWSI does provide individual connections to informal settlers in the West Zone under the BT project. As of July 2003, MWSI had set up at least 71,323 individual household connections. As a result, the beneficiaries were able to increase their water consumptions from about 6–7.5 cubic meters (when they bought water from vendors or collected water from the public faucets) to 27 cubic meters per month.[105] Therefore, it can be said that the individual connections under the BT project reduced both the charges and the hardship of the women as well as increasing the consumption of per capita water.

Before PPP governance, the MWSS had maintained public faucets for the informal settlers of the city so that in 1997, there were a total of 130 public faucets all over Metropolitan Manila. Both concessionaires continued the public faucet system. As of March 2003, MWSI and the MWCI maintained 402 and 533 faucets respectively. Both companies required that a person selected by the community association or the Barangay officials had to be in charge of the faucets. Every public faucet covered 475 people, that is, up to 50 households.[106]

Where there were no water pipe connections, the public faucet system was no doubt a better arrangement for the informal settlers and marginalized women. However, they had to pay more for the public faucet system than for the individual connection because they had to pay extra for the "faucet manager," who was in charge of organizing queues and collecting payments per container as well as remitting the collected charges to the Barangay officials or to the MWCI and MWSI staff.

Water is not available 24 hours per day at the public faucets and there are no regular operating hours. The positive side is that collecting water from the public faucets is cheaper than vended water.[107] But unfortunately MWSI has decided to gradually stop the service of public faucets because of mismanagement, such as not paying the collected bills to the company staff, either by the faucet managers or by the Barangay officials, and in some cases charging of exorbitant rates by the manager.[108]

The selling of bulk water is a major new strategy undertaken by the MWCI to drastically expand its water coverage in the East Zone. The aim of providing bulk water to the informal settlements was to reduce supply costs as well to ensure adequate economic return in areas where providing services was traditionally perceived as high risk and subject to low financial gain.[109] Under the group tap system, the concessionaire provides bulk water to sub-contractors, household unions, and water cooperatives.[110] Supplying water through household unions and water cooperatives ensures more participatory capabilities of the customers when it comes to the issue of dealing with the company. However, marginalized women probably cannot exercise their political capabilities through these organizations because these unions and cooperatives are not women-centered and are not organized to ensure their participation.

Inocencio and David classify two types of services: a community managed water connection and a privately managed water connection. In the community managed connection, the entire community forms an association to deal directly with the company for paying the bulk water bills and establishing its own distribution and fee collection system. An example of this type of water distribution system is the Durian community in Quezon City. The 228 member households of the community chose to establish a bulk water delivery system instead of a group tap scheme to avoid a high connection charge.[111] They reached an agreement with the MWCI that the whole community would receive the service of bulk water through just one mother meter. Under this system, the per household charge was set at roughly $83 (3,854 Filipino pesos), and the installation charge was at least $21. The community association collected the installation charge 3 months before the supply project was installed.[112]

This project ensured better quality water to the informal settlers at a comparatively cheaper price (Table 4.7). One household spent roughly from $16.92 to $20 per month for water before the project was implemented. The introduction of this project reduced the water price per household in 2001 to between 90 cents and roughly $3 per month. However, this community paid twice as much for water per household compared to the households with independent connections. As a result, the MWCI earned higher revenue per cubic meter than for the water they supplied to independent connections.[113]

In a privately managed water allocation system, the MWCI sells water to informal settlers via private sub-contractors. The advantage to the company is that it can supply water to the many households through just one mother meter. It is the sub-contractor's responsibility to manage sub-meters and sub-connections. The private contractor is also in charge of providing the necessary investment for setting up the network inside the informal settlements. The poor customers and marginalized women are in a real disadvantaged position under this distribution scheme because they pay much more than the customers receiving water from individual connections; David and Inocencio estimate that they pay at least 12 times more under this scheme.[114]

TABLE 4.7.
Water Rates under the MWCI's Bulk Water Project in May 2001

Consumption (cubic meters)	Price per Cubic Meter (Cents)
First 10	12
Next 10	14
Next 10	16
Next 10	18
Next 10	20
Next 10	22
Next 10	24
Next 10	26
Next 10	28
Next 10	30
Next 10	32

Source: Arlene B. Inocencio and Cristina C. David. "Public-Private-Community Partnerships in Management and Delivery of Water to Urban Poor: The Case of Metro Manila." Philippine Institute of Development Studies (PIDS) Discussion Paper Series No. 2001-18. August 2001: 18.

Another major disadvantage is that since no authority is in charge of regulating the private resellers, the quality of water might have been undermined.[115] A well-known example of questionable sub-contracting was the sale of water by a steel fabricating company, Inpart Engineering, to more than 20,050 low-income households in six communities in eastern Metropolitan Manila. They also obtained a contract for providing services to medium-sized government tenement housing in Sta. Ana, a franchised area of MWCI.[116] The purpose of mentioning this example here is twofold: to show (1) the variation of subcontracting and (2) that the reliability of water quality may not meet the national standard under this type of subcontracting.

PPP Governance, Water Supply Mechanisms, and Marginalized Women

Management of the water supply under PPP governance has brought a mixed result for marginalized women. On a positive note, there is no doubt that more women came under water service networks "despite the trouble accounts" of the scheme itself.[117] They benefited from the various connection mechanisms—such as individual connections, group taps, and community and privately managed distribution systems—under the TPSB, the BT and the STM projects. Various methods of water allocation "proved effective in enhancing and hastening access" to supplied potable water.[118] Although the number of connections and supply both increased, the increased supply was not equitably distributed; hence, women who are receiving water from non-individualized connections are not only receiving less water but are also paying more per unit of water.[119]

PPP governance has had further adverse effects on marginalized women who reside in the more dangerous zones of the city. The water companies were not eager to supply water there because these settlements were considered temporary and the people living there might relocate any time due to demolition decisions made by the municipalities or local authorities. Although the settlements in hazardous zones are more vulnerable to demolition, many of them "had existed for a long time."[120] The companies nevertheless consider investing in the dangerous zones highly risky because of the relocation uncertainty. If, after large investments, the settlers had to relocate, the companies would lose thousands of pesos.[121]

The settlers' major sources of potable water are large water vendors, illegal connections, dug wells, and open shallow wells. Many of the illegal connections were closed after the two concessionaire companies took charge of water distribution. The vendors increased their price when the availability of water sources became limited. As a result, marginalized women living in the dangerous zones suffer the most from PPP governance in Metropolitan Manila.

However, the water supply situation was already bad under the state-led governance. In "the new situation, onerous as it was, it was still considered an improvement."[122] Therefore, it could be said that the marginalized women's capabilities to access supplied water resources increased considerably (although not sufficiently) under PPP governance in Metropolitan Manila. Under the PPP governance, although their capabilities increased in terms of access and price, this increase is still not sufficient to meet their daily needs. They are not capable of obtaining the necessary amount of water under the various types of service and price structures. Moreover, some women still do not have the capability to access supplied water resources.

Marginalized Women and the Price of Water

PPP governance did not establish equitable capability among consumers, over either the supplied water resources or the prices. Marginalized women and low-income residents do not enjoy the same benefits of supply compared to those who are relatively well-off and have individual connections. They pay 10–25 times higher rates for the same amount of water compared to wealthier consumers. In Metropolitan Manila, where it might be necessary to provide subsidies to marginalized women's households, the rich households tend to receive better financial backing, and hence have better access to water compared to low-income residents.[123]

The PPP governance experience in Metropolitan Manila refutes the popular myth that the "poor are unwilling and cannot afford to pay the full cost of (supplied) water."[124] Poor people and women paid even more when water was allocated under the state-led governance because during that time, the lack of water availability in their neighborhoods forced them to buy water from the vendors at much higher prices. For example, marginalized people in the Tondo area used to pay 10 times more for per liter of water compared to their relatively wealthy neighbors. PPP governance ensures water availability to them through communal standpipes and in some cases, through individual connections, although they still have to pay roughly four times higher tariffs than the well-off consumers.[125]

The major allegation against managing water under PPP governance in Metropolitan Manila is that the price of every cubic meter of water goes up very high. Both companies increased water tariffs quite significantly. The RO was not able or willing to prevent the tariff hike. It is ironic that even for projects undertaken for informal settlers, they charge relatively higher tariffs. As a result, informal settlers pay more for supplied water than do the legal residents of the city.

As of January 2006, the average price per cubic meter of water increased more than 1000 percent from the bid rate, from 4 cents to 40 cents (Table 4.8).[126] The major reason for the price increase was the government's permission to let the companies recover foreign exchange losses that had originally been decided to be recovered over the 25-year period of the contract. As a result, about two thirds of the rate increase occurred solely between October 2001 and January 2003 (Table 4.8).[127]

Sub-contracting is another cause of increasing prices, resulting in four times higher tariffs than the companies' regulated rates. One reason is that the bulk water consumers are categorized as "semi residential" instead of "residential."[128] The semi-residential consumers are charged more than residential customers, who have individual connections. As mentioned, they have to pay extra money for the treasurer/inspector/manager, who supervises the faucets. Further, the individual connection fee was very high for marginalized women, which made it very difficult for them to obtain one; as of October 2003, to obtain a connection 25 m from a water main line, the MWCI charged about $132 per connection and MWSI charged about $107.[129]

Thus under PPP governance, those with the lowest monthly income among city dwellers have to pay the highest price per unit of water. The RO did not exercise its regulatory authority over pricing and service performance.[130] Marginalized women do not have much choice because when

TABLE 4.8.
Increase in Tariff between 1997 and 2006

Period	Tariff (per cubic meter)
Under State-led Governance	Cents 18
1997-1998 (Bid rate)	4
1999 (1st increase)	5
2000 (2nd increase)	6
Jan-March 2001(3rd increase)	6
Apr-Nov 2001[ADR adjustment] 4th increase	7
Nov. 2001 Contract Amendment (5th increase)	8
2002 (with FCDA) (6th increase)	13
Rate Rebasing (7th increase)	28
Increase in FCDA (1.25% of basic rate)—Aug. 25, 2003 (8th increase)	30
Increase in FCDA (2.8% of basic rate)—Oct. 7, 2003 (9th increase)	31
Increase in FCDA (1.58% of basic rate)—Jan. 1, 2004	32
Jan. 2005 (Php 2.00 as last installment of 2002 rebased rate plus Php 0.18 FCDA)	36
January 2006 (CPI and FCDA)	40

FCDA = Foreign Currency Differential Adjustment, ADR = Appropriate Discount Rate, CPI = Consumer Price Index. Source: South, "Profiting from People's Lives."
Source: "Profiting from People's Lives: Metro Manila's Water Privatization Saga." 18 Oct. 2006. *Jubilee South.* 20 July, 2008. <http://www.jubileesouth.org./upload1/fdc_low.pdf>.

it comes to buying water, they have to pay a much higher price to the vendors.[131] Therefore, we can say that although the capabilities of marginalized women in terms of their ability to purchase supplied water have increased, this increase is very moderate.

Marginalized Women and the Quality of Water

Quality of water is an important determinant for the capabilities of marginalized women over supplied water resources. The quality determines its uses. If the quality is not up to the level of drinking, it reduces their "well-being achievements" because poor quality may cause water-borne diseases. Moreover, women need to spend extra time boiling the water. Water quality is mainly "gauged by the number of coliforms and specifically fecal coliforms."[132] The Concession Agreement requires the compliance of the concessionaires with the Philippine National Drinking Water Standards as published by the Department of Health (Section 5.1.4).

Both companies were serious about providing better-quality water to their customers and both have surpassed the Philippine National Standards for Drinking Water, which basically follow the same standards set up by the World Health Organization (WHO). After introducing PPP governance, the number of tests increased 10- and 8-fold in the East and West Zones, respectively.[133] The MWCI was able to reduce the amount of coliform from 7 percent in 1997 to 0.4 percent in 2003 (Table 4.9). For MWSI, the reduction was from 5 percent to 0.8 percent (Table 4.10). In 2003, the MWCI's coliform compliance was 99.6 percent and fecal coliform compliance was 99.6 percent; MWSI's was 99.2 and 99.2 percent, respectively (see Tables 4.10 and 4.11). The Philippine National Standards for Drinking Water require that at least 95 percent of samples collected in a particular year should be coliform and *E. coli* free. Under the state-led governance, the MWSS was not able to meet the standard.[134] The MWCI has met the standards since 1998 and MWSI since 2000 (Tables 4.9 and 4.10).

As far as the quality is concerned, unlike DWASA, the MWCI was successful in providing quality water to its customers, which according to them "surpassed the minimum requirements under national standards for water quality." As a result, they also claimed that in the East Zone, the rate of waterborne diseases dropped significantly.[135] Their statement was also supported by the RO's annual reports. In the 2003 report, they mentioned that both companies were successful in maintaining the high standard of supplied water.[136]

TABLE 4.9.
MWCI's Service Area: Microbiological Quality

	2003	2002	2001	2000	1999	1998	1997
Coliforms:							
Total Number of Determinations	6,738	6,234	6,040	5,586	5,104	4,652	639
Number Containing Coliforms	25	21	25	19	36	91	45
% Containing Coliforms	0.4	0.3	0.4	0.3	0.7	2	7
% Compliance	99.6	99.7	99.6	99.7	99.3	98	93
Fecal Coliforms:							
Total Number of Determinations	6,738	6,234	6,040	5,586	5,104	4,652	639
Number Containing Fecal Coliforms	5	21	25	19	36	91	45
% Compliance	99.6	99.7	99.6	99.7	99.3	98	93
Ave. frequency Compliance, %	100	100	102	107	106	108*	75.6*
95%—12 Months Satisfactory Compliance	Yes	Yes	Yes	Yes	Yes	Yes	Failed

* Twelve-month phase-in period requested by the company. Source: MWSS: Regulatory Office, 2003 Annual Report 16.

TABLE 4.10.
MWSI's Service Area: Microbiological Quality

	2003	2002	2001	2000	1999	1998	1997
Coliforms:							
Total Number of Determinations	7,233	7,649	8,739	8,577	8,742	6,520	910
Number Containing Coliforms	58	52	41	45	267	205	43
% Containing Coliforms	0.8	0.7	0.5	0.5	3	3	5
% Compliance	99.2	99.3	99.5	99.5	97	97	95
Fecal Coliforms:							
Total Number of Determinations	7,233	7,649	8,739	8,577	8,742	6,520	910
Number Containing Fecal Coliforms	58	52	41	45	267	205	43
% Compliance	99.2	99.3	99.5	99.5	97	97	95
Ave. frequency Compliance, %	107	100	101	108	98 Failed	132	85 Failed
95%--12 Months Satisfactory Compliance	Yes	Yes	Yes	Yes	Failed	Failed	Failed

Source: MWSS Regulatory Office, 2003 Annual Report 16.

In 2003, the two concessionaires conducted a total of 98,828 tests (much higher than in Dhaka) from the samples they collected from the treatment works, service reservoirs, and distribution areas. Seventy-four percent of the samples collected were from the distribution areas, most of which were from consumers' faucets; 99.5 percent of the tests demonstrated compliance with the 1993 Philippine National Standards for Drinking Water. Among the conducted tests, 166 samples failed to meet the fecal coliform standards. The RO claimed that these were isolated cases, whereas the overall quality of the water was very high. However, during the period of 1997 to 2003, compared to MWCI, the MWSI's quality standards were a little lower.[137] Initially, they were also not successful in meeting the 12-month satisfactory compliance level.

The RO report also mentions some incidents of dirty water being supplied by the companies despite showing an overall positive outlook. The water supply incidents were mainly reported in the areas for which the MWSI is in charge of providing water. The RO reports that failure to detect leaks was the main reason for supplying dirty water, despite compliance with the standards.[138] However, these were isolated incidents; the overall quality of water met the basic national standards. Therefore, it can be said that the marginalized women's capabilities over the quality of water (i.e. capability of obtaining good quality water) were enhanced under PPP governance.

To conclude, in the PPP water governance in Metropolitan Manila, the marginalized women could not participate in the decision-making spaces of the companies. There was no room for them to decide for themselves.

Instead, a paternalistic pattern of distribution is followed regarding the allocation of water. All decisions are made in closed spaces by economically powerful actors, although legally these spaces are invited spaces. This group of people maintains their authority regarding the distribution of water through the visible power structures of their companies. The companies are not interested in promoting the actual capabilities of the marginalized women regarding their ability to participate in the governance mechanism. The marginalized women's agendas receive less priority in the decision-making process of the companies. There are also no deliberative, reflexive mechanisms through which women can participate in the decision-making process. Therefore, it is clear that under the PPP governance, the marginalized women in Metropolitan Manila do not have political capabilities or political freedoms—that is, capabilities or freedoms to participate either individually or as a group in the governance mechanism. However, in some cases, the PPP governance provides limited opportunities for participation at the local level. For example, under the TPSB and the BT projects, group taps and community managed distribution systems open up avenues for limited participation. The major distinction between the company and the local level participation is that through local level participation, women cannot exercise their political capabilities over the issue of supplying water to the entire group of marginalized residents of the city; however, in some cases, it ensures exercising their limited capabilities in their own neighborhoods.

Despite their overall lack of participation, due to the companies' goal of ensuring more profit through widening services to more people, a good number of marginalized women came under the services. The decision to expand services to the residences of informal settlements came as the outcome of a paternalistic form of decision making—making decisions by the powerful people at the top without involving the common people in this process. Marginalized women and economically vulnerable citizens pay more money for water than their relatively wealthier neighbors; however, at the same time, their level of consumption of water increased under the PPP governance mechanism. Moreover, the quality of water was also improved. In spite of not increasing their political capabilities, it could be said that in terms of quantity, price, and quality, the capabilities of marginalized women were relatively increased under the PPP governance as a result of the paternalistic pattern of distribution.

Notes

1. Shane Rosenthal, "The Manila Water Concessions and Their Impact on the Poor." 1 Feb 2001. Hixon Center for Urban Ecology and Yale School of Forestry

and Environmental Studies. 21 June 2007 <http://www.yale.edu/hixon/research/pdf/
SRosenthal_Manila.pdf>.

2. Virgilio C. Rivera, Jr., "The Experience of Manila Water Company under the
MWSS Privatization." Regional Conference on Universality of Infrastructure Services:
Financing, Delivery and Regulatory Issues, November 9-10, New Delhi: India Habitat
Center, 2006, p. 4.

3. The government announced that the tariff rate would not be increased for the
next 10 years (Rivera 9).

4. Using these standards, the Philippine authority estimates that at least 36
percent of the total population of the country is poor. Some scholars claim that
this poverty figure is "grossly understated." The Family Income and Expenditure
Survey in 2002 revealed that despite the government's claim of reducing poverty,
the overall living conditions of the urban poor deteriorated during the time the
survey was conducted. Teti Argo and Aprodicio A. Laquian, "The Privatization
of Water Services: Effects on the Urban Poor in Jakarta and Metro Manila." *The
Inclusive City: Infrastructure and Public Services for the Urban Poor in Asia*, Ed.
Aprodicio A. Laquian et al. (Washington, D.C. Baltimore. Woodrow Wilson
Center Press, Johns Hopkins University Press, 2007) 240. Republic Act 8425 and
the Social Reform and Poverty Alleviation Act classify the "poor" as families or
individuals whose earnings fall beneath the poverty level and who at the same time
cannot afford to meet their essential minimum needs in a sustained way (Argo
and Laquian 228).

5. Argo and Laquian 228.

6. Junio M. Ragaragio, "The Case of Metro Manila, Philippines" In *Global
Report on Human Settlements 2003, The Challenge of Slums* (London: Earthscan,
UN-Habitat, 2003) 22 March 2008 <http://web.mit.edu/sigus/www/NEW/challenge-
course/pdfs/pdfscities/Manila.pdf>.

7. Ragaragio.

8. Ragaragio.

9. Asian Development Bank, "Delivering Piped Water on a Small Scale: Results
of ADB's Water Supply Service Market Survey in Manila" (Manila: Asian Development Bank, Oct. 2007) 23 March 2008 <http://www.adb.org/Water/Water-Briefs/
delivering-piped-water.asp>.

10. Carmelita N. Ericta, "Change in Spending Pattern Among Filipino Families Seen in 2006" (Manila: National Statistics Office, 2006 Family Income and
Expenditure Survey, 9 Oct. 2007) 23 March 2008. < http://www.census.gov.ph/data/
sectordata/2006/ie0605.htm>.

11. Ragaragio.

12. Editorial, "A Slum-Free Metro Manila," 4 Sept. 2007. *The Manila Times*,
21   March   2008   <http://www.manilatimes.net/national/2007/sept/04/yehey/
opinion/20070904opi1.html>.

13. Metropolitan Manila consists of 12 cities, 5 municipalities and 1694 Baran-
gays, governed by their respective local government units.

14. Ragaragio.

15. Ragaragio.

16. An ADB report showed that in Metro Manila, 10,000 families lived on the banks of the Pasig River, 32,000 along the banks of its tributaries and streams, and 45,000 along the railroad tracks. These all were considered as the dangerous zones. Asian Development Bank, "Regional Profiles," ADB Water for All Program (Quoted in Argo, Teti and Aprodicio A. Laquian. "The Privatization of Water Services: Effects on the Urban Poor in Jakarta and Metro Manila." *The Inclusive City: Infrastructure and Public Services for the Urban Poor in Asia,* Ed. Aprodicio A. Laquian et al. (Washington, D.C. Baltimore. Woodrow Wilson Center Press, Johns Hopkins University Press, 2007), pp. 228.

17. MSN Encartra, "Manila" 22 March 2008 <http://encarta.msn.com/encyclopedia_761578132/manila.html>.

18. Results from the 2010 Census of Population and Housing, National Statistic Office, Republic of the Philippines. 7 August 2012 <http://www.census.gov.ph/data/census2010/index.html>.

19. An estimated 3.4 million people in Dhaka versus roughly 2.3–3.1 million in Manila live in slums.

20. The national average is five to six members per household (Ragaragio).

21. Metropolitan Manila Development Authority 22 march 2008 <http://www.mmda.gov.ph/mainhtml>.

22. Rosenthal. For the number of informal households in Metropolitan Manila, see Table 4.1.

23. Ragaragio.

24. Ragaragio.

25. Giok Ling Ooi and Kai Hong Phua, "Urbanization and Slum Formation," *Journal of Urban Health: Bulletin of the New York Academy of Medicine* 8.1 (2007) 29.

26. Ragaragio. My fieldwork experience in various slums suggests that the unemployment rate could be higher in slums than the overall average of the city. I saw many men and women in the slums during work hours and some of them informed me that they were in the slums now because they had no jobs.

27. Government authorities usually do not want to provide services in these areas because it may be "interpreted as recognition of the illegitimate tenure of informal settlers." The fear of the authorities is that the recognition and the improvement of the living conditions of the marginalized people may attract more people from the countryside to these locations. Moreover, it is also difficult to lay down water pipes inside the settlements because of inadequate space and congested living situations (Argo and Laquian 229).

28. MWSS Regulatory Office: Information Kit 1.

29. MWSS Regulatory Office: Information Kit 1.

30. Argo and Laquian 226.

31. In 1997, at the introduction of market-led governance, there were roughly 770,000 domestic water connections within the MWSS service areas (Rivera 6).

32. Cristina C. David, "MWSS Privatization: Implications on the Price of Water, the Poor and the Environment." Discussion Paper Series No. 200-14. (Manila: Philippine Institute for Development Studies, April 2000) 6.

33. While in the SEA region, there were an average of 2.6 staff per thousand connections, in Manila it was 9.8. However, in Dhaka, the number was double (18.5 per

thousand connections). Compiled from Arthur C. McIntosh and Cesar E.Yniguez, Eds., *Second Water Utilities Data Book: Asian and Pacific Region* (Manila: Asian Development Bank, 1997).

34. Raul Fabella, "Shifting the Boundary of the State: The Privatization and Regulation of Water Service in Metro Manila" (Manchester: Working Paper Series, Center on Regulation and Competition, March 2006) 16.

35. Carla A. Montemayor, "The Manila Water Privatization Fiasco and the Role of Suez Lyonnaise/Onedo" (Bantay Tubig: Summit for Another World, May 2003) 1.

36. Rivera 4. Executive Orders 286 and 311 implemented this Act, which encouraged the adoption of market-led governance as the state's major path for economic growth and development, "to engage or undertake the financing, construction, operation and maintenance of infrastructure and development projects," including the sectors related to water supply and sewerage (MWSS Regulatory Office 1).

37. MWSS Regulatory Office 1.

38. In 1994, a Malaysian firm wanted to purchase the MWSS as a government-to-government transaction. The government-appointed committee turned down their proposal because the committee considered selling the MWSS to be illegal. According to them, it would be virtually suicidal "to negotiate such a large transaction and one that involved a commodity as political as potable water." Mark Dumol, *The Manila Water Concession: A Key Government Official's Diary of the World's Largest Water Privatization, Directions in Development* (Washington, D.C.: World Bank, 2000) 9.

39. David 8. In turn, the International Finance Corporation employed French consulting firm Sogreah and the UK's National Economic Research Associates to handle technical issues and to formulate the economic regulation model (Rivera 8).

40. Rosenthal.

41. David 9. The West Zone is located alongside the coastal area of Manila Bay, where the groundwater depletion lowered the water level causing higher cost for pumping water and the intrusion of saline water into the zone. The total area of the West Zone is 208.74 square miles. As of June 2007, among the total Metro Manila population of 12.8 million, 8.1 million resided in the West Zone. The total area of the East Zone is 95.57 square miles and as of June 2007, the total population of that zone was 4.7 million. The business district Makati is located in the East Zone. MWSI, 12 June 2008 <http://www.mayniladwater.com.ph/our_services.asp>.

42. Rivera 10.

43. In addition to pre-qualifying for the bidding process, the international partners needed to demonstrate experience and expertise in water supply and sanitation services. The local sponsors also needed to show their financial solvency, managerial competency, and a minimum $100 million capital fund (Rivera 10–11). Furthermore, the Filipino company was required to show experience of generating $33 million in revenue through one or more infrastructure businesses, such as water supply, communications, power, construction, or real estate. It should also have at least $67 million in equity. The experience of working in water supply treatment and distribution, wastewater treatment and sewerage services, metering, leakage control, customer service and billing, and design and construction management for system expansion were essential for a partner foreign company. Further, 2 years of experience in supplying

water and sewerage services to a city of at least 2.5 million inhabitants, setting up 1 million connections and 6,000 miles of main pipe lines, the experience in generating $30 million in annual revenues from water and sewerage services, and an asset of $1 billion in equity were vital for pre-qualification. Both Filipino and foreign companies had to be a single company, not an association of companies, although for "a special purpose subsidiary," more than one company was allowed (David 9).

44. The MWCI is a consortium of the following companies: the Filipino corporation Ayla, the British utility company United Utilities Pacific Holdings, BPI Capital Corporation, the largest U.S. engineering company Bechtel, and the Japanese conglomerate Mitsubishi Corporation. Ayla leads this consortium. MWCI employees hold 6.3 percent of the company's shares through its Employees Stocks Program. On 31 May 2004, the International Finance Corporation (IFC) became one of the key shareholders of the company (Manila Water 2005 Annual Report 38). For the shareholding structures of these two concessionaires at the time of the formation, see Tables 4.6 and 4.7. For the details of the financial statement of this company, see Manila Water 2005 Annual Report 38–75. MWCI's franchise area includes Mandaluyong, Marikina, Pasig, Pateros, San Juan, Taguig, Makati, and parts of Quezon City and Manila. It also provides water to Antipolo City and the Rizal towns of Angono, Baras, Binangonan, Cainta, Cardona, Jala-Jala, Morong, Pillia, Rodrigues, Tanay, Taytay, and San Metro. The seven business areas of MWCI are Balara, Cubao, Makati, Marikina, Pasig, San Juan–Mandaluyong, and Taguig-Pateros-Rizal (MWSS Regulatory Office 2).

As of 31 December 2004, the stock holders of the MWSI were Benpers Holding Corporation (flagship of the Lopez Group of Companies), Ondeo Services (a French company), Lyonnaise Asia Water (Holdings), Pte. Ltd. (also a French company), and the Metropolitan Bank and Trust Company. The MWSI inherited 90 percent of the MWSS's previous debts. Due to the financial crisis and their failure to repay the company's foreign loan, on 11 Dec. 2006 the ownership of Maynilad was handed over to the all-Filipino partnership of D. M. Consunji, Inc. (DMCI) and Metro Pacific Investments Corp. (MPCI), and Lyonnaise Asia Water Limited (LAWL). They acquired 83.9 and 16 percent of the shares of the company respectively. These companies replaced the almost a decade-long partnerships of previous shareholders and paid the MWSI's remaining foreign debt of $240 million in January 2008 (MWSI, "Corporate Profile," 2 June 2008 <http://www.mayniladwater.com.ph/corporate_profile.asp>). See also Anand Chiplunkar, Ma. Christina Duenas, and Mai Flor, *Maynilad on the Mend: Rebidding Process Infuses New Life to a Struggling Concessionaire* (Asian Development Bank 2008) 1 and "Philippines' Maynilad Water Set to Repay $240 mln Debts" (Reuters, 13 Jan. 2008). 2 July, 2008 <http://in.reuters.com/article/asiaCompanyAndMarkets/idINMAN2471120080113>. For the details of the MWSI's financial crisis, see David L. Llorito and Meryl Mae S. Marcon, "Bad Financing Policies add to Maynilad Woes" March 28, 2003. *The Manila Times.* 2 July 2008 <http://www.manilatimes.net/others/special/2003/mar/28/20030328spe1.html>.

In December 2006, the newly constructed MWSI gained the right to operate the West Zone concession after "it put in a whopping $447 million bid for the 84 percent stake" of the MWSS. The consortium formally took control of Maynilad on 24 January 2007. MWSI, "Attaining Sustainable Water Management," 14 June 2008 <http://www.mayni-

ladwater.com.ph/>. MWSI is responsible for providing water and wastewater services in the cities of Manila (except San Andres) Pasay, Paranaque, Caloocan, Muntinlupa, Las Pinas, Valenzuela, parts of Makati, and Quezon City, including the municipalities of Navotas and Malabon. Its franchise area also covers Cavite City and the Cavite municipalities of Bacoor, Imus, Kawit, Noveleta, and Rosario. They have four business areas: Northeast, Northwest, Central, and South. (MWSS Regulatory Office 2).

45. Fabella 4.

46. Rosenthal.

47. Fabella 30.

48. As of 2011, a total of 1,833 staff members worked for the company as supervised workers (262) and regular employees (1,571). Among the regular employees there were 52 males and 32 females in senior management position, 540 males and 336 females in middle management positions, and 53 males and 72 females in rank-and-file position. The number of female employees was much higher in MWCI (28%) compared to DWASA (10%); *Sustainability Report 2011*, Manila Water, 2011, p. 26).

49. MWCI, *Manila Water's Corporate Governance Manual*, Article I, 1.5.

50. As of 2011, the price per share was 1 Filipino peso or 2 cents. The company issued 2,005,443,965 common shares in 2011. MWCI, *Manila Water: 2011 Annual Report*, (Manila: Manila Water Company, Inc., 2011) 65.

51. Besides MWCI, Frenando Zobel De Ayala has been serving as President and COO of Ayala Corporation; Chairman of Ayala Land Inc; Co-Chairman of Ayala-Foundation, Board Member of Integrated Micro-Electronics, Globe Telecom, Bank of the Philippine Islands and Pilipinas Shell Corporation; Vice Chairman of Habitat for Humanity International; Member of the World Economic Forum, INSEAD East Asia Council and World Presidents' Organization; member of the Board of Directors of Kapit Bisig para sa Ilog Pasig Advisory Boarand Pilipinas Shell Foundation. James Augusto Zobel De Ayala is also serving as Chairman and CEO of Ayala Corporation; Chairman of Globe Telecom, Inc., Bank of the Philippine Islands, and Integrated Micro-Electronics Inc.; Vice Chairman of Ayala Land, Inc.; Co-Vice Chairman of Mermac, Inc., and the Ayala Foundation. MWCI, 2011, 42.

52. The ten other directors are Gerardo C. Ablaza. Jr. (Filipino), Antonino T. Aquino (Filipino), Delfin L. Lazaro (Filipino), John Eric T. Francia (Filipino), Ricardo Nicanor N. Jacinto (Filipino), Keiichi Asai (Japanese), Simon Gardiner (British), Thomas Keevil (British), Jose L. Cuisia, Jr. (Filipino, Independent Director), Oscar S. Reyes (Filipino, Independent Director). Solomon M. Hermosura (Filipino) serves as Corporate Secretary. For information regarding their affiliation with other companies besides MWCI, see MWCI, 2011, 20–21.

53. Jose L. Cuisia, Jr. and Oscar S. Reyes are currently working as independent directors. Cuisia, Jr. is presently the Ambassador Extraordinary and Plenipotentiary to the United States of America and Vice Chairman of The Philippine American Life and General Insurance Company (Philam Life) Manila Water 2011, 43. Reyes is a director of the Bank of the Philippines Islands; member of theAdvisory Board of Philippine Long Distance Telephone Company and J. G. Summit Holdings and Chikka Holdings, Inc.; and director of Universal Robina Corporation, D. M. Consunji, Inc., and Pilipinas Shell Petroleum Corporation (Manila Water 2005, 21).

54. Manila Water's Corporate Governance Manual. Article I, 1.5.

55. Dumol 56.

56. Diana Mitlin, "Competition, Regulation and the Urban poor: A Case Study of Water" (Manchester: Center on Regulation and Competition Working Paper Series No. 37, Dec. 2002).

57. The World Bank Group, *Philippines: Meeting Infrastructure Challenges* (Washington, D.C.: The World Bank, 2005) 108.

58. Peter H. Gleick, Gary Wolff, Elizabeth L. Chalecki, and Rachel Reyes, "The Risks and Benefits of Globalization and Privatization of Fresh Water" (Oakland, California: Pacific Institute for Studies in Development, Environment and Security, 2002).

59. Fabella 30.

60. MWSS Regulatory Office. *Regulatory Office Information Kit* 1.

61. Fabella 29.

62. Article 11 of the Concessions Agreement stipulates the authority of the Trustee to set up the Regulatory Office (RO).

63. The president appoints the chair and the members of the Trustee Board. Some of them are chosen from the ex-officio members of cabinet secretaries, and as a result, "their pliability to presidential revealed preference may determine their future career path in government or in other government corporation" (Fabella 30).

64. World Bank, "Improving Water Supply and Sanitation" http://siteresources.worldbank.org/INTPHILIPPINES/Resources/DB15-WaterSector-June28.pdf (accessed August 16, 2012). Moreover, the failure of the RO to provide consistent sector data and "baseline figures on the extent and quality of coverage ... undermines the credibility of the regulatory process" World Bank, "Improving Water Supply and Sanitation" http://siteresources.worldbank.org/INTPHILIPPINES/Resources/DB15-WaterSector-June28.pdf (accessed August 16, 2012).

65. Bubut D. Palatto, Team Coordinator, FDC. Personal interview, Metropolitan Manila, November 2006.

66. Hemantha Withanage, Sri Lankan Environmental Scientist, NGO Forum, Quezon City. Personal interview, November 2006, and J. Ronald D. Masayda, Advocacy and Campaign Coordinator, NGO Forum, Quezon City. Personal interview, November, 2006.

67. Personal interview with a woman in Makati City, Metropolitan Manila, November, 2006.

68. Jocelyn C. Cuaresma, "Pro-Poor Water Services in Metro Manila: In Search of Greater Equity" (Manchester: Center for Regulation and Competition, 2004) 2.

69. For the service types, see Cuaresma 12. For the percentage of connections to low-income people, see MWSS Regulatory Office, *2002 Annual Report* (Manila: MWSS, 2002).

70. Cuaresma 3, 12.

71. Mustaq Ahmed Memon and Hidefumi Imura, "Public-Private Partnerships for Urban Water: Experiences of Manila, Philippines" (2nd Thematic Seminar, Kitakyushu Initiative for a Clean Environment, 4 Nov. 2002). According to the Philippine Institute of Development Studies (PIDS), the "amount of water for human survival depends on surrounding environmental conditions and human physiological char-

acteristics but the overall variability of needs across individuals is small." The PIDS determines that the minimal requirement of water is 10 cubic meters per month for a family of 6 members—that is, 55.55 liters per person per day—which is much higher than the universal WHO standards, which set the minimum daily per capita consumption at 5 liters, with 25 liters as the practical basic needs. Arlene B. Inocencio, Jose E. Padila, and Esmyra P. Javier, "Determination of Basic Household Water Requirements" (Manila: Philippine Institute of Development Studies, Discussion Paper Series No. 99-02, Revised, Feb. 1999) 3.

72.   Argo and Aprodicio, also, Roel Landingin, "Loaves, Fishes and Dirty Dishes: Manila's Privatized Water Can't Handle the Pressure" (Washington, D.C., Center for Public Integrity and the International Center for Investigative Journalism: The Water Barons, 7 Feb. 2003). 28 June 2008 <http://www.waterconserve.org/shared/reader/welcome.aspx?linkid= 20086&keybold=water%20privatization>.

73.   MWCI, 2011, 52, 23, 2. Ten years ago, in 1997, when MWCI took charge of supplying water to the Eastern Zone of the city, it supplied only 440 mld water per day MWCI, *Manila Water: 2007 Annual Report (Manila: Manila Water Company, Inc., 2007)* 10, 40. Non-revenue water refers to "water that is lost due to leakage, theft, pilferage and illegal connections." Orlando C. Hondrade, "Shattering Water Woes," *Corporate Planning Call*, Oct. 2006, p. 6.

74.   There is a dispute regarding the way the two concessionaires estimate the water coverage. Their way of measuring coverage is by employing a ratio of 9.2 consumers per connection. The French consultants established this way of calculating coverage to help the concessionaires prepare their financial bids. The 9.2 to 1 ratio provided the ground for exaggerating the claim of coverage for the companies. Moreover, there is an allegation by the MWSS that the companies are counting non-existent customers, which they both deny. For example, by the end of 2001, based on 184,782 connections, MWSI claimed it was serving 1.7 million people in Manila proper, which had only 1.4 million people according to the MWSS census. Similarly, based on 47,178 connections, MWCI claimed more than 450,000 customers in Manila's central district, Makati, which was 250,000 in MWSS's calculation. The MWSS also objected to the method of counting connections to asses their service targets. However, the companies refused to change the ratio for estimating coverage. Roel Landingin.

75. MWSI, "Capabilities and Facilities."

76. MWSI, *Maynilad 2010 Annual Report* (Manila: Maynilad Water Services, Inc. 2010) p. 3. The Angat Dam provided 97 percent of MWCI and 98 percent of MWSI water, whereas only 2 percent came from deep wells (Manila Water, 2011, p. 38). The water was treated in Las Mesa Treatment Plants: Plant1 and Plant 2. These plants together can treat 2,400 Ml/d of water. Plant 1's designed capacity is 1,500 Ml/d and plant 2's, 900 Ml/D. In June 2007, the plants were able to treat an average of 1,355 Ml/d and 872 ML/d respectively. MWSI has fifteen reservoirs, eleven pumping stations, and seven mini boosters. MWSI, "Capabilities and Facilities." Our Services. Maynilad Water Services, Inc. <http://www.mayniladwater.com.ph/our_services.asp> 12 June, 2008.

77.   Both the company's original target and the service obligation were to provide 24 hours water supply with 16 psi to all connections by 2007 (Chiplunkar et al. 5). During my stay in Makati city, which is one of the richest neighborhoods and a busi-

ness district in Manila, I was informed by the residents that even in that area due to low water pressure, they use pumps to lift water to their tanks. According to them, the pressure is not sufficient to supply water directly from the main pipelines. However, they are satisfied about the quality of water and the 24 hours availability.

78. Arlene B. Inocencio and Cristina C. David, "Public-Private-Community Partnerships in Management and Delivery of Water to Urban Poor: The Case of Metro Manila," Philippine Institute of Development Studies, Discussion Paper Series No. 2001-18 (2001) 5.

79. The company's target was to reach 97.1 percent of the population in the West Zone by the end of 2006 (Rosenthal). By 2007, it was able to reach only 73 percent of the residents and could not ensure 24 hours of water to all of them. Roughly 944,000 residents in the West Zone receive their water from private (not MWSI) water connections, deep wells, and water vendors (MWSI, "Capabilities and Facilities").

80. MWSI, 2010, p. 3.

81. MWCI, 2007, 19.

82. Arlene B. Inocencio and Cristina C. David. "Public-Private-Community Partnerships in Management and Delivery of Water to Urban Poor: The Case of Metro Manila." Philippine Institute of Development Studies, Discussion Paper Series No. 2001-18 (2001) 14. The Barangay-operated public faucets were provided temporarily at the initial stage of the introduction of market-led governance.

83. Cuaresma 6.

84. Virgilio C. Rivera, "How Private Sector Involvement Can Help the Poor: Lessons from Manila (East)," Conference on From Private Sector Participation in the Urban Water and Sanitation: Managing the Process and Regulating the Sector, December 5-6, Manesar, Haryana, India, 2001, qtd. in Cuaresma 6.

85. Inocencio and David 14. Under the MWSS's state-led governance, only legal residents in city were entitled to receive water connections in their households.

86. Mark A. Dumol, "The Design of the Manila Concessions and Implications for the Poor." PPIAF/ADB Conference on Infrastructure Development—Private Solutions for the Poor: The Asian Perspective (2001).

87. Cuaresma 7.

88. Personal interview with a woman in the Tondo District, Metropolitan Manila, November, 2006. See also David and Inocencio 14.

89. MWCI, *Annual Report 2011* (Manila: Manila Water Company, Inc., 2011), 3.

90. MWCI, 2007, 19.

91. MWSS Regulatory Office, *Information Kit* (Manila: MWSS) 2. The two concessionaires use different terminologies for connections. MWCI uses the terms "Regular Connections" and "Equivalent Household Connections." MWSI uses "Official Connections" and "Total Connections." These terms are defined as follows: "Official Connections/Regular Connections include billed services metered regular connections, bulk-metered connections, excluding connections downstream of the bulk meter and connections under special billing; e.g. raw water, water district, sea transport." "Total Connections/ Equivalent Household Connections include official connections plus connections downstream of bulk-metered connections." MWSS Regulatory Office. 2002 Annual Report.

92. Rosenthal. The MWCI encountered some problems in collecting monthly payments. The negative aspect of this project is that the community leaders usually enforce tougher rules on their members, such as disconnecting the service to those households who were unable to pay their monthly payments or charging penalties to the non-compliant members, acording to a United Nations report. There were also complaints of overcharging by the community leaders. United Nations ESCAP, "Water for Poor Communities in the Philippines," United Nations ESCAP, 3 July 2008. <http://www.unescap.org/pdd/prs/ProjectActivities/Ongoing/Best%20practice/Philippines.pdf>.

93. United Nations 26.

94. Cuaresma 14.

95. Rosenthal.

96. Inocencio and David 20.

97. Inocencio and David 20.

98. Inocencio and David 7.

99. MWSI, "Fact Sheet." *Corporate Planning* (March 2006) 3.

100. Rosenthal.

101. "Corporate Social Responsibility" Maynilad <http://www.mayniladwater.com.ph/about04-ct.html> (accessed August 15, 2012).

102. MWSI, 2010, p. 25.

103. Cuaresma 9.

104. Some vendors also collected water from official connections and public faucets. After buying the water, it was physically carried in cans using a wooden pole, pushcart, tricycle, or jeepney. Based on my conversation with women and informal settlers in Metro Manila, marginalized women in the informal settlements keep water in drums, which meet their entire family needs for 2–3 days. Although vended water was expensive, it was cheaper than bottled water. See also Cuaresma 15–16, and Arlene B. Inocencio, "Serving the Urban Poor Through Public-Private-Community Partnerships in Water Supply," Philippines Institute of Development Studies, Policy Notes No. 2001-10 (Sept. 2001).

105. MWSS-RO Report, qtd. in Cuaresma 12.

106. Cuaresma 15.

107. Based on my conversation with several women in various informal settlements in Metro Manila.

108. Inocencio and David 14.

109. Christophe Bosch, Kristen Hommann, Claudia Sadoff, and Lee Travers, "Water Sanitation and Poverty" http://www.intussen.info/OldSite/Documenten/Noord/Internationaal/WB/PRSP%20Sourcebook/18%20Water,%20sanitation%20and%20poverty.pdf (accessed, August 17, 2012).

110. Cuaresma 16.

111. Under the group taps scheme, MWCI installed meters at the doorway of the households' compound, and due to the distance from the main road to the compound in that particular area, the connection charge per household sometimes reached as high as $ 400. Inocencio and David 17.

112. The bill-paying date for every household was set between the 21st and 26th of every month and the treasurer pays the collected bills to the company on the 27th

(Inocencio and David 18). For how the price of water works under this scheme, see Table 4.9.

113. Inocencio and David 18. In June and July 2001, total water consumption for the Durian community under this project was 6,430 and 8,143 cubic meters (28 and 35 cubic meters per household). This scheme also reduced non-revenue water because the amount of water consumed or lost by any means would be billed to the mother meter, so the community organization appointed some individuals to guard the water sources continuously, which created pressure on the community members to pay extra money for water. This scheme also created pressure on the community to pay the bill on time, because non-payment would create the problem of disconnection of water services for the entire community. For the water rates under the MWCI's bulk water project, see Table 4.7.

114. Inocencio and David 19–20. In 2001, under this distribution mechanism, the low-income group people paid roughly $1.50 per cubic meter for water.

115. Inocencio and David. Cuaresma 18.

116. Inpart Engineering also provided water to Barangay Addition Hills in Mandaluyong city. In this project, Inpart Engineering invested in the construction of a 100,000-gallon water tank, water pipes, meters, faucets, hoses, and other equipment. The company worked on this project in coordination with former first lady Estrada's office (Cuaresma 19).

117. Argo and Laquian 241.

118. Cuaresma 21. However, neither company was successful in increasing the standard level of water pressure to 16 psi. The water pressure was only 3–5 psi when it was allocated by MWSS. (United Nations, "Water for Poor Communities"). According to the service obligations, the concessionaires are obliged to provide water 24 hours per day at 16 psi, in compliance with the WHO standard.

119. Only 20–25 percent of low-income households have individual water connections (Cuaresma 22). People with individual connections consume 4–5 times more water in Metro Manila than those who do not have connections in their households. Interestingly enough, of those with individualized connections, almost half relied on bottled water for drinking and cooking purposes. There is a direct correlation between water consumption and household income levels. The biggest consumers are those whose monthly household income is more than $1,041 and the least amount of water is used by consumers with monthly household incomes below $167. Moreover, the availability of individual connections provided the leeway for liberal use of water to the households. There is limited availability of individual connections for the marginalized women's households; hence, they have limited capabilities of "using expensive non-piped water, which they still pay for willingly." Marginalized women and low income households in Metro Manila usually have capabilities of using 5–8 cubic meters per month—the minimum monthly requirement for domestic and sanitation purposes. These households pay almost double the amount of households with individual connections. Asian Development Bank, "Delivering Piped Water on a Small Scale: Results of ADB's Water Supply Service Market Survey in Manila," Water Briefs (Oct. 2007). 4 July 2008 <http://www.adb.org/Water/Water-Briefs/delivering-piped-water.asp>.

120. Asian Development Bank 243.

121. Melissa Howell-Alipalo, "Water and Small Pipes: What a Slum Wants, What a Slum Needs" (Asian Development Bank, May 2007). 2 July 2008 <http://www.adb.org/Water/actions/phi/water-small-pipes.asp>.

122. Asian Development Bank, "Proceedings of the Regional Consultation Workshop on Water in Asian Cities—The Role of Civil Society," In *Water in Asian Citie— Utilities Performance and Civil Society Views* (Manila: ADB, 2004) 243.

123. Cuaresma 24.

124. Arthur C. McIntosh, *Asian Water Supplies: Reaching the Urban Poor* (Manila: Asian Development Bank, 2003) 1. In the Philippines, non-piped customers spent 16 percent of their household income for water compared with about 6 percent for those who have individual connections. In Metropolitan Manila, this ratio was much higher. The residents who had water connections with either of the two companies spent only 1.0 to 1.7 percent of their household income (Asian Development Bank 78). Besides the Philippines, in general, the economically marginalized urban residents living in the developing world paradoxically paid 10–25 times more for water than those who have the ability to have individual water connections in their households. Arif Hasan, "A Model for Government-Community Partnership in Building Sewage Systems for Urban Areas: The Experiences of the Orangi Pilot Project-Research and Training Institute, Karachi," *Water Science Technology* 45: 8 (2002) 199–216.

125. Asian Development Bank, "Proceedings of the Regional Consultation," 243.

126. In comparison to the MWSS rate, it was more than double (see Table 4.10). Although not accessible to the marginalized women of the city, the price of water was relatively cheaper under the state-led governance (Memon and Imura).

127. Landingin.

128. Sari-sari (convenience stores), vulcanizing shops, food stalls, small bodegas (except bonded warehouse), seasonal businesses, etc. are considered semi residential. But for supply and profit convenience, the water companies categorized the supply of bulk water to the informal households as supplying water to semi residents. For the classification of the customers and the water sold, see MWSS-RO, "Customer Service Regulation Complaints Services Monitoring Department, Five Year Accomplishment Report, 1997–2002," (MWSS-RO, Manila, 2002). In Metro-Manila, only roughly 20–25 percent of low-income and informal households have individual connections. Cuaresma 22.

129. Cuaresma 24.

130. Cuaresma 22.

131. For example, in 2006, in the island province of Cebu, water vendors sold P 250 per cubic meter water whereas in Metro-Manila, the average price was P 19.73. Jubilee South, "Profiting from People's Lives: Metro Manila's Water Privatization Saga." (18 Oct. 2008) <http://www.jubileesouth.org./upload1/fdc_low.pdf>. The water price is comparatively higher in the West Zone. MWSI charges roughly 65 cents per cubic meter to its customers, who have independent connections. This charge is a combination of a Basic Charge (45 cents per cubic meter), a Value Added Tax (VAT), a Currency Exchange Rate Adjustment (CERA, 2 cents), and an Environmental Charge (5 cents). The company also levied a fixed Maintenance Service Charge of from 3 cents to $1per connection depending on the meter size. MWSI, "More Affordable Water" (14 June 2008) <http://www.mayniladwater.com.ph/service_rates.asp>.

132. Fabella 11.

133. Fabella 11.

134. Fabella 11. The water quality was below the national standards between 1994 and 1996. United Nations, "Water for Poor Communities."

135. Fabella 12.

136. MWSS: Regulatory Office, 2003 Annual Report 15. This is the RO's last annual report. After that they did not publish any report regarding the performance of the concessionaires. I asked Randolph Sakai, acting deputy administrator (Financial Regulation of RO) about it; he was not able to inform me why they were no longer publishing the report.

137. MWSI claims that their water quality exceeds global and national standards, especially the one prescribed by the Department of Health's Philippine National Standard for Drinking Water. The Freedom from Debt Coalition collected water from affected areas and submitted the samples to the National Science Research Institute of the University of the Philippines. The tests revealed more than 16 fecal coliforms per 100 ml of water, which was more than seven times higher than the Philippine standard of 2.2 coliforms per 100 ml (South, "Profiting from People's Lives"). During my conversation with Jubilee South in the NGO office, Bubut Palattao, a leading Freedom From Debt Coalition activist, informed me that the claim of the quality by RO is questionable. However, she could not show any evidence regarding her claim. The perception I had after talking with people in various levels in Metro-Manila was that in comparison to MWSI, they believed that the water supplied by the MWCI was of better quality.

138. In 2003, the diarrhea outbreak occurred in the Tondo area. Upon the request of the chief regulator to DOH secretary, a fact-finding committee was created by the DOH to detect the number of incidents. This committee recorded 868 cases of diarrhea during October and November 2003 in the Tondo area. Eight died due to acute gastroenteritis. A DOH report identified the two waves of vibrio cholera and gastroenteritis cases during the period mentioned above and blamed the supply of dirty water for the outbreak (MWSS Regulatory Office 19–20). The first wave started on October 23 and the second wave on November 3. The DOH's report identified "person-to-person transmission" as the major cause for the second wave of the outbreak (MWSS RO 20). The highest number of diarrhea cases was detected in 1997 before the introduction of market-led governance. A total number of 109,483 cases were detected that year (Landingin).

5

Conclusion

Research of secondary materials before my fieldwork indicated that most of the marginalized women and the poor living in Dhaka and Metropolitan Manila did not have necessary access to supplied water resources. They also did not have capabilities to participate in the decision-making process. After investigating primary data and conducting interviews in both Dhaka and Metropolitan Manila, this study concludes that neither the state nor the Public-Private Participation (PPP) governance have ensured the political capability of marginalized women to participate in decision-making spaces. With regard to water resources, marginalized women do not have the basic material capability to access supplied water resources under the state-led governance in Dhaka, whereas their basic material capability did increase moderately under the PPP governance in Metropolitan Manila.

In DWASA, the elites of the city have relatively more capability to participate in decision-making spaces, although their capability to participate is also limited because the organization's decision-making process is controlled by civilian and technical bureaucrats. In Metropolitan Manila, the corporate elites monopolize the decision-making spaces of both companies (MWCI and MWSI), although in theory, these are invited spaces. Moreover, marginalized women and poor people do not have the capability to influence the Regulatory Office's decisions in their favor. Hence, they are not capable of participating in the decision-making spaces created by either the state-led or PPP governance systems in Dhaka and Metropolitan Manila.

This study uses three indicators—quantity, quality, and price—to measure the basic material capabilities of the marginalized women. In terms of quantity, marginalized women in Dhaka do not have the capability to access enough supplied water to meet their daily needs. DWASA has not been successful in bringing the economically marginalized population into its service networks. In contrast, under the PPP governance in Metropolitan Manila, marginalized women's capabilities have increased moderately; they have more capabilities to access the supplied water resources than their counterparts in Dhaka. Moreover, their capabilities have also increased compared to the time when water was managed by state-led governance.

The quality of water has also improved in Metropolitan Manila, whereas DWASA has not been able to improve water quality. However, the price of water has increased significantly under PPP governance; water is more expensive in Metropolitan Manila than in Dhaka. The increase in price has affected different groups of people unevenly. Although all people pay more per unit of water in Metropolitan Manila, marginalized women and the poor pay more than the other population groups. This is due to the various schemes the water companies (discussed in previous chapter) have used to supply water to poor people's households. However, marginalized women and the poor paid more for water even when water was cheaper under the state-led governance, because they had to buy water from vendors at much higher prices due to the unavailability of basic water services. They had to spend considerably more time collecting water from different sources.

In Dhaka, the price of water did not increase significantly under the state-led governance, but as a result of high water connection fees and the policy of DWASA to not provide connections to city residents they deem to be "illegal" (see previous chapter), the majority of marginalized women did not qualify to participate in the service networks. Therefore, despite the relatively lower price, marginalized women's basic material capabilities did not increase in terms of access to supplied water resources.

In Metropolitan Manila, women's capabilities increased moderately not as a result of their capabilities to participate in the decision-making spaces, but as an outcome of the paternalistic distribution of the water resources by the companies. They adapted this policy because it was a necessary part of the contract. Therefore, they widened their service networks to include the poor through various schemes that would fulfill their contract obligations as well as ensuring business profits. In this allocation process, marginalized women, poor people, or other customers could not play any role in distribution decisions; in other words, they could not exercise their political capabilities—an essential cornerstone of the capability approach.

The state-led governance of DWASA has not been successful in providing water to all city inhabitants. Mainly the poor and the marginalized women are deprived of receiving the minimum daily requirement of water under this governance mechanism. Although the state-led governance theoretically promised universal access to water resources, it was not successful in establishing marginalized women's capabilities to access supplied water resources in Dhaka. Instead, as a result of DWASA's policies, the elites are the chief beneficiaries of this governance system. The rest of the population does not receive its fair share of services.

This study finds that the needs of marginalized women and poor people are ignored by the state-led governance in Dhaka. Under the PPP system in Metropolitan Manila, more marginalized women and poor people have access to the services of water companies; it has increased the quantity, price, and quality aspects of their capabilities. However, their political capabilities have not increased under either of the governance systems. As mentioned earlier, the moderate increase of women's capabilities in Metropolitan Manila was not due to their capabilities to participate in the formal spaces, although their limited participation in informal spaces in some cases may have influenced the decisions taken in the formal spaces. Therefore, this study concludes that under both state-led and PPP governance, social justice has not been established in the supplied water sector.

Establishing social justice in water governance might require both material satisfaction and political participation. Political capability is a very important aspect of the capability approach. Individuals who can exercise the least political power might nevertheless have access to water resources, despite the prevailing inequitable political capability. As a normative theory, the capability approach defines development in terms of increasing both the political and the material capabilities of an individual. Instead of being a passive recipient of a good service, the goal of this approach is to create an equitable opportunity for all individuals to ensure their capability to make choices and to participate in the decision-making process. The issue is not whether every individual or every marginalized woman is participating in the decision-making process, but rather whether they have the capability to participate in the decision-making spaces—in Sen's words whether "the person is free to choose particular levels of functionings ... and that is not the same thing as what the person actually decides to choose."[1] Therefore, this study proposes that it is crucial to develop a choice-sensitive governance paradigm to involve all sections of the population in the governance system—with a special emphasis on marginalized women because they remain on the lowest rung of the social ladder—to ensure both the political and material capabilities of the people. In other words, this model is proposed to achieve what Sen mentions as "agency achievements" that would lead from people's, especially marginalized women's, political capabilities to their physical/basic material capabilities.[2]

An Alternative Paradigm: Marginalized Women–Centered, Deliberative, Reflexive Governance

This study concludes that the state-led and PPP governance systems are exclusionary in Dhaka and Metropolitan Manila. Sen believes that people should have the capability of making decisions for themselves, and for that, he advocates "democratic governance" where people can exchange their ideas and experiences and make decisions on the policies and priorities of society.[3] In theory, an ideal system would develop a governance mechanism with equitable participation of all people in the decision-making process. However, in reality people live in hierarchically differentiated locations (in terms of money, power, and technological know-how) in society and hence, their political and other capabilities vary. It is not possible for those who live on the lower rung of the social ladder to participate in any governance mechanism with equitable capability. It is therefore necessary to develop a more inclusive paradigm that creates a space (or provides access to the existing spaces) for marginalized women, who have the least capabilities to participate in the governance mechanism as well as to access water resources. Such a space would open up an avenue for them to exercise their political capabilities.

According to the capability approach, justice is served if the water governance is equitably responsive to all sections of the population in terms of ensuring both their political and material capabilities. Hence, it is necessary to create a governance system that would be more inclusive and less paternalistic. In Dhaka and in Metropolitan Manila, to ensure equitable political and material capabilities, the governance system needs to be marginalized women–centered because they are the most deprived group in these two cities. In a society where individuals "stand in structurally different positions in relation to one another," structural differentiation shapes dissimilar interests and postulates unequal vantage positions of individuals.[4] Unequal socio-economic, political, and structural relations privilege some segments more than others in obtaining resources. It is thus difficult to establish capabilities for the marginalized segments, where "social and economic injustices" prevail.[5]

Even the most industrially advanced, affluent societies fall short of economic, political, and social equalities. In the developing world, inequalities in general are much more intense. In an unequal society, enforcing "democratic governance" without taking affirmative measures for the marginalized segments may "reinforce more than undermine" inequalities.[6] This is also applicable to water governance. Most of the women I interviewed in Dhaka and Metropolitan Manila believed that their interests would be preserved in a better way if they could also participate in the governance process.

Dhaka and Metropolitan Manila are located in the developing world and the social gap between the rich and poor is much wider there than in the developed world. Hence, simply including poor women in the governance mechanism with relatively better-off social groups would not ensure their political capabilities. It would be almost impossible for them to compete with people who have better technological know-how and are equipped with superior economic and political capabilities. It is obvious that these more powerful people would dominate the space unless the system itself is centered on marginalized women. Therefore, as an affirmative measure, an alternative paradigm is needed to establish social justice in water distribution, where marginalized women's needs should be placed at the center of the governance and their participation in the decision-making spaces should also be ensured.

An affirmative action measure is vital in trying to incorporate relatively marginalized women into the spaces of water governance. To establish a relative social justice in the supplied water services in Dhaka and Metropolitan Manila requires a more inclusive, alternative paradigm for water governance that is marginalized women–centered, deliberative, and reflexive (referred to here as deliberative, reflexive governance). Redesigning the governance paradigm is necessary for improving the quality of participation and for fulfilling the conditions required to achieve both material and political capabilities. Governance systems should be redesigned by converting them into deliberative and reflexive as well as marginalized women–centered institutions. This model would ensure marginalized women's relatively equitable political and material capabilities.

The redesigned framework is fundamentally different from conventional paradigms because its basic objective is to take into account the needs of the marginalized women at the center of the decision-making process. In order to assess their demands, it is necessary to create a space (or to accommodate women in the existing spaces) within the conventional models of governance through which their needs can be articulated in the decision-making process.

Reflexive governance is an evolving new concept. Mainly, it refers to a form of governance that is self-introspective, with the ability to continue restructuring itself through systematic response.[7] The notion behind reflexivity includes two functions: organized inputs and "conscientious self-introspection."[8] More specifically, it engages various actors (often situated in contradictory locations) in examining and reassessing existing mechanisms, rules, and paradigms.[9] In this engagement process, power "struggles (among the different actors) may involve enacting reflexive governance."[10] The idea is to make decisions within the links of a reflexively reciprocal organization—that is, to take into account the multiplicity of inputs from the different actors situated in contradictory locations. Informal institutions, such as NGOs or women's groups, as well as formal and informal networking are important components in the development of reflexive mechanisms. John Grin has developed the concept of reflexive governance by introducing the idea that it also takes into account the transformation of the governance mechanism itself.[11] Reflexivity therefore implies that nothing is static—praxis, paradigms, and structures— all are subject to consideration and reconfiguration.

Reflexive governance requires participation. Its emphasis is on "the right of participation, empowerment, process monitoring and process conflict settlement."[12] As such the working definition for reflexive governance describes a strategy for organizing governance mechanism to establish recursive responsive networks between the stake-holders and the recipients of distributed services. Hence, it would be possible to include marginalized women in the reflexive structure of the governance mechanism and through this network they would be able to participate at least moderately in the decision-making process.

The conventional model of governance does not stand for creating or providing a space for marginalized women in particular (see Chapter Two). It also does not distinguish between the various recipients in terms of their locations in society. Instead, it mainly focuses on reflexive networks regardless of the individual's position in society. The inability to distinguish diverse recipients may favor some groups over others when it comes to the issue of receiving inputs. As seen in this study, the prevailing social and economic inequalities provide unequal benefits—both political and economic—to various groups.

In a hierarchical society, some groups have more resources, power, and influence than others. As a result, they are also more powerful in presenting their inputs to the governance system. They can thus exercise more political capabilities compared to less powerful groups. Marginalized women are the least powerful among the less powerful people. Without creating special networks to receive inputs solely from marginalized women, simply developing certain reflexive mechanisms may not provide them necessary access to the reflexive networks. Thus, to transform the existing governance mechanism into a reflexive system that is centered on marginalized women, it is necessary to develop certain networks to receive inputs directly from the marginalized women. As such this study proposes deliberative, reflexive governance as an alternative paradigm through which women in Dhaka and Metropolitan Manila would be able to establish their relative political capabilities by participating in the governance mechanism.

Besides creating special reflexive networks for marginalized women, to ensure their political capabilities it is also important to include the practice of deliberation in the reflexive networks of the governance system. Sen mentions the importance of public deliberation for achieving political capabilities that he refers to as "public discussion—between persons and across borders."[13] Deliberation between actors (service providers and recipients) is an important part of the decision-making process within the network of reflexive governance. Without deliberation or discussion, it would not be possible to implement reflexive networks. Deliberation means establishing dialogues between diverse actors—in this study, between the service providers and the recipients of water service, that is, marginalized women and other customers who are receiving services from the water board and companies in Dhaka and Metropolitan Manila respectively.

The purpose of dialogue is not to simply defend the existing situations; it should deal with the unequal capabilities of less powerful persons that persist in different segments of the population. Deliberation should also pave the way to solve this problem through recognizing the existence of unequal political and material capabilities; in this case, recognizing the unequal political and material capabilities of the marginalized women when it comes to the issue of making decisions regarding water distribution.

Creating (or providing) a space for deliberation between the different segments of people would open up an avenue to express their mutual interests and needs, and thus the marginalized women and poor people would obtain opportunities to articulate their demands. Open deliberation would engage the different segments in what James Bohman describes as "argument and counter-argument," which would create an environment of mutual respect among the different group members located on the different rungs of the social ladder.[14] Despite profound disagreements and dislike for the others, according to David Crocker, a "virtuous deliberator respects other group members."[15] Moreover, it helps to generate "a favorable attitude toward, and constructive interaction with, the persons with whom one disagrees."[16] Therefore, creating or providing a space for deliberation for the marginalized women would help them in interacting with the powerful segments of society and the stakeholders and thus would help them to realize their necessity for water.

Deliberative governance relies on a normatively legal and legitimate democratic procedure for rational conversation regarding social issues, and it offers policies or recommends policy changes to deal with them across a broad spectrum of society.[17] The major challenge for the marginalized women–centered, deliberative, reflexive governance is to create spaces for their inclusion, as they are the most underprivileged in a hierarchical social structure. Therefore, the task is to create a network of inclusion where they can exercise their political capabilities or freedoms, ultimately leading to "agency achievements"; in other words, they would also be able to gain material capabilities through exercising their political capabilities, not only through good bureaucratic or economic planning.

The inclusion of underprivileged groups in the formal networks creates an environment for exchanging opinions. Iris Young mentions that it provides an avenue to effectively express each other's concerns among those who not only have different opinions, but are also located in different socioeconomic contexts.[18] The important task is to create a sense of equitable political capabilities that would promote inclusion in the decision-making spaces. This situation would lead to David Crocker's notion of "reciprocity" and "accountability," that is, members of one group could propose and justify their suggestions in a way that other groups can comprehend and recognize.[19] He further elaborates that each deliberator should have "the right to make his voice heard and to contribute to the final decision."[20] Bohman argues that to make a contribution to the final decision, every participant should acquire equitable political capabilities for "political functioning" and real "social freedom"; for that, they have to develop minimal skills of public dialogue and debate.[21]

Crocker further mentions that a person is "politically poor" if he or she does not have the minimal skills of public dialogue.[22] In Dhaka and Metropolitan Manila, where marginalized women do not have the experience of participating in water governance, initially they may not have sufficient skill to engage in meaningful argument and counter-argument with the other stakeholders and technological bureaucrats. However, access to the decision-making space would certainly help them to develop persuasive rhetoric vis-à-vis framing and reframing a debate regarding the necessity of supplying water to the households of poor women and other impoverished people.

As mentioned, the major characteristic of the proposed deliberative, reflexive governance is that it is more inclusive than the conventional paradigms. As such, deliberative, reflexive governance reorganizes the allocation mechanism by incorporating alternative networks of distribution. In this alternative network, depending on the context, there might be a possibility for public-private-NGO coordination in resource distribution where economically marginalized women can participate in the process through deliberation and reflexive networks. This type of intervention in the governance mechanism might lead to political capabilities for marginalized women, which would then lead to improved material capabilities. This alternative paradigm recognizes the political capabilities of the marginalized women over the redistribution of resources, especially supplied water resources, which is ignored in conventional paradigms.

There is no universal paradigm or blueprint for the deliberative, reflexive governance. Socio, economic, cultural, and political phenomena as well as spatial and temporal variations would determine the patterns of this paradigm. The ostensible goal of the deliberative, reflexive governance is to put marginalized women at the center of the decision-making process, making decisions "over their own lives."[23] Structural reorganization is the prerequisite to providing access for marginalized women in the reflexive networks and participatory spaces.

Challenges for Marginalized Women–Centered, Deliberative, Reflexive Governance

The challenges for deliberative, reflexive governance are not only the inclusion of women in the process, but also the coordination of the marginalized women's priorities with the others, which may conflict. Establishing justice by ensuring water security for the poorest women is inherently a political task, involving complex interactions between the political, social, and economic institutions that shape the pattern of water services as well as the governance mechanism.[24]

Water governance is fundamentally different from other types of governance because on the one hand, water is a common property, and on the other hand, it could also be used as an economic good. Implementing deliberative, reflexive governance does not imply that the services should be free to all. The fact that services are free does not always assure their availability.[25] Similarly, free or inexpensive water might not assure its quality or availability. The challenge for water governance is to address fairness issues while ensuring cost effectiveness, as well as ensuring the effective participation of marginalized women and other citizens in the decision making-process. The goal is not only to increase operating efficiency but also to assure equitable material capabilities for all.

Deliberative, reflexive governance does not ignore the economic necessity of operational and managerial efficiency. Bakker has identified "three lows: low investment; low quality of services; and low revenue (and/or cost recovery) levels" in some water management systems.[26] An additional fourth low would be low levels of input from the water users, especially from marginalized women, in the decision-making process, as well as low or no water services to their households. Therefore, the challenge of water governance is to focus on five areas: investment, water quantity, water quality, revenue, and inputs. These are essential for safeguarding the supply of water resources to the marginalized women's households as well as for "safeguarding the right to safe water supply."[27]

Implementing deliberative, reflexive governance in the supplied water sector would be a complex and multi-faceted task. It is necessary to coordinate "economic instruments to re-allocate water" with the policy mandate of supplying water resources to every person, while paying special attention to the needs of marginalized women.[28] As this model has never before been implemented, it is difficult to say how successful it would be in coordinating the interests of poor women with relatively well-off customers. Success would be determined by the degree to which water providers in Dhaka and Metropolitan Manila could coordinate the interest of all these water users while providing poor women access to the spaces of governance by creating deliberative and reflexive networks. The aim of this model would thus be to implement Sen's capability approach in the water sectors in Dhaka and Metropolitan Manila by politically empowering the least powerful members of society.

Marginalized Women in the Supplied Water Sector

In order to exercise marginalized women's political capabilities, it is necessary to develop "governmentality from below," which Arjun Appadurai calls "coun tergovernmentality."[29] This study proposes deliberative, reflexive governance as countergovernmentality. Bakker describes the governance model as "a set of structures, functions and practices that defines who does what, and how they do it."[30] Similarly, a UN World Water Development Report notes that a "governance system determines who gets what water, when and how, and decides who has the right to water and related services and their benefits."[31] Good governance accomplishes desired objectives "in the right way."[32]

The prime goal for deliberative, reflexive governance is the establishment of marginalized women's basic material capabilities through enhancing their political capabilities. It is not a concrete scheme; instead it is a conceptual framework. It is vital that governance principles should be "home grown" and adaptive, as well as context-dependent.[33] Applications of this model should be diverse. Therefore, this study does not prescribe a concrete and universal normative model; rather, it makes broader and less specified claims. Moreover, although it does not make a strong universalistic claim regarding its scopes, structures, and mechanisms, deliberative, reflexive governance is nevertheless not completely free from universalistic claims. Despite its willingness to incorporate multiple organized interests, this normative governance system places the interests of the marginalized women at the center.

Deliberative, reflexive governance refers to a new type of governance structure that is capable of including marginalized women's inputs and feedback in the reflexive networks and is also able to integrate input from the stakeholders and technical experts. The "collective action" (of women and poor people) and reorganization of networks are key to this type of governance.[34] This paradigm should also be capable of creating sustainable management of water resources through coordinated networks of multi-sector partnerships, such as, depending on the context, public, private, non-governmental, and grassroots organizations, and water users, collaborating in the distribution process. Although this new paradigm is fluid and flexible in adapting policies and programs in different contexts, it is rigid about placing the interests of the marginalized women at the center.

It is important to consider the interior and exterior aspects of deliberative, reflexive governance. One important interior aspect consists of building networks among the stakeholders, the marginalized women, and other users to set up an institutional framework. Developing procedures for both the administrative and technical experts can also be considered interior aspects of governance. The role of the civil society and the government, as well as property laws associated with water governance, can be considered as exterior aspects of governance.[35]

To ensure material capabilities of the marginalized women, it is also important to develop a strong regulatory mechanism. Relying solely on the government regulatory authority might not assure appropriate distribution because the interests of government officials are different from those of marginalized women. Hence, it might be necessary to coordinate the role of the government authority with the local communities (or the grassroots organizations of women) and water-related NGOs.

As mentioned earlier, the aim of this study is not to develop a universal framework of governance. Therefore, instead of providing a concrete prescription for the state-led and PPP water governance in Dhaka and Metropolitan Manila, two outlines (Table 5.1 and Table 5.2) are provided only to demonstrate how DWASA and MWSS can include marginalized women–centered, deliberative, reflexive governance system into their existing mechanisms.

Sen is aware that a good governance mechanism is crucial for ensuring capabilities for all. He believes that "democratic governance" is the best form of governance, although he does not elaborately discuss the necessity of affirmative measures for ensuring the political and material capabilities of those who are disadvantaged in terms of exercising their political power and access to resources.[36] Despite his awareness of the unequal political and material capabilities of those who live on the lowest rung of the social ladder, Sen or other scholars do not directly address the capabilities of the economically marginalized women or how they can exercise their capabilities without enforcing affirmative measures. Therefore, this study argues for the necessity of developing a governance paradigm that would be centered exclusively on marginalized women but at the same time would not deny the political and material capabilities of other sections of the population. This study also argues that as marginalized women live on the lowest rung of the social ladder, if a governance system can provide the political and material capabilities to these poorest women, it would also be able to ensure the capabilities of the other people.

An individual's capabilities are related to the pattern of the governance system; that is, the governance pattern determines how much capability an

TABLE 5.1.
Deliberative, Reflexive Governance Paradigm for Public Governance (DWASA)

Agency:	
Assets Owner	DWASA (Public Enterprise)
Assets Manager	The Office of the Managing Director
Water Technicians	DWASA-appointed technical experts
Decision-Makers	DWASA officials and technical experts on the basis of the inputs from marginalized women, grassroots organizations and other sections of population
Regulatory Body	Proposed to create a govt. appointed body to work in coordination with the representatives of marginalized women, NGOS, and grassroots organizations
Political Capabilities:	
Level of Participation	Deliberative participation of the representative of the marginalized women, grassroots organizations and other sections of the population in the DWASA provided or created spaces
Actors of Participation	DWASA officials, marginalized women and other sections of population
Accountability	DWASA officials and technical experts to the marginalized women as well as to other sections of people
Decision-Making Space (Space of Power)	Invited (women, grassroots organizations' representatives, and other sections of population receive invitation to participate in the spaces created or provided by DWASA)
Form of Power	Visible power structures of DWASA
Reflexive-Networks	Obtaining inputs from marginalized women, other sections of people, and grassroots organizations
Implementation/ Responsibility	DWASA officials and their technical experts
Basic Material Capabilities:	
Outcomes/Goals	Ensuring marginalized women's necessary access to supplied water resources

TABLE 5.2.
Deliberative, Reflexive Governance Paradigm for PPP Governance in Metropolitan Manila

Agency:	
Assets Owner	MWSS (Public Enterprise)
Assets Manager	MWCI and MWSI
Water Technicians	MWCI and MWSI appointed technical experts
Decision-Makers	MWCI and MWSI boards of directors and technical experts on the basis of the inputs from marginalized women, grassroots organizations, and other sections of population
Regulatory Body	RO work in coordination with the representatives of marginalized women, NGOS, and grassroots organizations
Political Capabilities:	
Level of Participation	Deliberative participation of the representative of the marginalized women, grassroots organizations and other sections of population in the MWCI and MWSI provided or created spaces*
Actors of Participation	MWCI and MWSI officials, marginalized women and other sections of population
Accountability	DWASA officials and technical experts to the marginalized women as well as to other sections of people
Decision-Making Space (Space of Power)	Invited (women, grassroots organizations' representatives, and other sections of population receive invitation to participate in the spaces provided or created by MWCI and MWSI)
Form of Power	Visible power structures of MWCI and MWSI
Reflexive-Networks	Obtaining inputs from marginalized women, other sections of people, and grassroots organizations
Implementation/Responsibility	MWCI and MWSI officials and their technical experts
Basic Material Capabilities:	
Outcomes/Goals	Ensuring marginalized women's necessary access to supplied water resources

*The government can set-up a condition in the contract that the private companies have to incorporate the representatives of the marginalized women and those from grassroots organizations in their decision-making spaces. Women, grassroots organizations, and NGOs might need to organize campaigns to create pressure both on the government and the companies to provide marginalized women and other poor customers' access to their decision-making spaces.

individual can exercise. Therefore, based on my research, it is necessary to develop a governance system that would be centered mainly on marginalized or poor women, and that would give them opportunities to exercise both their political and material capabilities. Without developing a woman-centered governance system, it would not be possible to ensure the capabilities, especially political capabilities, of the poorest women under the good or democratic governance system, although it might be possible to achieve their material capabilities through such a system.

The findings of this research suggest that overcoming water users' low level of participation in conventional systems of governance is essential for water access to become both an efficient market commodity and a basic human right. This study could lead to future research as to whether the participation of marginalized women in water governance systems is necessary for the establishment of the principle of access to sufficient water as a basic human right.

Notes

1. Amartya Sen, "Human Rights and Capabilities," *Journal of Human Development* 6.2 (2005): 155.

2. Amartya Sen, "The Standard of Living: Lecture II, Lives and Capabilities," in *The Standard of Living*, ed. G. Hawthorn (Cambridge University Press: Cambridge, 1987) 28.

3. Amartya Sen, "Democracy as a Universal Value," *Journal of Democracy* 10.3 (1999).

4. Iris Marion Young, "Public Debate and Social Justice," *Maitreyee* 4 (February 2006): 2.

5. Young, "Public Debate" 3.

6. Young, "Public Debate" 3.

7. Adopted from Berejikian and Dryzek's concept of reflexive modernity; see Jeferey Berejikian and John S. Dryzek, "Reflexive Action in International Politics," *British Journal of Political Science* 30.2 (2000): 212–213.

8. Kim San Jun, "The Reflexive Consensus System: A New Governance Model." Paper presented at the 6th Global Forum on Reinventing Government: Toward Participatory and Transparent Governance. Seoul, Korea. May 24–27, 2005, 12.

9. Drawn from John Grin et al., "Practices for Reflexive Design: Lessons from a Dutch Programme on Sustainable Agriculture," *International Journal of Foresight and Innovation Policy* 1.1-2 (2004): 2.

10. Carolyn M. Hendriks and John Grin, "Contextualizing Reflexive Governance: The Politics of Dutch Transitions to Sustainability," *Journal of Environment Policy & Planning* 9.3-4 (2007): 333.

11. John Grin, "Reflexive Modernization as a Governance Issue—or Designing and Shaping Re Structuration," in *Reflexive Governance for Sustainable Development*, ed. Jan-Peter VoBV, Dierk. Bauknecht, and René Kemp (Cheltenham: Edward Elgar, 2006). VoBVoB and Kemp distinguish first and second orders of reflexivity. For

details, Jan-Peter VoB and René Kemp, "Sustainability and Reflexive Governance: Incorporating Feedback into Social Problem Solving." Paper presented at International Human Dimensions Programme on Global Environmental Change (IHDP) Open Meeting, Bonn. Oct. 9–13, 2005.

12. Marc van der Meer et al., "Adaptive and Reflexive Governance—Changing Boundaries of National Social-Economic Decision-Making in the Netherlands." Paper presented at IREC Conference. Utrecht School of Governance. Aug. 26–28, 2004, 16–17.

13. Sen, "Human Rights" 163.

14. James Bohman, *Public Deliberation: Pluralism, Complexity and Democracy* (Cambridge, MA: MIT Press, 1997) 90. See also James Bohman. "Deliberative Democracy and Effective Social Freedom: Capabilities, Resources, and Opportunities," in *Deliberative Democracy*, ed. James Bohman and William Rehg (Cambridge: MIT Press, 1997).

15. David Crocker, "The Capability Approach and Deliberative Democracy," *Maitreyee* 4 (February 2006): 6.

16. Amy Gutmann and Dennis Thompson, *Democracy and Disagreement* (Cambridge, MA: Harvard University Press, 1996) 79.

17. Sony Pelisesery and Sylvia I. Bergh, "Adapting the Capability Approach to Explain the Effects of Participatory Development Programs: Case Studies from India and Morocco," *Journal of Human Development* 8.2 (2007): 284.

18. Young, "Public Debate" 2.

19. David Crocker, "Deliberative Participation in Local Development." Paper presented at the International Conference of the Human Development and Capability Association. Groninger, Netherlands. Aug. 29–Sep. 1, 2006. 2 October 2007 <http://www.hd-ca.org>.

20. Crocker, "The Capability Approach" 5.

21. James Bohman, *Public Deliberation.*

22. David Crocker, "The Capability Approach" 6.

23. Irene Gujit and Meera kaul Shah, eds., *The Myth of Community: Gender Issues in Participatory Development* (London: IT Publications, 1998) 1.

24. It is a myth that poor people are not willing to pay for water. One study shows that poor slum dwellers in Dhaka are willing to pay for networked water to cover the expenses of supplying it. Nasima Tanveer Chowdhury, "Willingness to Pay for Water in Dhaka Slums; a Contingent Valuation Study," January 1999. IUCN 14 February 2005 <http://www.users.rcn.com/jhecht2/pubs-and-papers/SAsia.valuation.ch4.pdf>.

25. For example, medical services are supposed to be free for the poor in Bangladesh. However, in reality, the poor are deprived of the services when admitted to various public hospitals, due to the lack of availability of medical facilities. In addition, even when services are available, in reality, patients need to pay a significant amount of money for the services, especially for hospital admission fees, medicine, tests, food, and tips. Suhaila H. Khan, "Free Does Not Mean Affordable: Maternity Patient Expenditures in a Public Hospital in Bangladesh," *Pub Med Central.* 12 Feb., 2006. <http://www.pubmedcentral.nih.gov/articlerender.fcgi?artid=546230>.

26. Karen Bakker, "Good Governance in Restructuring Water Supply: A Handbook," *Federation of Canadian Municipalities.* 18 February, 2006 < http://www.sustainablecommunities.ca/Home/>.

27. World Water Assessment Programme, *Water a Shared Responsibility: The United Nations World Water Development Report 2* (Paris, New York: UNESCO and Berghahn Books, 2006) 66.

28. For the discussion of "economic instruments to re-allocate water," see Tony Allan, *The Middle East Water Question: Hydropolitics and the Global Economy* (London, New York: I. B. Tauris Publishers, 2001) 17.

29. Arjun Appadurai, "Deep Democracy: Urban Governmentality and the Horizon of Politics," *Public Culture* 14.1 (2002): 39, 36.

30. Bakker, "Good Governance."

31. UN World Water Development 47.

32. Bakker, "Good Governance."

33. UN World Water Development 20.

34. John T. Scholz and Bruce Stiftel, "The Challenges of Adoptive Governance," in *Adoptive Governance and Water Conflict: New Institutions for Collaborative Planning,* ed. John T. Scholz and Bruce Stiftel (Washington, DC: Resources for the Future, 2005) 1.

35. Rogers and Hall identify internal and external governance, where they consider property laws as part of internal governance. Peter Rogers and Alan W Hall, "Effective Water Governance," *TEC Background Papers* No. 7 (Stockholm: Global Water Partnership, 2003) 17.

36. Sen, "Democracy as a Universal Value."

Bibliography

Agarwal, Bina. "Participatory Exclusions, Community Forestry, and Gender: An Analysis for South Asia and a Conceptual Framework," *World Development* 29.10 (2001), pp. 1623–1648.

Agarwal, Bina et al. "Exploring the Challenges of Amartya Sen's Work and Ideas: An Introduction," *Feminist Economics* 9.2–3 (2003), pp. 3–12.

Ahmed, K. Iftekhar. "Urban Poor Housing in Bangladesh and Potential Role of ACHR," the Asian Coalition for Housing Rights [ACHR], Thailand, May 2007.

Ahmed, Sayeed Iftekhar. "Resurgence of Islam in Bangladesh Politics," *South Asian Journal* 11 (2006), pp. 149–162.

Aladin, Anwar, and Mohhamad Abu Taleb. "Eyi Pocha Pani-I Khacchhi" (We Are Drinking Polluted Water), 21 April 2009. *The Daily Ittefaq*, 22 April 2009 <http://www.ittefaq.com/content/2009/04/21/news0580.htm>.

Alam, Ahmed Nure. "Pani Noy Bish Pan Korchi: Rajdhani-soho Drihottoro Dhaka-er 1500 Borgo Km Elakar Pani Bisakto, Charpaser Nodigulo Bhoyaboho Dusone Aakranto" (We Are Drinking Poison Not Water: Including Greater Dhaka, Water Has Been Poisoned in 1,500 sq km of Area: The Level of River Pollution Around the City Is Very High), 15 Mar. 2007. *The Daily Janakantha*, 16 Mar. 2007 <http://www.dailyjanakantha.com/p1/html1>.

Alam, Imtiaz. "Growth and Poverty in South Asia," *South Asian Journal* 15 (2007), pp. i–iii.

Alamgir, Mahiuddin. "Participatory Development: The IFAD Experience." In W. Lineberry, ed., *Assessing Participatory Development; Rhetoric Versus Reality* (Boulder: Westview Press 1989), pp. 3-18.

Allan, Tony. *The Middle East Water Question: Hydropolitics and the Global Economy* (London, New York: I. B. Tauris Publishers 2001).

Alexander, John M. "Capability Egalitarianism and Moral Selfhood," *Ethical Perspectives* 10.1 (2003), pp. 3–21.

Alkire, Sabina, and Rufus Black. "A Practical Reasoning Theory of Development Ethics: Furthering the Capabilities Approach," *Journal of International Development* 9.2 (1997), pp. 263–279.

Alkire, Sabina. *Valuing Freedoms: Sen's Capability Approach and Poverty Reduction* (New York: Oxford University Press, 2002).

Appadurai, Arjun. "Deep Democracy: Urban Governmentality and the Horizon of Politics," *Public Culture* 14.1 (2002), pp. 23–43.

Argo, Teti and Aprodicio A. Laquian. "The Privatization of Water Services: Effects on the Urban Poor in Jakarta and Metro Manila." *The Inclusive City: Infrastructure and Public Services for the Urban Poor in Asia*, Ed. Aprodicio A. Laquian et al. (Washington, D.C. Baltimore. Woodrow Wilson Center Press, Johns Hopkins University Press 2007), pp. 224–248.

Arnstein, Sherry R. "A Ladder of Citizen Participation," *Journal of the American Institute of Planners* 35.4 (1969), pp. 216–224.

Authority, Dhaka Water Supply and Sewerage (DWASA). *Management Information Report* (Dhaka WASA: Dhaka, June 2006).

Authority, Dhaka Water Supply and Sewerage (DWASA). *Annual Report 2010–2011.* (Dhaka WASA: Dhaka, 2011).

Bakker, Karen. "Archipelagos and Networks: Urbanization and Water Privatization in the South," *The Geographical Journal* 169.4 (2003), pp. 328–341.

———. "A Political Ecology of Water Privatization," *Studies in Political Economy* 70 (2003), pp. 35–58.

———. "Good Governance in Restructuring Water Supply: A Handbook," *Federation of Canadian Municipalities.* 18 February, 2006 < http://www.sustainablecommunities.ca/Home/>.

Ballet, Jerome, Jean-Luc Dubois, and Francois-Regis Mahieu. "Responsibility for Each Other's Freedom: Agency As the Source of Collective Capability," *Journal of Human Development* 8.2 (2007), pp. 185–202.

Balota, Anges. *Water Advocates' Resource Book: Planning for Community-Based Integrated Water Resource Management, Vol. 3* (The Philippines: Tambuyog Development Center, Water Commons Institute, 2005).

Bank, Asian Development. "Diagnostic Water Market Assessment for Dhaka Water Supply and Sewerage Authority," *Asian Development Bank,* 2 Jun. 2007 <http://www.adb.org/Water/Tools/DWASA-TOR-digest.asp>.

Bank, Asian Development. "Proceedings of the Regional Consultation Workshop on Water in Asian Cities—The Role of Civil Society," In *Water in Asian Cities—Utilities Performance and Civil Society Views* (Manila: ADB, 2004), pp. 71–83.

Bank, Asian Development. "Delivering Piped Water on a Small Scale: Results of ADB's Water Supply Service Market Survey in Manila" (Manila: Asian Development Bank, Oct. 2007) 23 March 2008 <http://www.adb.org/Water/Water-Briefs/delivering-piped-water.asp>.

Bank, Asian Development. "Delivering Piped Water on a Small Scale: Results of ADB's Water Supply Service Market Survey in Manila," Water Briefs

(Oct. 2007). 4 July 2008 <http://www.adb.org/Water/Water-Briefs/delivering-piped-water.asp>.

Bank, World. *The World Bank: Participation Source Book* (Washington DC: The World Bank 1996).

Bank, World "Improving Water Supply and Sanitation" http://siteresources.worldbank.org/INTPHILIPPINES/Resources/DB15-WaterSector-June28.pdf.

Barlow, Maude and Tony Clark. "Who Owns Water?" *The Nation* 275.7 (2 Sept 2002).

Bhodro, Nikhil. "Rajdhanite Tibro Hocchhe pani Sonkot: Poristhiti Mokabelay Sorkarer Karjokor Uddok Neyi" (Water Crisis Worsens in the Capital: Government Does not have any Efficient Initiative to Tackle the Problem), May 29, 2005. *Weekly Ekota*, 30 May 2005 <http://www.cpbdhaka.org/Ekota83.pdf>.

Blackburn, James and Jeremy Holland. "General Introduction." In James Blackburn and Jeremy Holland, eds., *Who Changes? Institutionalizing Participation in Development* (London: International Technology Publications, 1998), pp. 1-8.

Billah, Wasek and Niaz Morshed. "Rajdhanite Pani Pan Kotoa Nirapod" (Drinking Water in Dhaka Is Not Safe), 24 Aug. 2008. *Prothom Alo*, 2 Sep. 2008 <http://www.prothom-alo.com/archive/news_details_home.php?dt=2008-08-24&issue_id=1023&nid=MTgzMzY=>.

Berejikian, Jeferey, and John S. Dryzek. "Reflexive Action in International Politics," *British Journal of Political Science* 30.2 (2000), pp. 193–216.

Bohman, James. *Public Deliberation: Pluralism, Complexity and Democracy* (Cambridge, MA: MIT Press, 1997).

Bohman, James. "Deliberative Democracy and Effective Social Freedom: Capabilities, Resources, and Opportunities" in *Deliberative Democracy*, ed. James Bohman and William Rehg (Cambridge: MIT Press, 1997), pp. 321–348.

Bosch, Christophe, Kristen Hommann, Claudia Sadoff, and Lee Travers. "Water Sanitation and Poverty" http://www.intussen.info/OldSite/Documenten/Noord/Internationaal/WB/PRSP%20Sourcebook/18%20Water,%20sanitation%20and%20poverty.pdf (accessed, August 17, 2012).

Brennan, Brid, Bernhard Hack, Oliveir Hoedeman, Satoko Kishimoto, and Phillip Terhorst. *Reclaiming Public Water! Participator Alternatives to Privatization* (The Netherlands: Transnational Institute, 2004).

Chiplunkar, Anand, Ma. Christina Duenas, and Mai Flor. *Maynilad on the Mend: Rebidding Process Infuses New Life to a Struggling Concessionaire* (Asian Development Bank, 2008).

Chowdhury, Nasima Tanveer. "Willingness to Pay for Water in Dhaka Slums; a Contingent Valuation Study," January 1999. IUCN 14 February 2005 <http://www.users.rcn.com/jhecht2/pubs-and-papers/SAsia.valuation.ch4.pdf>.

Citizen, Public. "Water Privatization Backgrounder," *Public Citizen*, 1 May 2007. http://www.citizen.org/ cmep/Water/activist/articles.cfm?ID=9589>.

Cooperatives, Ministry of Local Government, Rural Development and. *National Policy for Safe Water Supply and Sanitation 1998* (Bangladesh: Government of the People's Republic of Bangladesh, Ministry of Local Government, Rural Development and Cooperatives, 1998).

Cornwell, Andrea. *Making Spaces, Changing Places: Situation Participation in Development*, IDS Working Paper 170 (England: Institute of Development Studies, 2002).

————. "Whose Voices? Whose Choices? Reflections on Gender and Participatory Development," *World Development* 31.8 (2003), pp. 1325–1342.

Cornwell, Andrea and V. Coehlo, eds. *Spaces for Change? The Politics of Citizen Participation in New Democratic Arenas* (London: Zed Books, 2006).

Corporation, Dhaka City. *Dhaka City Corporation*, 14 Jan. 2007 <http://www.dhakacity.org/profile.html>.

Correspondent, Keraniganj (Dhaka). "Keraniganj Theke Protidin 50 Hazar Liter Pani Dhakay Asche" (Every Day 50 Thousand Liters of Water Supplied to Dhaka from Keraniganj), 27 April 2008. *Prothom Alo*, 30 Aug. 2008 <http://www.prothom-alo.com/archive/news_details_home.php?dt=2008-04-27&issue_id=906&nid=MTU2NDE=>.

Corton, Maria Luisa. "Benchmarking in the Latin American Water Sector: The Case of Peru," *Utilities Policy* 11 (2003) pp. 133–142.

Council, Water Supply and Sanitation Collaborative. *Global Water Supply and Sanitation Assessment 2000 Report* (United States of America : WHO, UNICEF, 2000).

Court, Julius. "Governance, Development and Aid Effectiveness: A Quick Guide to Complex Relationships," *ODI Briefing Paper* (London: Overseas Development Institute, March 2006).

Crocker, David. "The Capability Approach and Deliberative Democracy," *Maitreyee* 4 (February 2006) pp. 4–6.

————. "Deliberative Participation in Local Development." *Journal of Human Development*. 8 (3). 2007, pp. 431–455.

Cuaresma, Jocelyn C. "Pro-Poor Water Services in Metro Manila: In Search of Greater Equity" (Manchester: Center for Regulation and Competition 2004).

David, Cristina C. "MWSS Privatization: Implications on the Price of Water, the Poor and the Environment." Discussion Paper Series No. 200-14. (Manila: Philippine Institute for Development Studies, April 2000).

Deneulin, Severine. "Promoting Human Freedoms Under Conditions of Inequalities: A Procedural Framework," *Journal of Human Development* 6.1 (2005) pp. 75–95.

Dietz, Thomas et al., "The Drama of the Commons," In Elinor Ostrom et al., eds., *The Drama of the Commons* (Washington, DC: National Academy Press 2003), pp. 3-35.

Dreze, Jean and Amartya Sen. *Hunger and Public Action* (Oxford: Clarendon Press 1989).

————. *India: Economic Development and Social Opportunity* (Delhi: Oxford University Press, 1995).

Dore, Mohamed H. I. Joseph Kushner, and Klemen Zumer. "Privatization of Water in the U.K. and France—What Can We Learn?" *Utilities Policy* 12 (2004), pp. 41–50.

Drydyk, Jay. "When Is Development More Democratic?" *Journal of Human Development* 6.2 (2005), pp. 247–267.

Dumol, Mark. *Manila Water Concession: A Key Government Official's Diary of the World's Largest Water Privatization* (Washington DC: World Bank Publications 2000).

————. "The Design of the Manila Concessions and Implications for the Poor." PPIAF/ADB Conference on Infrastructure Development—Private Solutions for the Poor: The Asian Perspective (2001).

Dutt, Arup and Anis Rahman. "Loadsheding, Prochondo Gorom, Panir Tibro Sonkot" (Power Cut, Severe Heat and Acute Water Crisis), 27 April 2008. *Prothom Alo*, 30 Aug. 2008 < http://www.prothom-alo.com/archive/news details home. php?dt=2008-04-27&issue id=906&nid=MTU2NDA=>.

Easterly, William. *The White Man's Burden: Why the West's Efforts to Aid the Rest Have Done So Much Ill and So Little* (New York: Penguin Press, 2006).

Editorial. "A Slum-Free Metro Manila," Sept. 4, 2007. *The Manila Times.* 21 March 2008 <http://www.manilatimes.net/national/2007/sept/04/yehey/ opinion/20070904opi1.html>.

Encartra, MSN. "Manila" 22 March 2008 <http://encarta.msn.com/encyclope- dia_761578132/manila.html>.

Ericta, Carmelita N. "Change in Spending Pattern Among Filipino Families Seen in 2006" (Manila: National Statistics Office, 2006 Family Income and Expenditure Survey, 9 Oct. 2007) 23 March 2008. <http://www.census.gov.ph/data/sector- data/2006/ie0605.htm>.

ESCAP, United Nations. "Water for Poor Communities in the Philippines," United Nations ESCAP, 3 July 2008. <http://www.unescap.org/pdd/prs/ProjectActivities/ Ongoing/Best%20practice/Philippines.pdf>.

Evans, Peter. "Collective Capabilities, Culture, and Amartya Sen's Development As Freedom," *Studies in Comparative International Development* 37.2 (2002), pp. 54–60.

Fabella, Raul. "Shifting the Boundary of the State: The Privatization and Regulation of Water Service in Metro Manila" (Manchester: Working Paper Series, Center on Regulation and Competition, March 2006).

Finger, Matthias and Jeremy Allouche. *Water Privatization: Transnational Corpora- tions and the Re-Regulation of Water Industry* (UK: Spon Press, 2001).

Foldvary, Fred E. "Natural Monopolies," Jan 1999. *The Progress Report* (27 Feb 2005). <http://www.progress.org/archive/ fold74.htm>.

Gaventa, John. "The Scaling-Up and Institutionalization of PRA: Lessons and Chal- lenges," in James Blackburn and Jeremy Holland, eds., *Who Changes? Institutionalizing Participation in Development* (London: Intermediate Technology Publications 1998).

Gaventa, John and Andrea Cornwell. "Challenging the Boundaries of the Possible: Participation, Knowledge and Power," *IDS Bulletin* 37.6 (2006) 122–128.

Gaventa, John. "Finding the Spaces for Change: A Power Analysis," *IDS Bulletin* 37. 6 (2006) 23–33.

Ghai, Dharam. "Participatory Development: Some Perspectives from Grass-Roots Experiences," *UNRISD Discussion Paper* 3 (1988).

Giddens, Anthony. *The Transformation of Intimacy: Sexuality, Love, and Eroticism in Modern Societies* (California: Stanford University Press, 1993).

Giles, Mohan. "Beyond Participation: Strategies for Deeper Empowerment," In Bill Cooke and Uma Kothari, eds., *Participation: The New Tyranny* (London: Zed Books, 2001), pp. 153–167.

Gleick, Peter H., Gary Wolff, Elizabeth L. Chalecki, and Rachel Reyes. "The Risks and Benefits of Globalization and Privatization of Fresh Water" (Oakland, CA: Pacific Institute for Studies in Development, Environment and Security 2002).

Gleick, Peter et al. *The World's Water: The Biennial Report on Freshwater Resources, 2004–2005* (Washington and London: Island Press, 2004).

Goulet, Denis. *Development Ethics: A Guide to Theory and Practice* (London: Zed Books 1995).

Grin, John et al. "Practices for Reflexive Design: Lessons from a Dutch Programme on Sustainable Agriculture," *International Journal of Foresight and Innovation Policy* 1.1-2 (2004), pp. 126–149.

Grin, John. "Reflexive Modernization as a Governance Issue—or Designing and Shaping Re-Structuration," in *Reflexive Governance for Sustainable Development*, ed. Jan-Peter VoB, D. Bauknecht, and Rene Kemp (Cheltenham: Edward Elgar, 2006), pp. 57–81.

Group, the World Bank. *Philippines: Meeting Infrastructure Challenges* (Washington, D.C.: The World Bank, 2005).

Group, the World Bank. "Access to Safe Water," The World Bank (26 July 2012). <http://www.worldbank.org/depweb/english/modules/environm/water/print.html>.

Gujit, Irene and Meera kaul Shah, eds. *The Myth of Community: Gender Issues in Participatory Development* (London: IT Publications, 1998).

Gupta, Asim Das, Mukund Sungh Babel, Xavier Albert, and Ole Mark. "Water Sector of Bangladesh in the Context of Integrated Water Resources Management: A Review," *Water Resources Development* 21.2 (2005), pp. 385–398.

Gutmann, Amy and Dennis Thompson. *Democracy and Disagreement* (Cambridge, MA: Harvard University Press, 1996).

Hafiz, Mahmud. "MP Commissionarder Pani Rajnitir Hatiar: Somossa Somadhanae Char Bochore Kono Prokolpo Neya Hoyni" (Water is a Political Instrument for MPs and Commissioners: No Major Project was Undertaken in the Last Four Years to Solve the Problem), 7 May 2006, *The Daily Janakantha*, 8 May 2006 <http://www.dailyjanakantha.com/070506/p1/html5>.

Hasan, Arif. "A Model for Government-Community Partnership in Building Sewage Systems for Urban Areas: The Experiences of the Orangi Pilot Project-Research and Training Institute, Karachi," *Water Science Technology* 45: 8 (2002), pp. 199–216.

Hasan, Mehedi."Rajdhanir 60 Bhag Elaka Panir Jonno Hahakar: Dirghomeyadi Ebong Somonnito Porikolponar Tagid, Dainik Ghattir Poriman Der Koti Liter" (Sixty Percent of the City Experiences Water Shortage: Daily Water Shortage of 15 million Liters in the City, Long Term Coordinated Efforts Are Needed to Solve the Crisis). Apr. 19, 2007. *The Daily Ajker Kagoj*, 19 Apr. 2007 <http://www.ajkerkagoj.com/2007/April19/1st_page.html#16>.

———. "Dhaka-ke Paritakto Sohor Ghosona Kora Hote Pare: Ek Dosaoker Moddhe Bhu-Gorbhosto Panir Stor 40 Meter Niche Nemeche" (Dhaka Might Be Declared as a Deserted City: Underground Water Level Went Down 40 Meters in a Decade), 19 Jan. 2007. *The Daily Ajker Kagoj*, 22 Jan. 2007. < http://www.ajkerkagoj.com/2007/Jan19/1st_page.html#21>.

————. "Grismo Suru Na Hoteyi WASA-er Dainik Pani Ghati 55 Koti Liters, Dhaka-Basike Bachate Ekhoni 12 sh Koti Takar Prokolpo Hate Nite Hobe Sorkar-ke: Bhu-Gorbhosto Panir Stor Proti Bochor 10 Meter Kore Neme Jayoyar Asonka" (Even Before the Summer Season Begins, the Daily Water Crisis in the City Reached to 550 millions Liters per Day; Government should Immediately Take a Project of $172 m: It Is Apprehended that the Water Layer Will Go Down at the Rate of 10 Meter Per Year), 4 Apr. 2007. *The Daily Ajker Kagoj*, 7 Apr. 2007 <http://www. ajkerkagoj.com/2007April04/last_page.html#2>.

————. "Nogorir 40 Bhag Elakay Sorboraho Kora Hocchhe Moyla O Durgondho-jukto Pani: WASA-er Panite Payoya Geche Moricher Bichi, Balu and Chera Poly-thene." (DWASA Supplying Dirty and Odiferous Water to 40 percent of the City: Pepper Seeds, Sand Particles and Torn Polythene Found in the Supplied Water), 20 Apr. 2007. *The Daily Ajker Kagoj*, 20 Apr. 2007 < http://www.ajkerkagoj.com/2007/ April20/1st_page.html#13>.

Helal, Mansur. "Susko Mousumer Ageyi Rajdhanite Panir Sankot: Stor Neme Geche 46 Meter Niche, Barche Nogorir Tapmatra." (Capital's Water Level went Down 46 meters before the Dry Season Starts: the Average Temperature of the City Increas-ing). Jan. 24., 2007. *The Daily Ajker Kagoj*. 24 Jan. 2007. < http://www.ajkerkagoj. com/2007/Jan24/1st_page.html#17>.

Hendriks, Carolyn M. and John Grin. "Contextualizing Reflexive Governance: The Politics of Dutch Transitions to Sustainability," *Journal of Environment Policy & Planning* 9.3-4 (2007), pp. 333–350.

Hill, Carolyn J., and Laurence E. Lynn, Jr. "Is Hierarchical Governance in Decline? Evidence from Empirical Research," *Journal of Public Administration Research and Theory* 15:2 (2005), pp. 173–195.

Hondrade, Orlando C. "Shattering Water Woes," *Corporate Planning Call*, Oct. 2006.

Howell-Alipalo, Melissa. "Water and Small Pipes: What a Slum Wants, What a Slum Needs" (Asian Development Bank, May 2007). 2 July 2008 <http://www.adb.org/ Water/actions/phi/water-small-pipes.asp>.

Hussain, Sayed Sarwar and Ferdousi Ara. "Bangladesh Retail Food Sector Report 2004," 4 Feb. 2004. *USDA Foreign Agriculture Service*, 15 Jan. 2007 <http://www. fas.usda.gov/gainfiles/200402/146105367.pdf>.

Imam, Nazmul. "Panir Dese Panir Jonno Hahakar" (Crying for Water in a Water Affluent Country), 12 Apr. 2007. *Daily Naya Diganta*, 12 Apr. 2007 <http://www. dailynayadiganta.com/fullnews.asp?News_ID=17002&sec=2.>.

Inocencio, Arlene B. Jose E. Padila, and Esmyra P. Javier. "Determination of Basic Household Water Requirements" (Manila: Philippine Institute of Development Studies, Discussion Paper Series No. 99-02, Revised, Feb. 1999).

Inocencio, Arlene B. and Cristina C. David. "Public-Private-Community Partner-ships in Management and Delivery of Water to Urban Poor: The Case of Metro Manila," Philippine Institute of Development Studies, Discussion Paper Series No. 2001-18 (2001).

Inocencio, Arlene B. "Serving the Urban Poor Through Public-Private-Community Partnerships in Water Supply," Philippines Institute of Development Studies, Policy Notes No. 2001-10 (Sept. 2001).

Islam, Nazrul A. Q. M. Mahbub, Nurul Islam Nazem, Gustavo Angeles, and Peter Lance. *Slums of Urban Bangladesh: Mapping and Census, 2005* (Dhaka: Center for Urban Studies, National Institute of Population Research and Training, MEASURE Evaluation, 2005).

IWRM. "Tool Box," *Global Water Partnership* 19 Nov. 2006 <http://www.waterland.net/index.cfm/site/Toolbox%20-%20en/pageid/4663B313-A25C-8A9B-5C1C99D060C92B62/page/1/objecttype/mark.apps.nwp.contentobjects.tool/objectid/1991C019-0284-467B-9CCC9CC25D4EA057/index.cfm>.

"Integrated Water Resources Management," *Cap-Net* 16 Nov. 2006 < http://www.cap-net.org/iwrm_tutorial/mainmenu.htm.

Jansky, Libor, Dann M. Sklarew, and Juha I. Uitto. "Enhancing Public Participation and Governnace in Water Resource Management," in *Enhancing Participation and Governance in Water Resources Management: Conventional Approaches and Information Technology*, eds. Libor Jansky, Juha I. Uitto (Tokyo, New York, Paris: United Nations University Press, 2005), pp. 3–18.

Jessop, Bob. "The Governance of Complexity and the Complexity of Governance: Preliminary Remarks on Some Problems and Limits of Economic Guidance," in *Beyond Market and Hierarchy: Interactive Governance and Social Complexity*, eds. Ash Amin and Jerzy Hausner (Cheltenham and Lyme: Edward Elgar 1997), pp. 95-128.

Johnston, Barbara Rose. "The Political Ecology of Water: An Introduction," *Capitalism, Nature, Socialism* 14 (2003), pp. 73–90.

Jun, Kim San. "The Reflexive Consensus System: A New Governance Model." Paper presented at the 6th Global Forum on Reinventing Government: Toward Participatory and Transparent Governance. Seoul, Korea. May 24–27, 2005, 12.

Kamal, Mithun. "Pani Ghattir Poriman 100 Koti Liters: Rajhdhanite Pani Somossa Prokot" (Severe Water Crisis in the Capital: Water Shortage Is 1,000 mld per Day), 11 April 2006. *The Daily Inquilab*, 18 May 2006 <http://www.dailyinquilab.com/april1/index.htm>.

Kaufmann, Daniel, Aart Kraay, and Pablo Zoido-Lobatón. "Governance Matters," *Policy Paper 2196* (World Bank Institute, October 1999).

———. "Rethinking Governance: Empirical Lessons Challenge Orthodoxy," *Discussion Draft* (World Bank, March 11, 2003).

Kessler, Tim. "Who's Taking Risks? How the World Bank Pushes Private Infrastructure and Finds Resistance in Some Surprising Places," July 2004, *Citizen's Network on Essential Services*, 20 Jan. 2007 <http://www.servicesforall.org/html/infrastructure/Taking%20Risks-FINAL.pdf>.

Khan, Mizanur. "Water Crisis: WASA Blames Power Cuts, Depletion of Groundwater," 8 June 2005. *The Daily Star*, 8 Jul. 2005 <http://www.thedailystar.net/2005/06/08/d506082501121.htm>.

Khan, Morshed Ali. "Tanneries 'Kill' the Buriganga River," 11 Sep. 2006. *Asia Water Wire*, 24 Jan. 2007 <http://www.asiawaterwire.net/node/428>.

Khan, Suhaila H. "Free Does Not Mean Affordable: Maternity Patient Expenditures in a Public Hospital in Bangladesh," *Pub Med Central*. 12 Feb., 2006. <http://www.pubmedcentral.nih.gov/articlerender.fcgi?artid=546230>.

Kothari, Uma. "Power Knowledge and Social Control in Participatory Development." In Bill Cooke and Uma Kothari, eds., *Participation: The New Tyranny* (London: Zed Books, 2001), pp. 139–152.

Kumar, Sanjay and Stuart Corbridge. "Programmed to Fail? Development Projects and the Politics of Participation," *The Journal of Development Studies* 39.2 (2002), pp. 73–104.

Landingin, Roel. "Loaves, Fishes and Dirty Dishes: Manila's Privatized Water Can't Handle the Pressure" (Washington, D.C., Center for Public Integrity and the International Center for Investigative Journalism: The Water Barons, 7 Feb. 2003). 28 June 2008 <http://www.waterconserve.org/shared/reader/welcome.aspx?linkid=20086&keybold=water%20privatization>.

Lawson, Alastair. "Good Times for Bourgeois Bangladesh," 1 Jun. 2002. *BBC*, 15 Jan. 2007 <http://news.bbc.co.uk/2/hi/south_asia/2018535.stm>.

Llorito, David L. and Meryl Mae S. Marcon. "Bad Financing Policies add to Maynilad Woes." *The* March 28, 2003. *The Manila Times*, 2 July 2008 <http://www.manilatimes.net/others/special/2003/mar/28/20030328spe1.html>.

Martin, Narelle. "Corporations As a Means of Improving Water Quality: The Experience in Victoria, Australia," *Journal of Toxicology and Environmental Health: Part A*, 67 (2004) 1889–1899.

Memon, Mustaq Ahmed and Hidefumi Imura. "Public-Private Partnerships for Urban Water: Experiences of Manila, Philippines" (2nd Thematic Seminar, Kitakyushu Initiative for a Clean Environment, 4 Nov. 2002).

McGee, Rosemary "Unpacking Policy Actors, Knowledge and Spaces," in Karen Brock, Rosemary McGee and John Gaventa, eds., *Unpacking Policy: Actors, Knowledge and Spaces in Poverty Reduction in Uganda and Nigeria* (Kampala: Fountain Press 2004), pp. 1-26.

McIntosh, Arthur C. and Cesar E.Yniguez, Eds. *Second Water Utilities Data Book: Asian and Pacific Region* (Manila: Asian Development Bank, 1997).

McIntosh, Arthur C. *Asian Water Supplies: Reaching the Urban Poor* (Manila: Asian Development Bank 2003).

Meer, Marc van der et al. "Adaptive and Reflexive Governance—Changing Boundaries of National Social-Economic Decision-Making in the Netherlands." Paper presented at IREC Conference. Utrecht School of Governance. Aug. 26–28, 2004.

Metropolitan Manila Development Authority, 22 March 2008 < http://www.mmda.gov.ph/main.html>.

Mitlin, Diana. "Competition, Regulation and the Urban poor: A Case Study of Water" (Manchester: Center on Regulation and Competition Working Paper Series No. 37, Dec. 2002).

Montemayor, Carla A. "The Manila Water Privatization Fiasco and the Role of Suez Lyonnaise/Onedo" (Bantay Tubig: Summit for Another World, May 2003).

Muhammad, Anu. "Biplober Sopno Bhumi Cuba: Dhaka aar Havana" (Cuba: Revolutionaries' Dreamland: A Comparison between Dhaka and Havana), *Saptahik 2000* (Weekly 2000), Sept. 2007:9.

MWCI, *Sustainability Report 2011*, (Manila: Manila Water Company, Inc.) 2011.

MWCI, *Manila Water 2011 Annual Report 2012* (Manila: Manila Water Company, Inc.) 2011.

MWCI. *Manila Water's Corporate Governance Manual.*

MWCI. *MWCI Annual Report 2007* (Manila: Manila Water Company, Inc., 2007).

MWSI, *Maynilad 2010 Annual Report* (Manila: Maynilad Water Services, Inc. 2010)

MWSI. "Corporate Profile," 2 June 2008 <http://www.mayniladwater.com.ph/corporate_profile.asp>).

MWSI. "Attaining Sustainable Water Management." 14 June 2008 <http://www.mayniladwater.com.ph/>.

MWSI. "Fact Sheet." *Corporate Planning* (March 2006).

MWSI, "Capabilities and Facilities." Our Services. Maynilad Water Services, Inc. <http://www.mayniladwater.com.ph/our_services.asp> 12 June, 2008.

MWSI. "More Affordable Water," 14 June 2008 <http://www.mayniladwater.com.ph/service_rates.asp>.

MWSS Regulatory Office. *Regulatory Office Information Kit* (Manila: MWSS).

MWSS Regulatory Office. *2002 Annual Report* (Manila: MWSS, 2002).

MWSS-RO. "Customer Service Regulation Complaints Services Monitoring Department, Five Year Accomplishment Report, 1997–2002," (MWSS-RO, Manila, 2002).

Nahar, Begum Shamsun. "Gender, Water and Poverty Experiences from Water Resource Management Projects in Bangladesh," presented in *Regional Workshop on Water and Poverty*, Dhaka (22–26 Sept 2002).

Naznin, Afroza. "Kal Rajdhanibasike Grihobondo Korechilo Shittoprobah" (Yesterday City Dwellers Stayed in Their Houses Due to the Cold Wave). Jan. 5, 2007. *Ajker Kagoj*, 5 Jan. 2007 <http://www.ajkerkagoj.com/2007/Jan05/1st_page.html#7>.

Nussbaum, Martha. *Women and Human Development: The Capabilities Approach* (United Kingdom: Cambridge University Press, 2000).

———. "Capabilities As Fundamental Entitlements: Sen and Social Justice," *Feminist Economics* 9.2 (2003), pp. 33–59.

"One Water." 24 December 2008 <http://www.onewaterthemovie.org/>.

Ooi, Giok Ling and Kai Hong Phua. "Urbanization and Slum Formation," *Journal of Urban Health: Bulletin of the New York Academy of Medicine* 8.1 (2007), pp. 27–34.

Office, National Statistic, Republic of the Philippines. 21 March 2008 <http://www.census.gov.ph/data/pressrelease/2003/pr0312tx.html>.

Nations, The United. *Water for People, Water for Life: The United Nations World Water Development Report* (UNESCO and Berghahn Books, 2003).

Partnership, Global Water. "Effective Water Governance: Learning from the Dialogues" (Global Water Partnership, March 16–23, 2003).

Pelisesery, Sony, and Sylvia I. Bergh. "Adapting the Capability Approach to Explain the Effects of Participatory Development Programs: Case Studies from India and Morocco," *Journal of Human Development* 8.2 (2007), pp. 283–302.

Pogge, Thomas W. "Can the Capability Approach be Justified?" *Philosophical Topics* 30.2 (2002), pp. 167–228.

Position Paper of the South Asia Sub-Region. "Towards Reducing Poverty and Vulnerability in South Asia." Asia-Pacific Regional Document of the 4th World Water Forum (16–22 March 2006).

Pretty, Jules N. "Alternative Systems of Enquiry for Sustainable Agriculture," *IDS Bulletin* 25.2 (1994) 37–49.

Podymow, Tiina et al. "Health and Social Conditions in the Dhaka Slums," International Society for Urban Health, 21 March <http://www.isuh.org/download/Dhaka.pdf>.

Programme, World Water Assessment. *Water, a Shared Responsibility: The United Nations World Water Development Report 2* (Paris, New York: UNESCO and Berghahn Books, 2006).

Rabin, Masudujjaman. "Buriganga Ekhon Biser Adhar, Pani Sodhon Kore Pan Korche Dhaka-basi: Bisakto Shilpo-Borje Dushito Hocchhe Nodi" (Buriganaga Becoming a Poisonous River, the City Dwellers Are Purifying Water Before Drinking: Poisonous Industrial Waste Is the Main Cause of River Pollution), 16 Mar. 2007. *The Daily Inqilab*, 2 Apr. 2007 <http://www.dailyinqilab.com>.

Ragaragio, Junio M. "The Case of Metro Manila, Philippines," Massachusetts Institute of Technology (22 Mar 2008). <http://web.mit.edu/ sigus/www/NEW/challenge-course/pdfs/pdfscities/Manila.pdf>.

Rahman, Atiur, M. Ashraf Ali, and Farooque Chowdhury. *People's Report on Bangladesh Environment 2001: Main Report, Vol. 1* (Dhaka: Unnayan Shamannay, University Press Limited, 2001).

Rahnema, Majid. "Participation," in Wolfgang Sachs, ed., *The Development Dictionary: A Guide to Knowledge as Power* (London: Zed Books, 1992), pp. 127-144.

Ragaragio, Junio M. "The Case of Metro Manila, Philippines" In *Global Report on Human Settlements 2003, The Challenge of Slums* (London: Earthscan, UN-Habitat, 2003) 22 March 2008 <http://web.mit.edu/sigus/www/NEW/challengecourse/pdfs/pdfscities/Manila.pdf>.

Reuters. "Philippines' Maynilad Water Set to Repay $240 mln Debts" (Reuters, 13 Jan. 2008). 2 July, 2008 <http://in.reuters.com/article/asiaCompanyAndMarkets/idINMAN2471120080113>.

Rhodes, R.A.W. "Governance and Public Administration," *Debating Governance: Authority, Steering, and Democracy*, ed. John Pierre (New York: Oxford University Press, 2000), pp. 54–90.

Rivera, Virgilio C. Jr. "The Experience of Manila Water Company under the MWSS Privatization." Regional Conference on Universality of Infrastructure Services: Financing, Delivery and Regulatory Issues, November 9-10, New Delhi: India Habitat Center 2006).

Rivera, Virgilio C. "How Private Sector Involvement Can Help the Poor: Lessons from Manila (East)," Conference on From Private Sector Participation in the Urban Water and Sanitation: Managing the Process and Regulating the Sector, December 5-6, Manesar, Haryana, India, 2001.

Robeyns, Ingrid. "Sen's Capability Approach and Gender Inequality: Selecting Relevant Capabilities" *Feminist Economics* 9.2–3 (2003), pp. 61–92.

Rodriguez, Raul. "The Debate on Privatization of Water Utilities: A Commentary," *International Journal of Water Resources Development* 20 (2004), pp.107-112.

Rogers, Peter and Alan W Hall. "Effective Water Governance," *TEC Background Papers* No. 7 (Stockholm: Global Water Partnership 2003).

Rosenthal, Shane. "The Manila Water Concessions and Their Impact on the Poor." 1 Feb 2001. Hixon Center for Urban Ecology and Yale School of Forestry and Environmental Studies. 21 June 2007 < http://www.yale.edu/hixon/research/pdf/ SRosenthal_Manila.pdf>.

Rothfeder, Jeffrey. *Every Drop for Sale: Our Desperate Battle over Water in a World About to Run Out* (Washington, DC: International Thompson Publishing, 2001).

Saha, Arup. "Susko Mousume Pani Sankat Erate WASA Totpor" (WASA Taking Adequate Measures to Avoid Water Crisis During the Dry Season), 1 March 2008. *The Daily Jaijaidin*, 1 March 2008 <http://www.jaijaidin.com/details.php?nid=57426>.

Scholz, John T. and Bruce Stiftel. "The Challenges of Adoptive Governance," in *Adoptive Governance and Water Conflict: New Institutions for Collaborative Planning*, ed. John T. Scholz and Bruce Stiftel (Washington, DC: Resources for the Future 2005).

Scott, James C. *Seeing Like State: How Certain Schemes to Improve the Human Condition Have Failed* (New Haven and London: Yale University Press, 1998).

Sen, Amartya. "Equality of What?" In Sterling M. McMurrin, ed. *Tanner Lectures on Human Values* (Cambridge: Cambridge University Press, 1980), pp. 195–220.

———. "The Standard of Living: Lecture II, Lives and Capabilities" in *The Standard of Living*, ed. G. Hawthorn (Cambridge University Press: Cambridge, 1987), pp. 20–38.

———. *On Ethics and Economics* (Oxford: Blackwell, 1987).

———. *Development as Freedom* (New York: Knopf, 1999).

———. "Democracy as a Universal Value," *Journal of Democracy* 10.3 (1999), pp. 3

———. *Commodities and Capabilities* (India: Oxford University Press, 1999).

———. "Human Rights and Capabilities," *Journal of Human Development* 6.2 (2005), pp. 151–166 .

"Sharing Knowledge for Equitable, Efficient and Sustainable Water Resources Management," 2003 *Global Water Partnership* 19 Nov. 2006 <http://www.waterland. net/gfx/content/ToolBox%20text%20book%20Ver2%20Eng.pdf>.

Sharma, Manoj. "Capability Theory for Use in Alcohol and Drug Education Research," *Journal of Alcohol & Drug Education* 48-1 (2004), pp. 1–4.

Shiva, Vandana. *Water Wars: Privatization, Pollution and Profit* (Cambridge, MA: South End Press, 2002).

South, Jubilee. "Profiting from People's Lives: Metro Manila's Water Privatization Saga," 18 Oct. 2008 <http://www.jubileesouth.org./upload1/fdc_low.pdf>.

Sohel, Tanvir. "Dhaka-er Jonosonkhar 37 Bhag Bostibasi, 6 Mohanogore 54 Lakh: Ucheder Por Ghor-Kaj Dutoyi Harachhen Tara" (37 percent Population Live in the Slums in Dhaka and 5.4 million in Six Mega Cities: They Lost Both their Households and Livelihoods When They Were Evicted From Their Slums). Jan 29, 2007. *Prothom Alo*, 29 Jan. 2007 <http://www.prothom-alo.org/index.news.details. php?mid=MzM4MQ==>.

Soja, E. *Third Space: Journeys to Los Angeles and Other Imagined Places* (Cambridge, MA: Blackwell, 1996).

Soussan, John. *Water and Poverty: Fighting Poverty through Water Management* (Manila: Asian Development Bank, 2004).

Stewart, Frances. "Groups and Capabilities," *Journal of Human Development* 6.2 (2005), pp. 185–204.

Trawick, Paul. "Against the Privatization of Water: An Indigenous Model for Improving Laws and Successfully Governing the Commons," *World Development* 31 (2003), pp. 977–996.

Ullah, A. K. M. Jafar. "Country Report of Bangladesh: Management of Urban Water Environment," JICA Executive Seminar on Public Works and Management JFY 2004, National Institute for Land and Infrastructure Management, 27 Oct. 2006 <http://www.nilim.go.jp/english/conference/04.13th/7/13-7-2.pdf>.

UNDP. *Human Development Report 1998* (Oxford and New York: Oxford University Press, 1998).

UNICEF, WHO. "Meeting the MDG Drinking Water and Sanitation Target," (UNICEF, WHO 2004). 3 Feb 2005 <http://www.unicef.org/wes/mdgreport/disparities2.php>.

Uyan-Semerci, Pinar. "A Relational Account of Nussbaum's List of Capabilities" *Journal of Human Development* 8.2 (2007), pp. 203–221.

Veneklasen, Lisa and Valerie Miller, eds. *A New Wave of Power, People & Politics: The Action Guide for Advocacy and Citizen Participation* (UK: Practical Action Publishing 2007).

VoB, Jan Peter and René Kemp. "Sustainability and Reflexive Governance: Incorporating Feedback into Social Problem Solving." Paper presented at International Human Dimensions Programme on Global Environmental Change (IHDP) Open Meeting, Bonn. Oct. 9–13, 2005.

Webster, N. and L. Engberg-Petersen, eds. *In the Name of the Poor: Contesting Political Space for Poverty Reduction* (London: Zed Books, 2002).

White, Sarah C. "Depoliticising Development: The Uses and Abuses of Participation," *Development in Practice* 6.1 (1996), pp. 6–15.

WHO. "Minimum Water Quantity Needed for Domestic Use In Emergencies," *Technical Note* 3 (2005).

Williams, Glyn. "Evaluating Participatory Development: Tyranny, Power, and (Re) politicization," *Third World Quarterly* 25.3 (2004), pp. 557–578.

Wolfe, Marshall. *Participation: The View from Above* (Geneva: UNRISD 1983).

Young, Iris Marion. "Public Debate and Social Justice," *Maitreyee* 4 (February 2006) 2–3.

Appendix

Table A.1.
International Declarations and Conventions Recognizing Water As a Human Right

Articles 20,26, 29, 46, Geneva Convention III (1949)

Articles 85,89, 127, Geneva Convention IV(1949)

Articles 54,55, Geneva Convention Additional Protocol (1977)

Articles 5,14, Geneva Convention Additional Protocol (1977)

Preamble, Mar del Plata Declaration of the United Nations Water Conference (1977)

Article 14 (2) (h) Convention on the Elimination of All Forms of Discrimination Against Women (1979)

Article 8 of the United Nations Declaration on the Right to Development (1986)

Article 11, American Convention on Human Rights in the Area of Economic, Social, and Cultural Rights (1988)

Article 24 (2) (c), Convention on the Rights of the Child (1989)

Paragraph 18:47, Agenda 21 Report of the United Nations Conference on Environment and Development (1992)

Article I (10), Vienna Declaration, World Conference on Human Rights (1993)

Section 27 (1) (b), Bill of Rights of the Constitution of South Africa (1994)

Article 93 and 107 of the Beijing Platform of Action

Paragraphs 5 and 19, Recommendation 14 of the Committee of Ministers to Member States on the European Charter on Water Resources (2001)

General Comment 15 of the United Nations General Assembly (2002).

Source: Peter Gleick et al., *The World's Water: The Biennial Report on Freshwater Resources (2004-2005)* (Washington, Covelo, London: Island Press 2004) 206.

Appendix

Table A.2.
The Constitutions of the Various Countries that Recognize Water As a Basic Right

Burkina Faso—Article 2 of the Law of the 8th of February 2001.
Ethiopia—Constitution, 1995, Article 90.
Gambia—Constitution, 1996, Article 216 (4).
India—On the Basis of Article 21 of the Indian Constitution on the right to life, the
    Supreme Court of India considers water is a fundamental human right.
South Africa—Constitution, 1996, Section 27.
Uganda—Constitution, 1995, Article 14 of the National Objectives.
Zambia—Constitution, as amended in 1996. Article 112.

Source: Gleick et al. 207.

Table A.3.
Water-Related Diseases

Diarrhea: 4 billion cases per Year, 2.2 million deaths (1.8 m children) per year.

Arsenicosis: "Millions of people are potentially in danger from arsenic poisoning."

Cholera: Over 120,000 cases were reported in 2002.

Fluorosis: An endemic disease in at least 25 countries across the world. The total numbers of cases is unknown.

Guinea worm disease (Dracunculiasis): 50,000 cases were reported in 13 countries in Africa in 2002.

Intestinal Worms: 10 percent of populations in the developing world are infected by intestinal worms. About 400 million school-age children have been infected by roundworm, whipworm, and/or hookworm. About one quarter of the world's population has been affected by roundworm and whipworm.

Schistosomiasis: About 200 million people have been already infected worldwide; 20 million severely.

Trachoma: There are 6 million people blind worldwide due to trachoma.

Typhoid: About 12 million people are affected by typhoid every year.

HIV/AIDS: HIV-infected people are more susceptible to water-related diseases.

Source: UNICEF, "Common Water and Sanitation Related Diseases," *Water, Environment and Sanitation* http://www.unicef.org/wes/index_wes_related.html (accessed, 25 April 2005).

Table A.4.
Population Coverage in Asia Required by the 2015 International Development Target
(in millions)

	Water Supply		
	Urban	Rural	Total
2000:			
Total population	1352	2331	3683
Population with access	1254	1736	2990
Percent coverage	93%	74%	81%
2015:			
Target coverage	96%	87%	91%
Expected total population	1943	2404	4347
Target population to have access	1873	2097	3970
Target additional urban population to serve	619	361	980
Target increase in population to be served	49%	21%	33%

Source: Water Supply and Sanitation Collaborative Council, Global Water Supply and Sanitation Assessment
2000 Report (USA: WHO, UNICEF 2000) 32–33.

Index

About the Author

Sayeed Iftekhar Ahmed, Ph.D., is an independent researcher who has been a faculty member in the Department of Politics and International Affairs at Northern Arizona University as well as the Department of Political Science at Rajshahi University in Bangladesh. His writings cover water governance, Islamism, democratization, and development.